D1237550

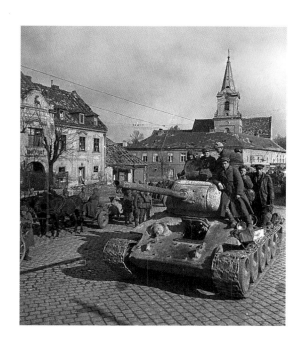

RED ARMY INTO
THE REICH

RED ARMY INTO
THE REICH

SIMON FORTY, PATRICK HOOK, & NIK CORNISH

CASEMATE

Published in the United States of America and Great Britain in 2021 by
CASEMATE PUBLISHERS
1950 Lawrence Road, Havertown, PA 19083, USA
and
The Old Music Hall, 106–108 Cowley Road, Oxford OX4 1JE, UK

Hardcover Edition: ISBN 978-1-63624-022-0
Digital Edition: ISBN 978-1-63624-023-7

A CIP record for this book is available from the British Library

Printed and bound in the Czech Republic by Finidr s.r.o.

Packaged by Greene Media Ltd
Design: Eleanor Forty

For a complete list of Casemate titles, please contact:

CASEMATE PUBLISHERS (US)
Telephone (610) 853-9131
Fax (610) 853-9146
Email: casemate@casematepublishers.com
www.casematepublishers.com

CASEMATE PUBLISHERS (UK)
Telephone (01865) 241249
Email: casemate-uk@casematepublishers.co.uk
www.casematepublishers.co.uk

Page 1: *T-34/85 of XXIII Tank Corps, passes the Church of the Holy Trinity in Kleinschwechat on the outskirts of Vienna.*

Pages 2–3: *"Tankovyy desant"—carrying troops onboard a tank—was a useful way of transporting troops quickly and helped ensure tank–infantry cooperation, but was a dangerous tactic: the men on the back made easy targets. Nevertheless, the Russians adopted it enthusiastically and even crafted handholds for the infantry.*

Below: *T-34/85s at the Dukla Pass, scene of bloody fighting in September and October 1944. German resistance here was vigorous and committed, leading to heavy casualties on both sides. The last months of the war would be anything but a triumphant progress for the Allies and the Red Army would have to fight hard, bloody battles in grim conditions for most of the way to Berlin.*

Nomenclature
To differentiate between them, Russian units have been Anglicized while German units have been left in their German form.

THE RED ARMY

The Workers' and Peasants' Red Army—Рабо́че-Крестья́нская Кра́сная Армия—was created after the 1917 Revolution. Its part in the Great Patriotic War— Вели́кая Оте́чественная война́—between June 22, 1941, and May 9, 1945, was flawed but in the end victorious. Invaded by its hitherto German ally, with an officer corps damaged by Stalin's purges, nevertheless it overcame its enemies thanks in no small part to the material assistance of its allies—particularly the United States, through Lend-Lease—and ended the war by taking Berlin. Over 34 million men and women served in the army and air forces, of whom the official war dead figure is 8,668,400 (although other estimates put it as high as 11 million). Of these as many as 3.6 million of 6 million PoWs didn't survive. Marshal Zhukov dedicated his memoirs "to the Soviet soldier. It is with his blood and sweat that the victory over the powerful enemy was gained. He knew how to face mortal danger, he displayed a supreme valor and heroism. There is no limit to the greatness of his exploit in the name of his Motherland."

Contents

Introduction

Hitler called it "the greatest bluff since Genghis Khan." He scoffed at the analysis by Generalleutnant Richard Gehlen, head of the *Fremde Heere Ost* (FHO), that informed Generaloberst Heinz Guderian's attempts to get Hitler to remove his gaze from the west and turn it to the more dangerous east. Gehlen's intelligence gathering had emphasized the overwhelming might of the Soviet forces ready for an attack on January 12. Their superiority, Guderian relates in *Panzer Leader*, Gehlen reckoned to be 11:1 in infantry, 7:1 in tanks and 20:1 in guns. At the meeting on December 24 Hitler refused to believe it and—in Guderian's estimation—squandered Germany's last few assets in the Ardennes and, later, Alsace-Lorraine. He refused to stop the Ardennes offensive or to allow the armies in the Courland Pocket to be transferred to help. The men that did become available were sent to Hungary whose oil, Hitler believed, was essential to Germany's war effort.

It was, almost certainly, too late anyway. Hitler's 1941 gamble to attack the Soviet Union had already backfired. On the defensive since 1942–43, and after June 1944 fighting on three fronts, most of the German generals knew that they were dead men walking. Hitler, whose little faith in the military hierarchy had been finally destroyed by the July 20, 1944 bomb plot, wasn't prepared to listen to dissent. Anyone who disobeyed was replaced, as were those who dared to argue with him. Guderian became one, eventually, after one disagreement too many toward the end of March 1945.

It had all seemed so very different in 1944 before the Allies landed in France, Rome had fallen and the Italians surrendered. And even after those reverses, there were no enemies knocking at the door of the Reich. The Allies' strategic bombing campaign was certainly wreaking havoc and destruction, but it didn't stop German productivity increasing sharply at the back end of 1944. And the wonder weapons—the V bombs and jet aircraft—were beginning to reach the front line. Surely the tide would inevitably turn?

It would not. Oil production and military manpower were the two most critical factors that would contribute to collapse. As Earl Ziemcke says in *Stalingrad to Berlin*: "[synthetic oil production] output had fallen during the summer. In September, because of the bombings, no synthetic plants had

Opposite: *"Glory to the heroes of the Patriotic War! Glory to Stalin's Falcons!" This 1941 poster is the work of P. Vandyshev and L. Torich in 1941.*

Above: *The Il-16 "Ishak" first flew in 1933 and was, at the time, a revolutionary aircraft but by 1943, when it was replaced, was long in the tooth. Nevertheless, it continued to be flown until the war's end and, in the hands of a good pilot, was extremely effective.*

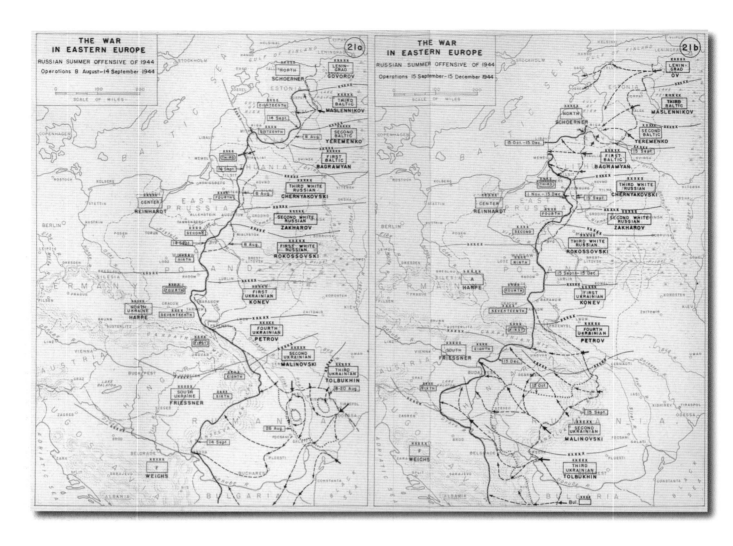

Above: *Summer 1944 saw the beginning of the end for German hopes in the east. Steady progress became major advances in the south and north as the Baltic states the USSR had acquired in 1940 were freed. The advances bottled up a large number of German troops in the Courland Pocket. They would still be there in May 1945. Hitler had instructed them to stay in the pocket in the optimistic hope that they would force the Russians to waste time and men to reduce the pocket. The troops were also planned to form the basis of a future counterattack. In the south, the change of initiative was exemplified by the retaking of the Crimea. It had taken the Germans five months to take Sevastopol—the Soviets retook it in five days.*

operated. The Romanian oil had been lost at the end of August ... Army Group South held the Hungarian fields at Nagykanizsa, but owing to the loss of the refineries at Budapest ... gasoline output was not enough to meet the army group's own requirements. In June 1944 the German Air Force had consumed 180,000 metric tons of gasoline; its total supply for the rest of the war amounted to no more than 197,000 metric tons."

German manpower—particularly trained troops—was also suffering from attrition. Between June and November 1944 the Wehrmacht lost nearly 1.5 million men, three-fifths on the Eastern Front. To cover this, Hitler helped paper over the cracks by setting up the *Volkssturm* (see pp. 50–51)—calling to the colors anyone aged between 16 and 60 not already serving. But new troops had to be trained and equipped. Few of the 1.5 million called up August–December 1944 would reach combat zones before January 1945. When they did, unsurprisingly, their quality was nowhere near that of the early war inductions. Clutching at straws, Hitler also allowed the constitution of the renegade Russian Liberation Army (see pp. 16–17) and combing through all units to provide more men who could serve at the front. He also activated the emergency units formed by the German military district headquarters—codenamed "Blücher" and "Gneisenau"—that provided another 200,000 men.

What this actually meant was, as Gehlen had pointed out, the Russians had superior numbers. He may have been overly pessimistic about the force ratios, but there was no denying that the Russians had near-overwhelming superiority: 414 divisions at the front as opposed to the Germans' 160 (although the Russian division had fewer men than a full-strength German equivalent so the disparity can be overstated). And as far as aircraft went, the Russians' 10,000 were opposed by 1,875, giving the Red Air Force air superiority, too.

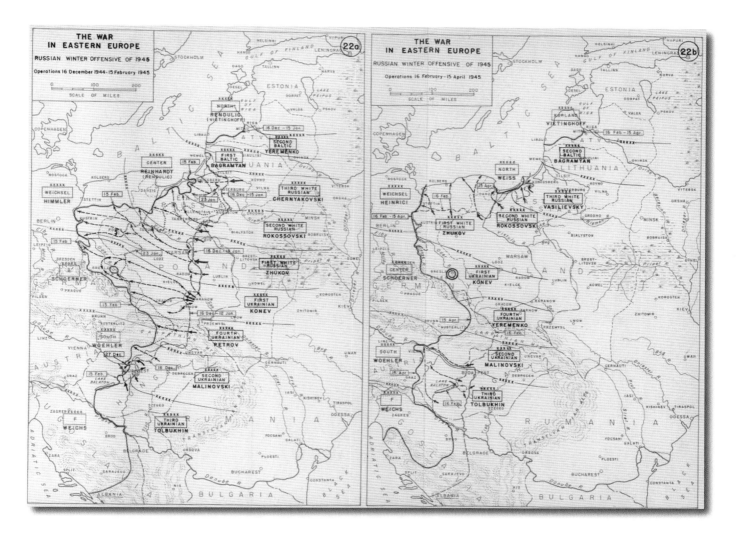

The result was a catastrophe for the Germans. Between January 12 and 17 the Russians broke out from their bridgeheads and flooded across the Vistula. Warsaw fell. Hitler reacted as only he could, blaming his generals, replacing many, and renaming their commands. To make matters worse, one of the replacements was Himmler, who only Hitler thought was worth a try. Of course, in very short order he proved he wasn't—and, in very short order, the front line was along the Oder. The Germans had lost Poland and the Red Army was camped 40 miles from Berlin. There were still some of Hitler's *Festungen* (fortresses) that held out—such as Posen (see pp. 98–99), and as the advance continued to the Neisse in February, Arnswalde, Breslau (pp. 94–95), and Küstrin (p. 110)—and a significant force continued to hold Courland (pp. 78–81)—but to all intents and purposes, the final act had arrived. All that was missing was the denouement.

Just at that moment a number of factors induced the Russian to halt: a thaw turned the roads to mud; the ill-designed Stargard counterattack, *Unternehmen Sonnenwende*, in Pomerania on February 15–18 was successful enough to jolt the Soviets; the Hron offensive, *Unternehmen Südwind* (see pp. 126–127), was much further south in Hungary, but cleared the Soviet Hron bridgehead. Enough was enough for the Russians. They decided to clear the flanks, attacking into Pomerania. There was no need for undue haste—the Allies were still west of the Rhine and there could be no question of them reaching the ultimate prize, Berlin, first.

The Soviet East Pomeranian/East Prussian offensives by the 1st, 2nd, and 3rd Belorussian fronts whittled away the German hold on the area between Königsberg and Stettin. The 3rd Belorussian Front (Gen Ivan Chernyakhovsky and then Gen Aleksandr Vasilevsky after the former's death) had been attacking toward Königsberg from mid-January. Between February 24

Above: *The collapse of the German front in the Vistula–Oder offensive slowed as the Russian forces stopped to regroup. Armchair generals have debated the rationale for the pause. Was it for military reasons to stabilize potential issues on the flanks or politically motivated to allow the Red Army to roll up the German defenses in central Europe and therefore ensure that they would be Soviet client states in post-war Europe. Whatever the reason, the pause meant that there were more defenses between the Oder and Berlin, so more Russians died—but by the time the final attack started, Hungary, Austria, and Czechoslovakia, were either under the Red Army's control or would be very soon.*

(Note: this map uses "White Russian" for the armies named as "Belorussian" in this book.)

9

and March 6 the 1st and 2nd Belorussian fronts (Marshal Georgy Zhukov and Marshal Konstantin Rokossovsky respectively) attacked north to the Baltic, cutting off Königsberg (see pp. 102–103) and Danzig (p. 107), surrounding Kolberg (p. 108). Next, those cities were taken, a process that took most of March. Finally, the east bank of the Oder was cleared near Stettin.

While Zhukov and Rokossovsky cleared Pomerania, Marshal Ivan Konev cleared Silesia. His advance through Lower Silesia between February 8 and 24 while protecting the flank of Zhukov's 1st Belorussian Front had ended with a bridgehead across the Neisse at Forst and the encirclement of Breslau (see pp. 94–95). Upper Silesia saw hard fighting as the 1st Ukrainian Front pushed south and cleared the Germans from this important industrial area between March 15 and 31. Some of the heaviest fighting took place around Lauban (Lubań) and Striegau (Strzegom), where German counterattacks encircled and massacred elements of the Third (Lauban) and Fifth (Striegau) Guards armies and then Oppeln where the 20. Waffen-Grenadier-Division der SS (estnische Nr.1) and 168th Infanterie-Division were encircled and crushed.

Hungary, Czechoslovakia, and Austria

The pause on the Oder–Neisse line in February and March 1945 allowed the Red Army to cement its control over central Europe from the Balkans to the heart of Germany. Held up at the end of 1944 by the Carpathian Mountains and the Arpad Line, and the Margit and Attila lines that ran through

southern Hungary and Slovenia, the Russians concentrated on taking Budapest which surrendered on February 13, 1945. The Germans' subsequent attempt to hold onto the Hungarian oilfields—the Plattensee (Lake Balaton) offensive—saw the Soviets allow their attackers to grind themselves down on prepared antitank defenses until the opportunity to counterattack presented itself. When it did, they threatened to surround elements of 6. SS-Panzerarmee forcing their retreat. Unlike Romania (August 1944) and Bulgaria (September 1944), Hungary wasn't able to swap sides (although it tried in March 1944), and its remaining armies were destroyed alongside their German allies as General Fyodor Tolbukhin's 3rd Ukrainian Front prepared for an offensive that took the Soviet forces from Budapest to Vienna by way of Bratislava (April 4). Vienna fell on the 10th, Brno on April 26 and Prague by May 8.

The political ramifications of this were immense. The Iron Curtain would come down over a great deal of eastern Europe. Had Berlin been taken in February and the Reich surrendered then, it's debatable whether the postwar political setup would have been as clearcut as it turned out.

The End

With any potential problems on either north or south flanks cleared by the end of March, the stage was set for the Russian envelopment of Berlin and the final days of the Reich. The offensive started on April 16. Having crossed the Oder, the main battle was on the Seelow Heights and lasted three days. The Germans under Heinrici defended brilliantly, but the assaulting forces were too numerous and too resilient after years of warfare to be beaten back. On April 20, the shelling of Berlin started. It continued until the surrender. On April 24 Busse's 9. Armee was surrounded in the Halbe Pocket and desperately attempted to break to meet up with 12. Armee only seven miles to the west. They finally accomplished it and some 25,000 men got out, but left behind as many as 30,000 dead, along with 10,000 civilians and 30,000 men of the Red Army. The remnants of the two German armies crossed the Elbe on May 5–8 and surrendered to U.S. forces.

By then Hitler was dead, having committed suicide on April 30. Early on May 2, the Reichskanzlei fell and a few hours later General Weidling surrendered the city. The Great Patriotic War against Germany was over.

Opposite, Above: *Red Army T-34/85 of the 62nd Guards Tank Brigade, part of the Fourth Guards Tank Army, 1st Ukrainian Front on a U.S. M9 low loader portion of a tank transporter supplied under Lend-Lease. It's in the Czech town of Trebon in front of the Church of the Virgin Mary and St Giles as part of the Prague offensive. The unit was awarded the Order of Suvorov II degree "by Decree of the Presidium of the USSR Armed Forces of April 26, 1945, for exemplary performance of command assignments in battles during the breakthrough of the German defense and the defeat of enemy troops southwest of Oppeln and the valor and courage shown at the same time."*

Opposite, Below: *They're coming! A lone German sentry keeps watch for any Red Army patrols. Soviet reconnaissance groups were a constant headache for their opponents and reconnaissance in large groups often presaged an attack.*

Above: *Hungary and its oilfields were of huge importance to the Germans in the last months of the war and they fought hard to keep hold of them. Festung Budapest was ravaged as a result.*

Partisan warfare

Below: *The Bandenkampf-abzeichen was an award made for fighting guerrillas and other such enemies usually behind the front lines. The award came in three levels depending on days spent in the field: bronze, silver, and gold for 20, 50, and 100 combat days respectively. Note the Hydra (multi-headed serpent) representing the "bandits" and the sunwheel swastika on the hilt. The badge was instituted on January 30, 1944, by Adolf Hitler. Of course, for a German soldier caught by a Partisan wearing one, it would be a death sentence or worse, if captured wearing one.*

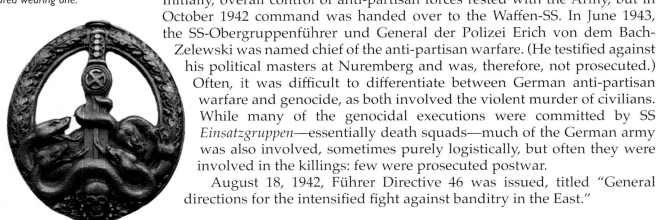

Below: *The Monument to the Fighters of the Revolution in Valjevo, Serbia is a piece by Vojin Bakić, a Croatian sculptor. It remembers the execution of a young Partisan, Stevan Filipovic, on May 22, 1942. His last words were:*

"Long live our great allies! Long live Comrade Tito! Long live the democracy of free peoples! Long live the leader and protector of the people and peasants, Comrade Stalin! Long live the brotherhood of Slavic peoples who will emerge victorious from this war."

Bitter, with no quarter given, anti-guerrilla operations were widespread in the territories conquered by the Germans, particularly in the Soviet Union and Yugoslavia—such as *Unternehmen Rösselsprung* (Knight's Move) aimed at Tito and his HQ at Drvar. This was the seventh major anti-partisan operation in Yugoslavia. However, it's important not to separate the anti-partisan war from the holocaust. The Jewish population was intentionally identified as Bolshevik and, therefore, partisans by the German leaders, and this allowed them to be killed in huge numbers—by the Wehrmacht as well as police units.

Reprisals for German deaths included destruction of entire communities (such as Oradour-sur-Glane in France or Lidice in today's Czech Republic). Initially, overall control of anti-partisan forces rested with the Army, but in October 1942 command was handed over to the Waffen-SS. In June 1943, the SS-Obergruppenführer und General der Polizei Erich von dem Bach-Zelewski was named chief of the anti-partisan warfare. (He testified against his political masters at Nuremberg and was, therefore, not prosecuted.)

Often, it was difficult to differentiate between German anti-partisan warfare and genocide, as both involved the violent murder of civilians. While many of the genocidal executions were committed by SS *Einsatzgruppen*—essentially death squads—much of the German army was also involved, sometimes purely logistically, but often they were involved in the killings: few were prosecuted postwar.

August 18, 1942, Führer Directive 46 was issued, titled "General directions for the intensified fight against banditry in the East."

"Banditry in the East has in the last few months grown to an unbearable extent and threatens to become a serious menace to the supplying of the front and the economic exploitation of the country. Before the onset of winter these bands must be practically routed out …

The destruction of banditry requires a vigorous campaign and the harshest measures against all who have a hand in organizing the bands or are guilty of aiding them. Detailed directions for combating banditry will follow.

In the theater of operations the Chief of the Army General Staff has the sole responsibility for combating banditry. In the performance of the ensuing tasks the police forces stationed in the theater of operations are subordinated to the respective theater commanders, in addition to the forces assigned for this purpose by the Army."

The response to this directive obvious left something to be desired, so Hitler followed it up on October 18:

"I feel that it is necessary to inform the various commanders of the reasons behind this order.

Many of our measures against this cruel and underhanded sabotage activity are ineffective simply because the German officers and their men are unaware of the extent of the danger and therefore do not take sufficiently decisive measures against these partisans, to help our front lines and thus the entire war effort.

Therefore it was necessary at some places in the East to organize German units to cope with this danger, or to entrust special SS formations with this task. Only where the fight against the partisans was waged with ruthless brutality were results achieved which relieved the troops fighting at the front.

In the entire East area, therefore, the war against the partisans is a fight of extermination on both sides.

Unless German warfare is to suffer serious setbacks as the result of such activities, the enemy must be given to understand that all sabotage troops will be exterminated to the last man without exception. That means that the chances of survival are nil. Therefore it can in no case be tolerated that sabotage, demolition or terrorist troops simply surrender, are taken prisoner, and are treated in accordance with the Geneva convention. On the contrary, they must be annihilated under all circumstances."

In a postwar analysis of the Russian campaign, SS-Obersturmbannführer Jochen Peiper, CO of 1. SS-Panzerdivision *Leibstandarte*, wrote while in Landsberg prison awaiting execution for war crimes (the sentence was commuted and he was freed in 1956):

"The Ukraine received us as liberator and waited for the proclamation of their independence. The shortsighted setup of our civil-administration created the enemy in the back, as also the partisan fighting and was in my opinion a decisive error. It is my conception that the backbone of the Soviet Army was broken in the Autumn of 1941. If the German politics and propaganda would have had the same force of impact as the Army, the war could have been brought to an end still in the same year.

A good treatment of the subjugated ones would have been the start for mass desertion of the enemy. Instead, the contrary was done. One thus created for the first time an 'emergency organization,' reconciling the national antagonistic trends and oppositions and handed Stalin the slogan for a unifying national goal."

Top: *Execution of hostages by hanging on the Eastern Front.*

Above: *SS troops crossing a mountain stream in pursuit of Yugoslav partisans. The soldier in the foreground is carrying an MG34 machine gun with a drum magazine, and the unit's supplies are being carried by pack mule.*

Lend-Lease played an important role in assisting the Russian war effort as both America and Britain delivered tanks, aircraft, and war matériel to the USSR, usually by means of the Arctic convoys to Murmansk. Around 13,000 armored vehicles came from U.S. Lend-Lease (including 7,000 tanks, of which nearly 2,000 were M3 mediums and 4,000 were Shermans) and over 427,000 trucks out of a Russian total inventory of 665,000 trucks. One top of this, clothing and raw materials should not be discounted. Britain's contribution was smaller, but between June 1941 and May 1945, it included around 5,250 tanks (including 1,380 Valentines from Canada) and over 5,000 antitank guns. And they helped!
(Source Report on war aid furnished by the United States to the U.S.S.R.; DC, 1945.)

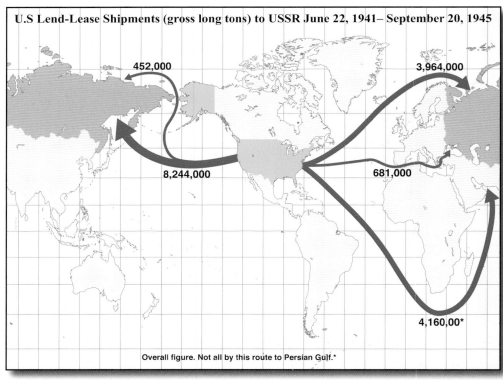

U.S Lend-Lease Shipments (gross long tons) to USSR June 22, 1941– September 20, 1945

452,000

3,964,000

8,244,000

681,000

4,160,00*

Overall figure. Not all by this route to Persian Gulf.*

Lend-lease

It is a matter of conjecture just how well the Soviets would have managed without the enormous assistance provided to them by the western allies. In financial terms, the numbers are still staggering today—back then they would have been beyond comprehension to most. The United States provided matériel that was worth a total of more than $50,000,000,000, while the British contributed a further $1,300,000,000 (these are the values at the time). The sums were represented in the form of every conceivable kind of armament, vast fleets of trucks, jeeps, and other transport equipment, as well as innumerable quantities of petroleum products, machine tools, raw materials, and desperately needed foodstuffs.

To cite a few examples: without the huge numbers of trucks it received, it is improbable that the Red Army could have moved with the speed and efficiency that it achieved on the battlefield. Previously foot-bound infantry became fully motorized. Likewise, the sheer distances involved in navigating the Soviet Union together with the relative lack of satisfactory roads, meant that railroads were critically important. Huge numbers of locomotives and rolling stock were specially constructed to fit the unusual Soviet track gauge and then shipped over.

Without the specialist chemicals which allowed the Soviets to convert their low quality petrol into aviation quality fuel, few of their aircraft could have flown; that alone would have made a massive difference to their combat capabilities.

Another incredibly important factor was the food that was delivered—on which large parts of the Red Army depended. Not only was it highly nutritious, but it was packed in such a way that it could last for long periods of time without deteriorating. Again, the consequences of this not being provided are incalculable.

Lend-Lease tanks made up 30–40% of the Russian heavy and medium tank strength in front of Moscow at the crucial moment of Unternehmen Barbarossa at the beginning of December 1941. Here are two examples of Lend-Lease tanks to Russia First, a British Valentine (1), suitably named!; 2 Seen alongside a IS-2 as part of Second Guards Tank Army, a U.S. M4A2 76(W).

3 A convoy of Studebaker US6 trucks—the Lend-Lease version of the "Deuce and a half"—in Russia. They would receive some 152,000, many via the Persian Corridor.

4 The Russians also received a number of U.S. landing ships, including the 16 LSI (L)s used during the invasion of the Kuril Islands in August 1945. Five were destroyed by Japanese coastal artillery during landings at Shumshu, including this one, LSI(L)-554.

5 Unveiled in 2006, this is the memorial to the Lend-Lease link between Ladd Field, Fairbanks, Alaska and Siberia. Over 8,000 aircraft flew across the Bering Straits 1942–45. There's a plaque to the Women Airline Service Pilots involved in the process.

Fellow travelers

Unsurprisingly, each side had some strange bedfellows. Politics, religion, revenge—the rationale behind those who supported the Axis and Allies is not always easy to understand or comfortable to live with today now that the true extent of the awful crimes committed during the period are well known. For example, many inhabitants of what is now Ukraine welcomed the German Army as liberators. After the Holodomor and the genocide of the 1930s, that's hardly surprising. But Stalin's brutal purges paled besides the *Einsatzgruppen* and indiscriminate mass killings perpetuated by the advancing Germans.

Home-grown fascist organizations such as Hungary's Arrow Cross and the Croat Ustaše flourished. On the other side, so did the communist guerrillas in countries like Italy, Yugoslavia, and Russia—although in Yugoslavia the clashes between the pro-monarchist Chetniks and the Partisans led to great complications exacerbated by religion.

It is, again, unsurprising that the violently anti-Zionist Grand Mufti of Jerusalem would support the Nazis, and that political opponents of the Russian regime would provide fertile ground for German support. One obvious form of collaboration was the SS-Freiwilligen and other Waffen-SS units made up of "volunteers" mainly from subjugated countries. The voluntary aspect of these units, however, is conjectural and was recognized postwar when those of the Baltic states—Latvia, Estonia, and Lithuania—were exempted from the overall treatment of the other Waffen-SS. Probably the most unfortunate of these were the XV. SS Cossack Corps, who surrendered to the British in Austria and were repatriated to the Soviet Union and almost certain death. The lack of enthusiasm for their task is shown by how many of these SS units were relegated to functions behind the main lines. The only country not to supply units was Poland.

The bulk of the troops that fought alongside the Germans came in two forms, the *Ostlegionen*—such as the ROA, Croat infantry divisions, and the

various ethnic legions (Armenian, Georgian, Azerbaijani etc)—and the Hiwis (*Hilfswilliger* volunteers) and *Ostbataillone*—which were recruited from Russian (or other) PoWs. As the PoWs' death rate ran at nearly 60 percent, and serving with the Germans included food, it is understandable that many—up to a million—preferred that option. The numbers involved are certainly sizable. Nigel Thomas put the level of Hiwis in German 6. Armee at Stalingrad at 25 percent. Postwar, there was little understanding or sympathy shown to them. Hiwis were branded "former Russians" and sent to the gulag or killed.

The eastern troops saw action in both east and west—indeed, one of the last battles in the west saw Georgians of Infanterie-Bataillon 882 *Königin Tamara* fighting with the Germans on the island of Texel until stopped by the Canadians on May 20. This bloody little war within a war saw 565 Georgians, 812 Germans, and 120 Dutch die. On May 5, 1943, the Ostruppen accounted for 10 regiments, 170 battalions, 221 companies, and 11 platoons / sections, the bulk being used as infantry with a sizable construction element.

The Russian Liberation Army had a checkered existence. Hitler was against the idea of a Russian army of liberation but Himmler persuaded him in fall 1944 that it was worth using the men they had. On January 28, 1945, all Russian divisions were transferred directly under the command of KONR—the Committee for the Liberation of the Peoples of Russia. The army only fought one major battle on the German side: on the Oder on April 11, 1945. Thereafter, when push came to shove, in Prague on May 6, 1945, the ROA fought alongside the Czech resistance fighters against the Germans and were instrumental in preserving the city. Vlasov, hoping that his men would not have to be returned to the Soviets, tried to surrender to the Americans. Eventually he was repatriated, tried, and—along with eleven of his officers— executed by the Soviets on August 2, 1946. Vlasov, for understandable reasons, raises different emotions in the Czech Republic, where his men's actions helped liberate Prague, than in Russia where he is, of course, seen as a traitor.

Above left: *Ukrainian volunteers of the SS Galicia division (14. Waffen-Grenadier-Division der SS [galizische Nr. 1]) marching outside the courthouse in Sanok to receive their troop flag.*

Above: *The Grand Mufti of Jerusalem [Amin al Husseini] saluting Bosnian volunteers of the Waffen-SS.*

Below: *The infamous Russian Army of National Liberation— RONA—was headed by Bronislav Vladislavovich Kaminski. He took control of the security of Lokot Oblast in Belorussia on the German side (he had spent time in Stalin's gulag) eventually ending up with 10,000 men, tanks, and field guns. The Kaminski Brigade retreated with the Germans. In June 1944 they became part of the Waffen- SS as the Waffen-Sturm- Brigade RONA. They were heavily involved in suppressing the Warsaw Uprising, but they got greedy and started stealing goods from their victims. This is what is said to have led to Kaminski's execution, but the likelihood is that Himmler preferred Vlasov as commander of the Russian contingent to Kaminski.*

Above: *A U.S. military assessment of the European landscape says, "It is anticipated that in the European theater, water obstacles 100m wide will be encountered every 35–60km; between 100 and 300m wide every 100–150km; and more than 300m wide every 250–300km. Further, they anticipate that 60 percent of all water obstacles will be less than 20m wide." The Vistula proved no obstacle to this German pontoon bridge in 1939.*

Right: *Another bridge over the Vistula. This is a through-girder type with a 10ft clear roadway. The girders are constructed of steel-lattice pyramids. The decking is 6-inch timber plank.*

Below right: *German troops cross a river in a powered storm boat. Carried and launched by eight men, with four needed for the motor. The boat is steered by pivoting the motor on the bracket which attaches it to the stern. The helmsman stands in the stern gripping two handles at the front of the motor.*

Opposite, Above: *Finnish infantry unit with anti-tank guns loaded into boats from the pier in the northern part of Lake Ladoga, in Karelia. Nowhere were bridge-building skills and the availability of boats more important than in Finland which is dotted with thousands of lakes and watercourses.*

Opposite, Below: *Heavier vehicles—such as this ISU-152— were often best carried on a pontoon ferry.*

Crossing rivers

Just as in the west, eastern Europe is criss-crossed by rivers, some mighty, such as the Don, Dnieper, and Danube; others were smaller but no less of an obstacle to an army on the move, especially as armored vehicles grew in size and weight. For the Germans, in retreat, the problem was when to blow the bridges; the Red Army had to cross them—usually under fire. The U.S. Army's immediate postwar *Handbook on USSR Military Forces* says this about Soviet bridging engineers:

"An independent light bridging battalion is capable of building a 200–250ft pontoon bridge of 5–14-ton capacity in 70–90 minutes. It consists of HQ and HQ company, three light bridging companies, and transport and service units. Each light bridging company has three platoons with 18–23 men in each. Strength of a light bridging battalion is approximately 250 officers and enlisted men.

The independent light (16T) bridging battalion is capable of constructing a 500ft pontoon bridge in 2 hours. It consists of three companies of four platoons each. Strength of this battalion is c. 300 officers and enlisted men. Two such battalions may be combined to form a light bridging regiment capable of erecting a 1,350ft pontoon bridge in 2 hours. Strength of the light bridging regiment is approximately 750 officers and enlisted men.

The independent medium (30T) bridging battalion is capable of erecting a 325ft pontoon bridge in 2.5 hours. It consists of two companies of four bridging platoons each. Its strength is c. 300 officers and enlisted men. The engineer park of each tank and mechanized corps is allotted sufficient pontoon materials to build a 30-ton bridge 300ft long.

A heavy (60–100-ton) bridging regiment is capable of constructing a 340ft pontoon bridge in 3 hours. It consists of two heavy pontoon battalions of four heavy pontoon companies each. Its strength is c. 700 officers and enlisted men."

The Soviet leaders

By January 1945 Stalin's armies were poised to roll up the remnants of the Wehrmacht in the east. They had the men and the equipment and, most importantly, the resolve to finish the task in spite of the fanatical defense. With a superiority in numbers of about 4 to 1, this was no steamroller and simply winning by numbers as so much western literature—particularly that provided by captive German generals—would have you believe. The Soviet war machine of 1945 was sophisticated, cunning, and ably led. Backed by powerful artillery and heavy armor, in Zhukov, Konev, and Rokossovsky the Red Army had a set of experienced commanders who were used to winning. There was little, if anything, the Germans could do to stop them.

Leningrad Front (Marshal Leonid A. Govorov)
Armies—First and Fourth Shock; Sixth and Tenth Guards; Forty-second and Fifty-first; Fifteenth Air.

1st Belorussian Front (Marshal Georgi K. Zhukov)
Armies—Third and Fifth Shock; Eighth Guards; Third, Thirty-third, Forty-seventh, Sixty-first and Sixty-ninth; First and Second Guards Tank; First Polish; Sixteenth Air.

2nd Belorussian Front (Marshal Konstantin K. Rokossovsky)
Armies—Second Shock; Nineteeth, Forty-third, Forty-ninth, Sixty-fifth, and Seventieth Army; Fifth Guards Tank; Fourth Air.

3rd Belorussian Front (Colonel General Ivan Chernyakhovsky to Feb; Marshal Aleksandr M. Vasilevsky to April; General Hovhannes Bagramyan)
Armies—Second and Eleventh Guards; Forty-eighth and Fiftieth; First and Third Air.

1st Ukrainian Front (Marshal Ivan S. Konev)
Armies—Third and Fifth Guards; Sixth, Thirteenth, Twenty-first, Twenty-eighth, Thirty-first, Fifty-second and Fifty-ninth; Third and Fourth Guards Tank; Second Polish; Second Air.

2nd Ukrainian Front (Marshal Rodion Malinovsky)
Armies—Seventh Guards; Fortieth, Forty-sixth and Fifty-third; Sixth Guards Tank; First Guards Horse-Mechanized Group; First and Fourth Romanian.

3rd Ukrainian Front (Marshal Fyodor I. Tolbukhin)
Armies—Fourth and Ninth Guards; Twenty-sixth, Twenty-seventh and Fifty-seventh; First Bulgarian; Fifth and Seventeenth Air.

4th Ukrainian Front (Gen. Army Andrey I. Yeremenko)
Armies—First Guards; Eighteenth, Thirty-eighth and Sixtieth; Sixth Air.

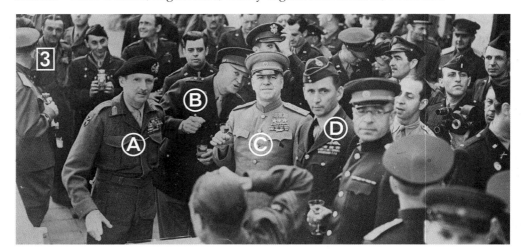

1 Stalin and Molotov.
2 Konev and memorial (in Kirov).
3a–d Montgomery, Eisenhower, Zhukov, and
Tedder.
4 Yeremenko.
5 Tolbukhin memorial (Yaroslavl).
6 Zhukov and memorial (Manege Square).
7 Rokossovsky.
8 Malinovsky memorial (Khabarovsk).

The Soviet soldier

Often derided as cannon fodder, the Russian soldier proved hardy, durable, brave, and—ultimately—successful. A contemporary German assessment—with all their prejudices—said:

"No one who belongs to the Western sphere of culture will ever be able to understand the Russian completely, or to analyze the character and soul of this Asiatic who has grown up on the far side of the border of Europe. The Russian is unfathomable. He swings from one extreme to the other without our being able to recognize the reasons for his behavior. It is possible to predict from experience how practically every other soldier in the world will behave in a given situation—but never the Russian. The characteristics of the Russian soldier, like his vast country, are strange and full of contradictions. There were units which one day repulsed a strong German attack with exemplary bravery, and on the next folded up completely. There were others which one day lost their nerve when the first shells exploded, and on the next allowed themselves, man by man, literally to be cut to pieces. The Russian is generally impervious to crises, but he can also be very sensitive to them. He has no fear of a threat to his flanks, but at the same time he can be most touchy about the flanks. He disregards all the old established rules of tactics, but he clings to the absolute letter of his own precepts. ...

"Disregard for human beings and contempt of death are other characteristics of the Russian soldier that are incomprehensible to us in such a degree. The Russian soldier climbs with complete indifference and cold-bloodedness over the bodies of hundreds of fallen comrades, in order to take up the attack on the same spot. With the same apathy he works all day long burying his dead comrades after the battle. He looks toward his own death with the same resignation. ... The Russian soldier endures cold and heat, hunger and thirst, dampness and mud, sickness and vermin, with the same equanimity. With his simple and primitive nature, all sorts of hardships cause but few reflexes within his soul. His emotions run the gamut from animal ferocity to the utmost kindliness; odious and cruel in a group, he is friendly and ready to help as an individual.

"There can be no doubt that the sum of these most diverse characteristics makes the Russian a superior soldier, who, under the direction of an understanding leader, becomes a dangerous opponent. It would be a serious error to underestimate the Russian soldier, even though he does not quite fit into the picture of modern warfare and up-to-date fighters.

"In judging the basic qualities of the Russian it should be added that by nature he is brave, as he has well demonstrated in the course of his history. In 1807 it was the Russian soldier who for the first time, at Eylau, made a stand against Napoleon after the latter's victorious march through Europe."

Above: The modern photographs of the Soviet soldiers on pp24–25 are from the archives of the British reenactment society of the 1st Battalion, 42nd "Vistula" Order of the Red Banner Guards Rifle Regiment, part of the 13th Guards Rifle Division. The banner of the 13th Guards Division is held at Central Army Museum, Moscow.

Above right: General Rodimtsev, commander of the recently formed 13th Guards Rifle Division, receives the division's new Guards Banner, March 1942.

Center right: The 50mm company mortar Model 1938 was improved in 1939 and 1940, resulting in a reduction of weight and tube length. In 1941 a new design, the PM41, appeared but it was generally superseded by more powerful 82mm mortars and by mid-1944 50mm mortars were dropped from infantry divisional TO&Es.

Below right: The M37 Sorokapyatka—little forty-five—was a 45mm anti-tank gun that was replaced in service by the longer-barreled M42 in 1942. However, with 37,354 units built from 1937 to 1943, the M37 could still be seen in the field in 1944–45.

Opposite, Below: Although many in the west considered the Red Army to be behind the times, the truth was very different, for their senior staff were always looking for ways to gain an edge. One of those they exploited was the creation of special units which fought at night. These helped keep the front-line momentum going 24 hours a day by taking over from worn-out men who had been going since daybreak. This put extreme pressure on the Axis defenders. An example of how seriously they took this concept was that while preparing for the East Prussia Offensive, within each division of nine battalions, three were dedicated to fighting in the dark. As if that were not enough, conventional troops also received extensive nocturnal training, with V Guards Rifle Corps of the Thirty-ninth Army working exclusively at night. Several battalions became specialized at night-time pursuit operations and/or as advanced detachments.

The Vistula–Oder campaign saw much use of such units, with the taking of the heavily defended Meseritz fortified area between Posen (Poznań) and Küstrin being a good example. In this action, on the night of January 29/30, the 44th Brigade used the cover of the dark to covertly creep into the complex. By the time the Germans realized what was going on it was too late, and Soviet tanks had established themselves in secure positions.

Zhukov was a staunch advocate of fighting at night, making full use of it whenever he deemed it appropriate. One of his favorite techniques was to use massive arrays of AA searchlights to illuminate German defense positions (not always a success) while his troops launched carefully planned and prepared assaults. More often, however, the Red Army made use of stealth by moving in complete darkness, or hid their men's presence with artillery barrages and/or smoke screens.

Soviet logistics units moved a huge amount of supplies at night. Despite the Soviet air force controlling the skies, Stavka saw no reason to lose any munitions that come so far over heavily damaged terrain that lacked good roads and railways. Furthermore, immense convoys of lorries pointed to the places where operations were to take place, therefore why advertise such locations? Jochen Peiper said: "The darker the night, the heavier the rain, and the stronger the snow storm, the more infallible an attack of the Russian can be expected."

The Russian infantryman was known as a Peshkom (footslogger), Streltsi (rifleman) or Frontovik (front fighter)—or Ivan to the Germans. A simple and capable soldier he or she—and there were a lot of women, over 800,000 in the Russian armed forces—was tenacious and tough, with a deep love of country, but still fearful of the commissar and his network of informers. The soldier's obligation was to fight to the death no matter what. If they didn't, their family would suffer. The soldier's uniform was well-designed and good for all seasons but often ill-fitting and of poor quality. The winter uniform was considered far superior to that of the Germans, especially the valenki; compressed felt boots. They were worn as an alternative to boots in sub-zero temperatures, allowing extra insulation to be worn inside (additional foot wraps, straw, paper). They could be worn with rubber galoshes/overshoes, covering only the foot, otherwise during times of thawing the Valenki would soak up moisture and be rendered useless.

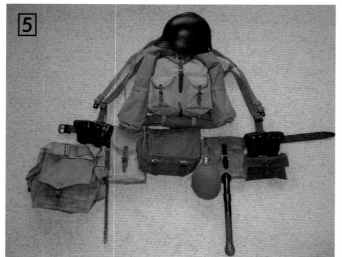

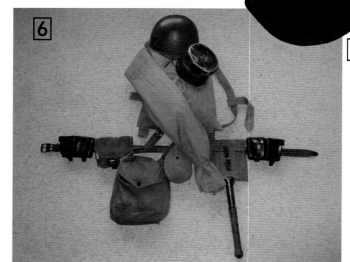

Opposite:

1 This wartime shot shows a youthful *peshkom* or *strelstsi carrying a PPSh-41 submachine gun wearing a pilotka, kirza SK boots, and an M41 shinel greatcoat*. Made of gray heavy wool with a hook front instead of buttons, large collar, slash pockets at the waist, internal pocket, and back belt, it was cut to length. When not in use it was rolled and worn over the non-firing shoulder, usually the left, with a strap securing the ends.

2 The plasch palatka *(raincoat tent) was used as a rain cape, ground sheet, shelter half, and stretcher, and had many other uses—in conjunction with the* shinel *it was used as bedding.*

3 The M43 gymnastiorka *pull-over blouse or field shirt.* was made of wool for winter and cotton for summer. Officers had two-buttoned breast-pockets (as here); other ranks had none. It had a high collar and half-length, five-buttoned front. It went with M35 or M43 breeches—there was no significant difference between the two.

4 Soviet camouflage dress was used from the start of the war—particularly by engineers, snipers, and airborne troops. The first style was the maskirovochnyi kamuflirovannyi kostium *or MKK, more often known as the* amoeba pattern. *It was also produced as a one-piece, the* maskirovochnyi kombinezon *or MK. In 1941, the leaf pattern was introduced, with different variations for summer and fall. The next variation was the* tritsvetnyi maskirovochnyi kamuflirovannyi kostium *or TTsMKK uniform that had two green foliage patterns on a yellow-tan base (as here).*

5 Obr 1938 field equipment.
• *Top:* Obr 1936 kaska *(helmet—note the comb on top),* Obr 1938 rioksak, plashch palatka, *tent poles, rope and pegs in small pouch attached to the bottom of the rioksak.*
• *Bottom:* L–R, Soomka Protivogaznaya *(respirator bag), leather belt (remyen),* web Y straps, Obr 1937 leather ammo pouch, bayonet and frog, RGD-33 *grenade pouch, ration bag, water canteen (*flyaga*—often made of glass with a heavy duty canvas cover closed by a button or wooden toggle), infantry shovel, leather ammo pouch and canvas reserve ammo pouch. Note: The anti-gas cape and salopettes would have been strapped to the top of the* rioksak *on top of the rain cape. Also, the bayonet frog was not a common issue item. It was usual for the bayonet to be permanently attached to the rifle.*

6 This image shows the basic layout for the mid/late-war rifleman's belt equipment: an EM pattern leather belt, two pairs of ammo pouches, a grenade pouch (heavy-duty canvas of variable colors, three pockets for the F1 grenade), a water canteen, gas mask bag, shovel, rain cape, simple backpack, and a mess tin.

7 The SSh-39 helmet took over from the SSh-36 (see **6**); in 1942 the SSh-40 was adopted. It had three rivets a little lower down than the SSh-39. (See p. 27.)

Right: *Our reenactor wears:*
• *The iconic* telogreika *jacket was an olive/khaki cotton, cotton wool-padded jacket designed to be worn under the greatcoat. It had a five-button front, button cuffs, minimal collar, rear belt adjustment, and was practical and cheap to produce. Two patterns were in use: the M41, issued 1941–42 only had a fall collar, same as M35* gymnastiorka. *The M43, as seen here, has a short standing collar.*
• *M35 trousers/breeches made of tight-weave olive/khaki cotton—commonly called* sharovaris.
• *M35* pilotka *sidecap made of tight-weave olive/khaki cotton. The prewar colored piping was discarded for this simpler design with a Red Star cap badge.*
• *Kirza SK high boots. Nicknamed "shit trampers," they were made from leather (the foot part), of rubber (the sole), and the upper part/stock is made of the synthetic* kirza *material—pimpled artificial leather (synthetic latex-soaked layers of stiff canvas) which was a cheap replacement for natural leather.*

He is armed with a PPS-43 SMG (as the weapon had automatic fire only, it was nicknamed "Balalaika," after the musical instrument), F1 grenade at the ready (held in left hand), and an SVT bayonet acquired as close-quarter fighting knife. His economy-made web belt has a pouch for three 35-round magazines. He carries an ecomomy-made gasmask bag, which may have contained 24-hour dry rations, extra ammunition, and grenades. There's a liberated German MG42 in the background. The Red Army summer uniforms were usually issued from May onward, so during the last days of the war, the majority of Soviet troops were still wearing winter uniforms, as the image reflects.

1 These soldiers have just been awarded the Order of Glory 2nd class to go with the 3rd. Note, too, the Guards badges (as **left**) worn correctly over the right breast pocket flap and in line with its upper left edge. Soldiers in Guards units were referred to as Gvardeytsy (guardsmen) and singularly as Gvardeyeets (guardsman). They are wearing Ushanka fur or artificial fur caps with tie up/down ear flaps. Note the different magazines for their PPSh-41 SMGs—one 71-round drum mag and two 35-round box mags. The NCO second from right has adapted a rifle sling for his PPSh-41. He is wearing a M35 pocketed gymnastiorka together with M43 shoulder boards. This was common during the intermediate period when the M43 pattern tunics were initially introduced (spring 1943) and its eventual general widespread issue. M35 pattern tunic collars were modified in the field and the fall type collars removed and adapted to appear like M43 tunic collars. The NCO at far right may well have done this. The NCO in the center appears to be wearing a U.S. Lend-Lease supplied waist belt.

2 The Berlin Reichstag amid the detritus. The Russian soldier has a PPSh-41 SMG around his neck, wears a cap (pilotka) and carries a myeshok duffel rucksack which would have held his essential items—washing kit, rations, and baccy.

3 Wearing an amoeba camouflaged smock and a SSh-40 helmet, this soldier has an RGD-33 grenade tucked into his belt. It's an offensive grenade with a narrow blast area. A fragmentation sleeve could be added to improve the kill radius thus making it a defensive grenade. It had a 4 to 5-second fuse. (See also p. 160.)

4 On the march these infantrymen carry their rolled greatcoats wrapped into a skatka bedroll. The simple myeshok did not lend itself to the greatcoat being wrapped around the outside like the earlier M36, M38, and M41 rucksacks and was worn as a bedroll over the left shoulder, sometimes wrapped inside the rain capes/tent halves (plashch palatka) or the rain cape was carried inside the rucksack itself. On occasion when a rucksack was not issued, personal possessions would be stored within the skatka bedroll. They wear caps (pilotka); note spike bayonets (shtiki) and DR-27 LMG.

Below: *A Red Army sniper, M.A. Passar was a hunter by trade, hailing from Far East Passar. He was credited with 237 kills mainly during the battle of Stalingrad where he served with the 117th Rifle Regiment. Born in 1923 he died in January 1943. He was awarded two Orders of the Red Banner, one posthumously. He's posed here holding his M91/30 Mosin-Nagant PE/PEM sniper's rifle with an unlikely affixed bayonet. He's wearing Kirza boots with puttees. These had several advantages over the high boots: they weren't so sweaty and puttees reduced the amount of detritus getting into the boot. Also, they dried quickly and gave better support to the ankle. Russians also tended to use portyanki—foot wraps, rectangular or triangular cloths that were easy to wash and dried quicker than socks (see p. 252).*

1 Mosin-Nagant M91
(of 1891).

2 Mosin-Nagant M91/30
(of 1930).
Cal—7.62mm.
Magazine, fixed—5 rounds.
Action—bolt at 90% to the body.
Range—550yd (500m) effective.
Rugged and reliable, it had a separate bayonet (3 and 4). About 37 million of all were produced 1891–1965.

5 *The Soviets, with German training and expertise, had an established sniping program before "Barbarossa." The most common scope (around 300,000 made) was the PU "short cut" scope. With x3.5 magnification and a fixed focus, it was simple to fit, basic, and robust, although to fit the M91/30 the bolt had to be modified. Also used was the PE x4 power scope (see page 27). Longer than the PU, it used optics copied from Zeiss and an adjustable eye-piece. The PEM had fixed magnification and focus for ease of production.*

6 *The carbine version of the Mosin, the M44, had a shorter barrel and permanently mounted folding cruciform bayonet.*

7 The Tokarev SVT-40 semi-automatic (self-loading) rifle.
Cal—7.62mm.
Mag—detachable, 10 rounds.
Action—gas-operated short-stroke piston.
Range—550–1,100yds (500–900m).
A complex weapon, unreliable and difficult to maintain. About 2,650,000 SVT-38 and -40 were produced.

1 PPSh-41 SMG—probably the most effective SMG of the war because it was so easy to mass-produce: some 5 million examples made.
Cal—7.62mm.
Mag—71-round drum or 35-round curved box.
Action—Blowback, open bolt.
Range—65–219yd (150–200m) effective.
Rate of fire—900-1,000 rpm.

2 and **3 PPS-43 SMG.**
Cal—7.62mm.7.62mm
Mag—35-round double-feed curved box not compatible with PPSh.
Action—Blowback, open bolt.
Range—110–219yd (100–150m) effective.
Rate of fire—100rpm effective; 600–700rpm max.
Low-cost, stamped from sheet steel, its metal stock folded onto the top of the weapon. Over 2.5million were produced, it was ideal for AFV crew.

4 M1895 Nagant revolver.
Cal—7.62mm.
Mag—7-round cylinder.
Action—double/single: cock and trigger (Officers); trigger only (the rest).
Range—50yd (46m) effective.
The Nagant took time to load and had a heavy trigger pull. Over 2 million produced.

5 TT-33 Tokarev semi-automatic pistol and holster with spare magazine.
Cal—7.62mm.
Mag—8-round detachable box.
Action—recoil to cycle the action.
Range—55yd (50m) effective.
Robust, it was a heavy hitter. Over were 1,330,000 produced.

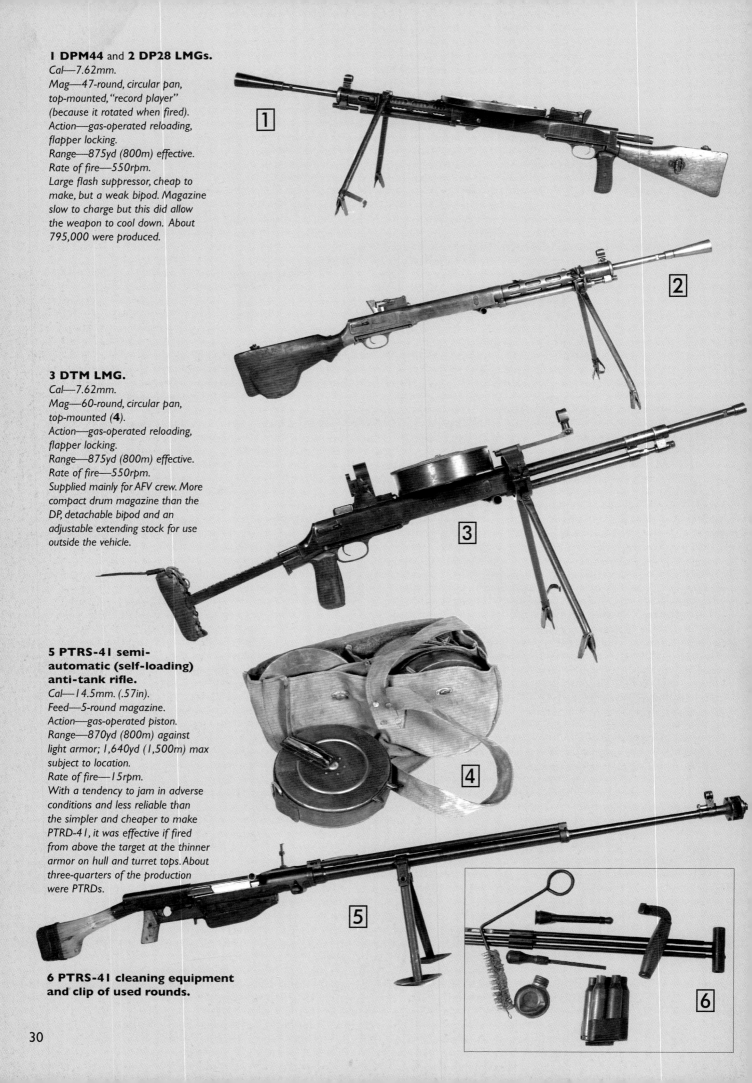

1 DPM44 and **2 DP28 LMGs.**
Cal—7.62mm.
Mag—47-round, circular pan, top-mounted, "record player" (because it rotated when fired).
Action—gas-operated reloading, flapper locking.
Range—875yd (800m) effective.
Rate of fire—550rpm.
Large flash suppressor, cheap to make, but a weak bipod. Magazine slow to charge but this did allow the weapon to cool down. About 795,000 were produced.

3 DTM LMG.
Cal—7.62mm.
*Mag—60-round, circular pan, top-mounted (**4**).*
Action—gas-operated reloading, flapper locking.
Range—875yd (800m) effective.
Rate of fire—550rpm.
Supplied mainly for AFV crew. More compact drum magazine than the DP, detachable bipod and an adjustable extending stock for use outside the vehicle.

5 PTRS-41 semi-automatic (self-loading) anti-tank rifle.
Cal—14.5mm. (.57in).
Feed—5-round magazine.
Action—gas-operated piston.
Range—870yd (800m) against light armor; 1,640yd (1,500m) max subject to location.
Rate of fire—15rpm.
With a tendency to jam in adverse conditions and less reliable than the simpler and cheaper to make PTRD-41, it was effective if fired from above the target at the thinner armor on hull and turret tops. About three-quarters of the production were PTRDs.

6 PTRS-41 cleaning equipment and clip of used rounds.

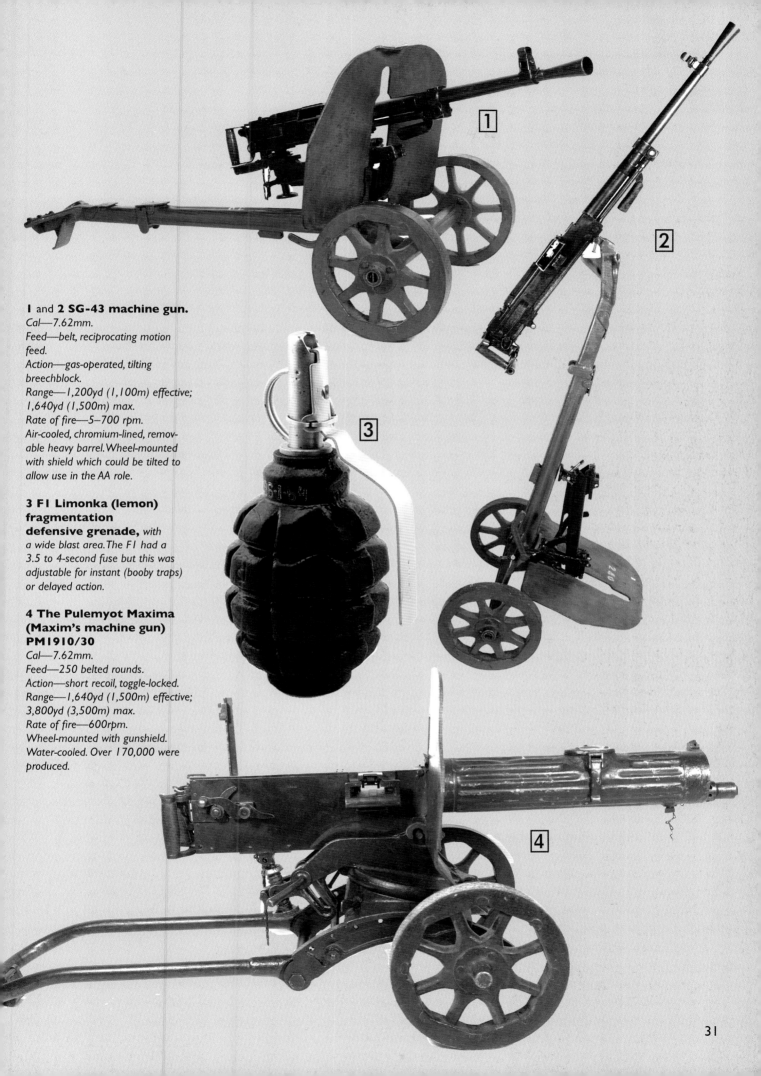

1 and **2 SG-43 machine gun.**
Cal—7.62mm.
Feed—belt, reciprocating motion feed.
Action—gas-operated, tilting breechblock.
Range—1,200yd (1,100m) effective; 1,640yd (1,500m) max.
Rate of fire—5–700 rpm.
Air-cooled, chromium-lined, removable heavy barrel. Wheel-mounted with shield which could be tilted to allow use in the AA role.

3 F1 Limonka (lemon) fragmentation defensive grenade, *with a wide blast area. The F1 had a 3.5 to 4-second fuse but this was adjustable for instant (booby traps) or delayed action.*

4 The Pulemyot Maxima (Maxim's machine gun) PM1910/30
Cal—7.62mm.
Feed—250 belted rounds.
Action—short recoil, toggle-locked.
Range—1,640yd (1,500m) effective; 3,800yd (3,500m) max.
Rate of fire—600rpm.
Wheel-mounted with gunshield. Water-cooled. Over 170,000 were produced.

Above: *A Red Army infantry group advances along a woodland road. The machine gunners are serving a Maxim M1910/30 weapon. Upgraded in 1930, one of the innovations was the introduction of the corrugated water jacket visible here. The wheeled Sokolov carriage is unchanged but here the shield has been removed. The submachine gun is the PPS-42/43 that featured a banana-shaped magazine.*

Above right: *One of the best HMGs of the war, the Soviet DShK Model 1938 weighed in at 75lb and a whopping 346lb on its wheeled mount. It fired 12.7mm (.50in) rounds to around 2,500 yards. It was fed by a drum magazine holding 30 rounds or could be belt-fed. It was the main Soviet HMG of the war and is still in service today.*

Below right: *Soviet infantry enter a burning town and, by their demeanor, clearly expect no opposition. The Maxim machine gun is being towed on a Sokolov wheeled mount.*

Above: A Soviet mortar team of 3rd Ukrainian Front are congratulated by their spotter on a successful shoot. This 120mm model was issued in units of six per rifle regiment and could achieve 15 shots per minute up to a range of 5,500m in the hands of a veteran crew.

Left: The Red Army employed a number of 82mm mortars. The 82-PM-41 had built-in wheels to help mobility—the main difference between it and the Model 1937. Note on their backs the Mosin-Nagant M38 carbines, the usual weapons for gun and mortar crew.

Below left: Headed by a captured VW Kübelwagen, a unit of Katyusha (the nickname is thought to come from the girl featured in a patriotic song dreaming of her soldier love at the front) BM-13 rocket launchers, mounted on Lend-Lease Studebaker US6 truck pass through a town in Bulgaria. (See also pp. 38–39.)

Soviet armor

There's always so much written about German armor that it's easy to underplay the role of Soviet armor. As with the Western Allies, whose Shermans and Cromwells weren't a match for Tigers and Panthers, one on one, quantity, bravery, and initiative, ensured that the Germans' great strengths were negated. In the end, the availability and serviceability of Soviet armor counted for more than impressive armor and a big gun.

The T-34 everyone knows about, and in its later form with the 85mm gun it was a match for all but the heavier German tanks. However, with 1,200 rolling off the production lines each month, 22,500 were completed by the end of the war, as against fewer than 6,500 Panthers and 2,000 Tiger I and IIs.

With its heavy armor and 122mm main gun, the IS-2 Model 1944 was more than capable of taking on the heaviest German tanks. Indeed, in a series of engagements in January 1945 around Kielce and Lisow, IS-2s were involved in wiping out a company of sPzAbt 424's Tiger IIs.

Like the Germans, the Soviets made use of tank destroyers—from the lighter SU-76M to the heavyweight ISU-152, although the latter had a very slow rate of fire and was best employed in ambushes or as SP artillery.

3 *T-34/85 in Gliwice (see also p. 92). Jochen Peiper was a fan of the T-34. "This medium-heavy tank with the American Christie drive assembly represented an exceptionally able solution. Main characteristics are: speed, covering of space, and a great suitability for all types of terrain by virtue of favorable ground pressure. With these qualities, our tanks never could compete. ... The heavy oil motor was a very much superior one to the German gasoline motor in performance and economy. Due to its additional fuel tank, the T-34 drives without stopping 350km (on a fairly good road). The speed lies between 60–70km/h and it traverses terrain and bridges where other lighter tanks fail without exception. Of advantage is also the low silhouette and streamlined construction. The 7.62cm gun is very good. The quantity of ammunition carried along is amazing. ... If one likes to talk about the decisive weapon of the Eastern front, then the honors unquestionably have to go to the T-34."*

4 *IS-2s in Berlin. The assault on Germany's capital saw small units of around five IS-2s supported by a company of assault infantry, with sappers and flamethrowers. When Berlin fell, more than 67 IS-2s had been destroyed in action, many by the "Faustniks" (Panzerfaüste).*

5 *The SU-76M (the original version ceased production after only 560 had been built because of unreliable engines) was based on a lengthened version of the T-70 light tank chassis and armed with a 76mm gun—the M1942, ZiS-3. Its simple construction and sturdiness made it the second most produced Soviet AFV of the war (after the T-34)—over 13,700 SU-76Ms built.*

6 *An SU-85, covered with infantrymen, drives through Hungary during the winter of 1944–45. This vehicle was basically created to counter the Panther and Tiger tanks deployed by the Wehrmacht in 1943. It married the proven chassis of a T-34 with an 85mm gun.*

Soviet artillery

Jochen Peiper's view on Soviet artillery was that, "After wasting their effect in the beginning, the Russians adopted the basic German principles. The massing of fire and the creation of centers of artillery positions became more and more apparent. The attacks of the last year were always preceded by a long and continuous preparatory barrage. The fire control disclosed a very systematic guiding line. Dugouts and field fortifications, which could not have been pierced by the highly sensitive artillery ammunition of the Western powers, was usually destroyed by the insensitive Russian shells by delayed explosions. In spite of it, the results were mostly in no comparison to the mass-scaled commitment. However, Russian artillery has learned a lot and is in my opinion in a state of definite development."

He emphasized the effect of the Katyusha:

"The Russians employed them during the last year of the war in large numbers. A medium-sized Studebaker truck was used which carried as superstructure a sliding rail device, which in turn carried, I believe, 14 medium-sized mortars. [16 x 132mm on the BM-13-16]. *The opponent committed this weapon in an extremely quick and flexible manner.*

Although the morale effect is greater than the damage done, our attacking infantry was often forced to dig in and give up its objective. This was especially true at night when they shot a mixture of explosives and flaming oil. Due to the easy concentration of the mobile vehicles, it was possible to cover a large area and great distances with a dense fire distribution. I have experienced salvos where on a width of 800m one impact was located next to the other! The 'Stalin Organ' never could stop a tank attack, however, it did succeed in separating the infantry following up."

Left: *A Soviet rocket barrage. Unusually these launching systems have been removed from their transport. This suggests that counter battery fire is unlikely or that the vehicles were unnecessary as this firing pattern was likely to be reproduced as the target was a fixed one, such as a fortress complex.*

Below left: *Soviet gunners using a German PaK 40 7.5cm anti-tank gun against its former owners. The use of such so-called (by the Russians) "trophy" weapons was limited by the lack of spares and ammunition. Nevertheless, any gun is a good gun in certain situations.*

Below: *This mortar, the 280mm M1939 Br-5, was the heaviest artillery piece deployed by the Red Army. Information about the combat operations of this weapon is limited as its use was indicative of an offensive. 45 of this type were built at the famous Barrikady factory in Stalingrad. They were used at the sieges of Posen and Königsberg as well as the assault on Küstrin.*

1 A female air armorer poses for the camera as she prepares to rearm the wing mounted 23mm VYa cannon. This weapon had originally been designed for use in a tank. It was not an ideal weapon for an aircraft as it was heavy and required a very deliberate angle of approach as the rounds had a tendency to ricochet.

2 An Il-2 flight pulls out from an attack on Axis transports. By 1944 the Red Air Fleet commanded the sky over the Eastern Front. Capable of carrying payloads as diverse as rockets, anti-tank bombs, and 37mm anti-tank guns, it was a formidable enemy.

3 Ivan Kozhedub is credited with over 60 solo victories—the highest scoring Soviet and Allied fighter pilot of World War II.

The Red Air Force

The Luftwaffe's initial superiority in 1941–42—over 3,000 Russian aircraft destroyed in three days, many without leaving the ground—should not hide the fact that Soviet airpower ended the war on top. The Soviet Air Force (*Voyenno-voz-dushnyye sily*—VVS) had become one of the largest and most effective in the world and the reason for this wasn't just numbers and bravery—although, of course, both helped. When the Russian offensive started on January 13, 1945, the five armies were supported by 7,700 aircraft. As the front lines moved forward, the VVS had to construct forward strips, sometimes even making use of German autobahns. The Germans desperately brought aircraft to the east from the west, but it was no use. As Premchand Sanu Kainikara says:

"In the battle for Berlin which lasted two months and ended the war in Europe, the Luftwaffe fought with desperation and distinction, flying more than 1,100 sorties a day with a daily loss in excess of 200 aircraft until all airfields were overrun by the Allied forces. The Russians were by then averaging 15,000 sorties daily and in April alone the Soviet Air Force carried out 215,000 combat flights, dropping about 45,000 tons of bombs on enemy targets. During the seventeen-day Berlin operations, the VVS flew 91,384 sorties, fought 1,317 air combats, and claimed 1,232 enemy aircraft destroyed in the air and on the ground, for a loss of 527 aircraft."

4 Il-2 Shturmovik ground attack aircraft warm up their engines. These aircraft are flying in support of 1st Ukrainian Front. The workhorse of the Soviet air forces' ground attack machines, the Il-2 was feared by Axis ground forces who nicknamed it the "Black Death."

5 The Yakovlev Yak-3 reached front-line units during summer 1944. It proved to be a great success. This is a preserved Yak-3U, the last of the line that didn't enter production because the war ended.

6 The Yakovlev Yak-9 entered service in October 1942 and first saw combat in late 1942. The Yak-9U entered service in late 1944 and helped win air superiority for the Red Air Force. This one is seen having crash-landed in Sweden on August 30, 1944.

7 Tupolev Tu-2 light bombers. Mass produced in Siberia from late 1941, the Tu-2 was a fast light bomber that was popular with its four man crews as it could sustain considerable damage and still remain airborne. By 1945 there were 279 such aircraft deployed at the front, mainly with VI Aviation Corps operating over the northern sector of the drive into Germany.

Armored trains

The Western Front had its railroad guns and one or two armored trains were used to police the Mediterranean shores, but it was in the east, with its greater distances and bandit country, that they flourished. Used initially to keep the supply lines open and to help fight partisans, latterly the Germans found them useful in their defensive battles. They were sturdy and, even when damaged, could be repaired or rebuilt unless they had been derailed or the lines cut behind them. The Germans had looked to increase the numbers significantly in 1944, intending to build eight BP-44s, 16 heavy scout car trains, 46 armored pursuit cars, and five armored railcars. The worsening war situation and loss of steel mills in the Ukraine meant that few of these were completed although construction continued into 1945.

The Russians were also major builders of armored trains. In 1941 they had 26 light and 11 heavy armored trains with 47 locomotives, 85 light and 27 heavy wagons. Many were lost in the first months of *"Barbarossa"* and were—in typical German fashion—taken into their inventory. The Russians rebuilt and quickly built up the number of trains—by November 1942, 78 new ones were ready. From late 1942, 21 of the final standardized design, the BP-43 using T-34 76.2mm turrets, were built. The Soviet force settled at 61 battalions, each usually of two trains.

Right: *Command car of German BP-44 armored train at Bratislava's Rendez Railway Museum. Eleven BP-42s were built and a number were reconfigured to this standard before it was decided to add extra anti-tank firepower producing the BP-44. The BP-42 trains were configured with two ATG-2 armored tenders, ATG-3 artillery wagons housing 7.2cm or 10cm howitzers, an ATG-5 infantry wagon, an ATG-4 command wagon, then an ATG-6 2cm Flakvierling wagon. Additionally, there were two tanks, carried in ATG-7 tank-carrier wagons (often Czech 38Ts) and then at both ends were ATG-8 pusher cars loaded with ballast and track-mending equipment. In the BP-44, the pusher cars were replaced with ATG-9 Panzerjäger wagons carrying PzKpfw IV turrets.*

Below right: *The one-off Panzertriebwagen Nr.16 (PzTrWg 16) appeared in late 1942 and fought until the end of the war, patrolling southwest Poland until it was captured at Neustadt during the advance of Soviet 61st Army. It was powered by a WR550D14 diesel locomotive and was armed with Putilov 76.2mm Mod. 02/30 turreted field guns. From mid-1944 T-34 turrets were added.*

Above: *Originally named Eva, the renamed Botond fought in the Soviet Union during 1941–43 against partisans around the Bryansk Forest. Later, it took part in Unternehmen Frühlingserwachen around Lake Balaton. It was armed with a 36M 20mm AP gun, a 22M 8cm field gun, and two 31M 8mm machine guns.*

Left: *A Red Army BP-43 armored train negotiates a repaired railroad line. BP are the Cyrillic initials for armored train, the number is the year of initial production. This model included an armored locomotive, two-four wagons each carrying a single T-34 turret with a 76mm gun and an anti-aircraft wagon with either heavy, 12.7mm machine guns or two light, 20mm anti-aircraft guns. German destruction of railroad tracks made the operation of such weapon's systems problematic, consequently their use was often restricted to anti-partisan operations behind the front line, particularly in Ukraine where nationalist groups fought on into the mid-1950s.*

Below: *A wrecked BP-42 German train lies abandoned in a siding. A Soviet engineering officer and others can be seen inspecting the turret and other parts of this weapon's system. Beyond the last wagon an unarmored locomotive is visible.*

1 *The men at the top. Increasingly Hitler tried to control every troop movement and every engagement. The men around him couldn't tell him to stop. Here, L–R, Großadmiral Erich Raeder, GFM Walther von Brauchitsch, GFM Wilhelm Keitel, and Reichsführer-SS Heinrich Himmler—the latter tried to run an army group but turned out to be inept.*

2 *Generaloberst Heinz Guderian ended the war being sent on sick leave after clashing with Hitler in his role as Acting Chief of the General Staff of the OKH. (Art by Wolfgang Willrich.)*

3 *The last Chief of Staff of the OKH, General der Infanterie Hans Krebs committed suicide in the Führerbunker on May 2, 1945.*

4 *Generaloberst Gotthard Heinrici (R) replaced Himmler as Commander-in-Chief of Heeresgruppe Weichsel but was dismissed for disobeying orders on April 29. He's seen with GFM Günther von Kluge who committed suicide when accused of involvement in the July 20 Bomb plot.*

5 *Brutal GFM Ferdinand Schörner (left, while still a general and seen with Finnish Oberstleutnant Wahren) was promoted to his rank and named the last Commander-in-Chief of the OKH in Hitler's testament.*

6 *To the left, clad in a Waffen-SS camouflage smock, stands Obergruppenführer Josef "Sepp" Dietrich. He commanded Hitler's bodyguard and, in the end, the Leibstandarte in the field. His last command was 6. SS-Panzerarmee during the retreat to Vienna.*

7 *General der Infanterie Theodor Busse commanded 9. Armee in 1945, fighting at the Seelow Heights before being trapped in the Halbe Pocket.*

The German leaders

While most German army training and leadership were of the highest level operationally, these abilities and professionalism did not reach the top where politics, cronyism, and complicity in genocide were more likely paths to high office. Hitler had always had doubts about the army. He allowed the rise of the SS, and as the Soviet Union held and then pushed the invaders back, by 1944 Hitler's mistrust of his army generals—exacerbated by the failed July 20 Bomb plot—led to the increasing involvement of political figures in running the military. Guderian in *Panzer Leader* talks often about Hitler's arbitrary and often illogical hiring and firing. While many of the men running armies and army corps were extremely capable, they were unable to stop the Allies' encroachment closer and closer to Germany. And as the inexorable end got nearer, so more of the generals were replaced by hard men who tried to fulfill Hitler's every command. The result was death, destruction, and total defeat.

8 *Generaloberst Georg-Hans Reinhardt was given command of Heeresgruppe Mitte in August 1944 and was retired in January after being pushed out of Poland into northern Prussia.*

9 *General der Artillerie Helmuth Weidling commanded the defenses of Berlin from April 23. He surrendered the city to Soviet General Vasily Chuikov on May 2.*

10 *Lothar Rendulic played an important role in the fighting in Scandinavia, commanding 20. Gebirgsarmee from June 1944, Heeresgruppe Kurland (Courland), and Heeresgruppe Nord from January to March 1945. Postwar he was found guilty of murdering hostages in Yugoslavia but was acquitted for the scorched earth tactics in Finland.*

The German soldier

On March 15, 1945, the U.S. War Department produced its TM-E 30-451, Handbook on German Military Forces. Its opening section on the German soldier discusses its continued defiance in the face of the overwhelming likelihood of defeat:

"When the German Panzer divisions struck out across the Polish frontier at dawn on 1 September 1, 1939, no one could predict the scope, intensity, and duration of the armed conflict which they were precipitating. The German Army then was fresh, vigorous, expansive, and obviously superior to its contemporaries. Its weapons were new and shiny; its tactics and techniques—the old doctrines adapted to the new conditions—were untried; its officers and men were young and full of enthusiasm. A career of easy conquest seemed to open up before it.

After five and a half years of ever-growing battle against ever-stronger enemies, the German Army in 1945 looks, at first glance, much the worse for wear. It is beset on all sides and is short of everything. It has suffered appalling casualties and must resort to old men, boys, invalids, and unreliable foreigners for its cannon fodder. Its weapons and tactics seem not to have kept pace with those of the armies opposing it; its supply system in the field frequently breaks down. Its position is obviously hopeless, and it can only be a question of time until the last German soldier is disarmed, and the once proud German Army of the great Frederick and of Scharnhorst, of Ludendorff and of Hitler, exists no more as a factor to be reckoned with.

Yet this shabby, war-weary machine has struggled on in a desperate effort to postpone its inevitable demise. At the end of 1944 it was still able to mount an offensive calculated to delay for months the definitive piercing of the western bulwarks of Germany. Despite the supposed chronic disunity at the top, disaffection among the officer corps, and disloyalty in the rank and file, despite the acute lack of weapons, ammunition, fuel, transport, and human reserves, the German Army seems to function with its old precision and to overcome what appear to be insuperable difficulties with remarkable speed. Only by patient and incessant hammering from all sides can its collapse be brought about.

The cause of this toughness, even in defeat, is not generally appreciated. It goes much deeper than the quality of weapons, the excellence of training and leadership,

PANZERGRENADIER

These three of a series of drawings on the theme of Panzergrenadiere are by German artist Walter Gotschke (1912–2000) on order of the magazine Signal in 1942. He was part of a Propaganda-Kompanie on the Russian front. The Panzergrenadiers highlight the top echelon of infantry, whose transportation and weaponry meant they could keep up with the slashing attacks by armored units. Of course, it paints a slightly rose-tinted view of German mechanization. In fact, even by the end of the war when the Allies were using specialized vehicles—the Kangaroos—to deliver troops to the battlefield, the German Army in the main moved on foot with much of its artillery horse-drawn. Some Panzergrenadier units were fortunate enough to be equipped with SdKfz 251 halftracks, but most were trucked. In 1943, of the 226 Panzergrenadier battalions, only around ten percent were carried in halftracks.

45

UNIFORMS

By 1939 the German uniform was practical and functional but as the war progressed and materials became scarce, something had to give and everything was pared to the minimum. Take the stages of development of the Feldbluse (jacket) as an example. The M36 was the traditional feldgrau (field gray) with dark bottle-green collars and shoulder straps with the national emblem (Hoheitsabzeichen) above the right breast pleated pocket. It had a five-button front and was tailored to fit. The M40 had no green collar or shoulder straps.

The M41 had six buttons but was made from inferior synthetic and/or recycled materials. The M42 saw the pocket pleats removed. The M43 was simpler still with no proper lining. The M44 was shortened and was a drab greenish-brown referred to as Feldgrau 44.

Pants, too, changed over time, progressing from the M36 slate gray (steingrau) M36 to the superior M43 with reinforced seating, belt loops, and narrower corded ends for gaiters and ankle boots.

The iconic jackboot (Marschstiefel) was expensive. The M37 ankle boot was cheaper to make as it used less leather, but was initially only used during training and light duties. As shortages increased, the M44 ankle boot became standard issue to all, with putties or gaiters to protect the ankle.

Oversized fur or sheepskin overcoats were often made locally to a standard pattern. Almost all were reversible, had huge pockets, fur or heavy wool collars, and buttoned in most cases by means of wooden toggles. Designed to go over all webbing and belt-order, it could be cut to length. Color was the natural hide, more often a dirty off-white.

Hooded snow suits, some reversible, with mitts were issued and for some ski-troops (Skijäger), buttoned balaclavas, cylindrical neck warmers, and heavily lined, trigger friendly mitts were essential additions. As with all armies, anything better was used; Soviet winter footwear and clothing being especially prized.

the soundness of tactical and strategic doctrine, or the efficiency of control at all echelons. It is to be found in the military tradition which is so deeply ingrained in the whole character of the German nation and which alone makes possible the interplay of these various factors of strength to their full effectiveness.

The German Army of 1939 was a model of efficiency, the best product of the concentrated military genius of the most scientifically military of nations. A study of the German Army of 1945, however, older and wiser, hardened and battle-tested, cornered and desperate as it is, will show best how this military science and military genius operate in the practical exigencies of long-drawn-out total war."

This does not emphasize strongly enough the main fears of the German troops: what the Bolshevik hordes would do to their country and womenfolk should they be victorious; what the Gestapo would do to their families if they were seen to have failed in their duties—*Sippenhaft*, the so-called "blood loyalty," that allowed the Nazis to make a person's relations and family liable for punishment and death should that person fail to live up to their duty; and the fear of direct action against them, personally: over 50,000 German soldiers were executed during the war for desertion or insubordination.

Foreign troops

The Germans were reasonably successful in raising "volunteers" from captured enemy soldiers. Some of these were simply "Hiwis"— *Hilfswilliger*, auxiliary volunteers who were willing to help wherever needed. Others were recruited to fight. The Germans assumed initially that their motivation was political. While some were, indeed, motivated to fight against communism and Soviet Russia, that was far from being the main reason, as a postwar report outlined:

"the bulk of the volunteers … I am convinced, did not enlist to fight for the cause but solely for the purpose of gaining personal advantages, immediately or within the near future. Many of these men attempted to demonstrate strongly an idealism which neither existed nor governed their actions. Distress, simply, prompted most of them to change sides. The horrible conditions prevailing in most of the camps induced them to consider this last hope, with complete disregard for all possible consequences. The prospect of good food, clothing and all the privileges of a German soldier as compared to the hunger, cold, and sickness which were certain if they remained captive for a longer period of time, was the motive for their enlisting."

1 Der Spieß—Hauptfeldwebel, company sergeant-major—identified by his double Kolbenringe (piston rings) on his forearms. He's wearing a "crusher" cap, jackboots, and an M40 jacket.

2 This soldier carries an MP 40 and wears a lightweight camouflage smock, with tan and water (Sumpfmuster) pattern outside and white inside.

3 and **4** German war artists were important for propaganda. These muddy soldiers are from Soldatenblätter für Feier und Freizeit—a Knapsack publication. The MG34 gunner wears a locally made winter coat and Russian boots.

DIE
POLIZEI
IM FRONTEINSATZ

1 The German infantry squad was the building block of the army; in turn, it was built around the machine gun team.

2 Time for a new barrel. Note the two tank destruction badges on his right sleeve.

3 Two of Himmler's enforcers—the SS and the Ordnungspolizei. The "Orpos" were directly involved in the Nazis' genocidal activities working with the Einsatzgruppen. Note the police-issue M35 Bergmann SMG.

4 Trench scene in Russia. Note rifle-grenade attachment— Gewehrsprenggranate—for the Kar98k.

5 Weary soldiers during a pause in the action. Note the carry bags for the M24 grenades.

6 By 1944 there were huge variations in uniform. Hooded snow suits, some reversible, with mitts were issued and for some, such as ski-troops (Skijäger), there were buttoned balaclavas, cylindrical neck warmers, and heavily lined, trigger friendly, mitts.

7 German Gebirgsjäger are identified by the Edelweiss badge (on cap) which was used by both army and SS troops. These men are moving a 75mm GebK 36 mountain gun by horse in the mountains of Albania. The country was liberated by partisans by the beginning of December 1944.

Opposite: *Some Volkssturm units fought well—the 3/115 Siemensstadt Battalion in Berlin made up of 770 mainly WWI veterans is always held up as an example. 26 of them won the Iron Cross. Other units, more sensibly, slipped away into the shadows discarding weapons and uniforms when the Allies arrived. The Red Army regarded them as semi-terrorists and treated them in the same manner that the Germans had treated Soviet partisans—with little mercy. These photos show the German propaganda view of the Volkssturm preparing for combat:*

1 and **2** *Berlin—taking the oath, November 1944.*

3, 4 *Parading with Panzerschreck and Panzerfäuste.*

5 *A youthful Volkssturmmann with an MP 40.*

6 *Training with an MG34.*

7 *Learning how the Panzerfaust works.*

8 *Older weapons were impressed into service.*

9 *Trenches were prepared.*

Above: *Allied propaganda leaflet—"Read and pass on to your comrades! Volkssturm—a new Hitler adventure! ...What does it mean?*
- *Hitler has no faith in the Wehrmacht*
- *Hitler will allow the lost war onto German soil and the families of soldiers will pay the price.*
- *Senseless annihilation."*

Volkssturm

Hitler's decree on the formation of the Volkssturm

On September 25, 1944, it was decreed that every male between 16 and 60 not engaged in war work should join the *Volkssturm* (People's Storm):

"After five years of tough struggle, as a result of the failure of all our European allies, the enemy is on some fronts near or on the German borders. He is trying hard to smash our Reich, to destroy the German people and their social order. His ultimate goal is the extermination of the German race.

As in the autumn of 1939, we are again completely alone facing our enemies. Then, in a few years we succeeded in solving the most important military problems through the first large-scale deployment of our German people's power, and in securing the existence of the Reich and thus Europe for years to come. While the enemy now believes they can strike the last blow, we are determined to carry out the second large-scale mission of our people. We must and we will succeed, as in the years 1939 to 1941, by relying exclusively on our own strength, not only to break the enemy's will to destroy, but to throw it back again and keep it from the Reich until a peace that safeguards the future of Germany, its allies and thus Europe is guaranteed.

We oppose with the total commitment of all German people the desire of our Jewish international enemies to annihilate us.

In order to strengthen the active forces of our Wehrmacht and in particular to wage relentless struggle wherever the enemy wants to set foot on German soil, I therefore call on all German men who are capable of armed forces to engage in combat. I order:

1. In the districts of the Greater German Reich, the German Volkssturm is to be formed from all men capable of arms between the ages of 16 and 60. They will defend their home soil with all weapons and means, as far as they appear suitable.

2. The Gauleiter in their districts is responsible for setting up and managing the German Volkssturm. Above all, they should make use of the most capable organizers and leaders of the tried and tested institutions of the party, the SA, SS, the NSKK and the Hitlerjugend."

Their first "uniform" was an armband (**Below**). Determined that Germans would fight the Bolsheviks to the last man, as head of the Replacement Army, Reichsführer-SS Heinrich Himmler controlled the organization; Bormann was in charge of the administration. The results were, predictably, mixed, so much so that on January 28, 1945, Hitler had to issue another order:

"The experiences in the East show that Volkssturm ... units used independently have only very little fighting strength and can be smashed quickly. The fighting strength of these units, which are usually strong in numbers but insufficiently armed for modern fighting, is incomparably higher when they are used within the framework of the field army. I therefore order that when Volkssturm units as well as troops of the field army are available in a combat sector, mixed combat groups (brigades) are to be set up under unified command, so as to give support and backbone to the Volkssturm units."

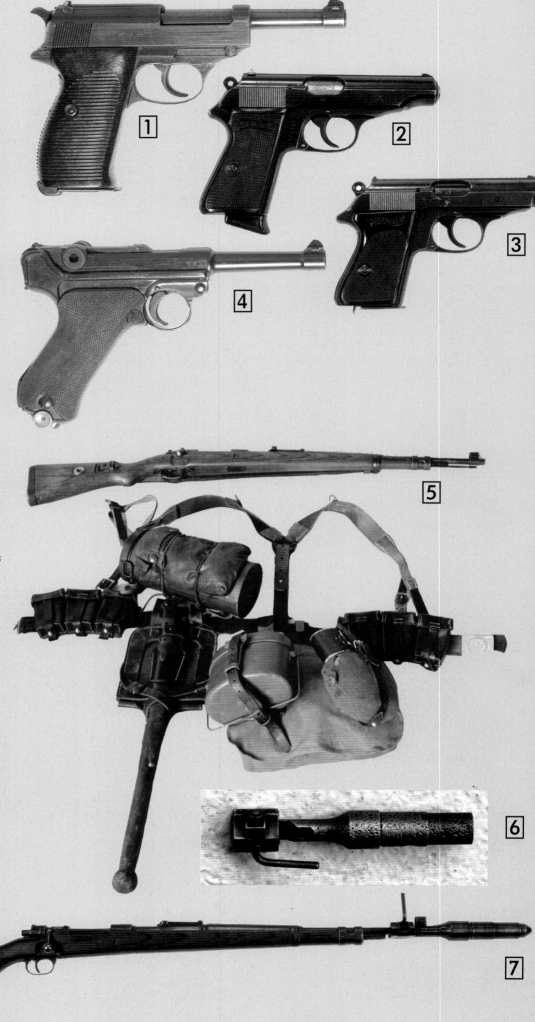

1 Pistole 38 (P38)
Cal—9mm.
Mag—detachable, 8 rounds.
Action—Short recoil, locked breech.
Range—55yd (50m).
In 1938 the P38 was adopted as the standard sidearm of the Wehrmacht. Designed with mass production in mind, the P38 demanded far less skilled labor than did the Parabellum 08.

2 Walther PP pistol
Cal—7.65mm.
Mag—detachable, 8 rounds.
Action—blowback.
Range—55yd (50m).
The standard pistol of the German Luftwaffe.

3 PPK pistol
Cal—7.65mm.
Mag—detachable, 7 rounds.
Action—blowback.
Range—30yd (25m).
The PPK, like the PP, was widely used by Germany's armed forces and was also produced in France, Hungary, and Turkey.

4 Parabellum Pistole '08 Luger
Cal—9mm.
Mag—detachable, 8 rounds.
Action—Short recoil, toggle-locked.
Range—55yd (50m).
Originally produced in Berlin, from 1914 weapons were produced at Erfurt where the lug for the famous shoulder-stock was added.

5 Karabiner Kar 98k carbine
Cal—7.92mm.
Mag—integral, 5 rounds.
Action—Mauser turn bolt.
Range—550–1,100yds (500–900m). In the early 1930s the design was simplified to facilitate mass production, and the resulting weapon was adopted as the standard rifle for the new Wehrmacht in 1935. It was produced by the millions. It could also fire a rifle grenade (6 and 7).

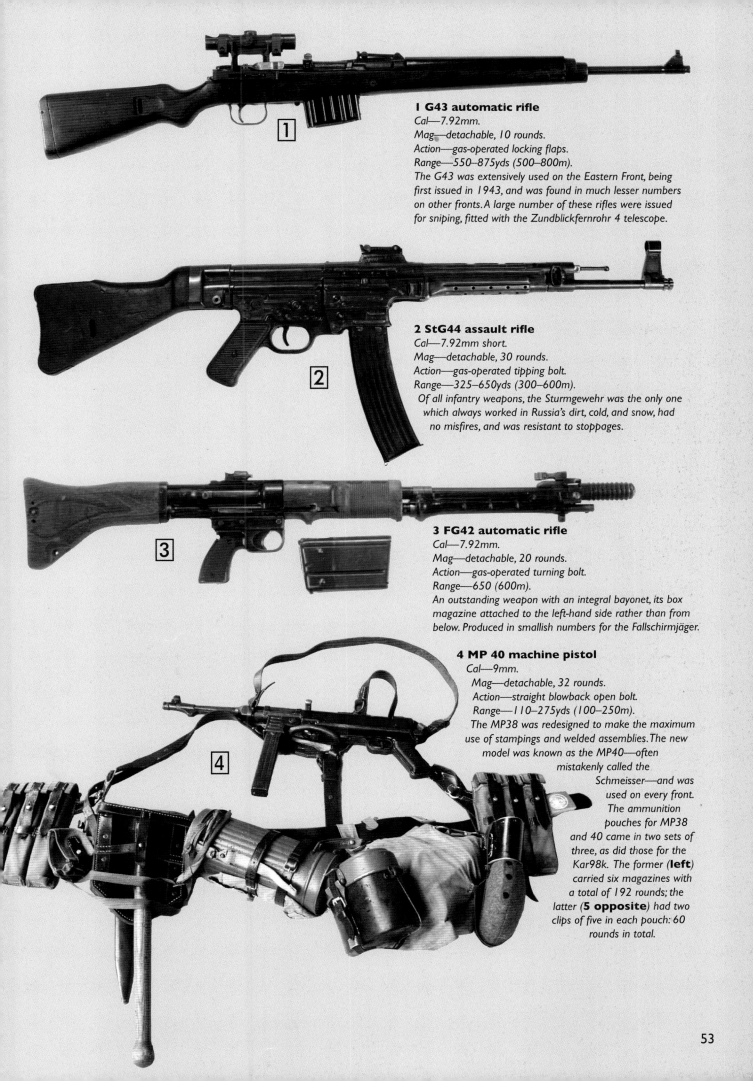

1 G43 automatic rifle

Cal—7.92mm.
Mag—detachable, 10 rounds.
Action—gas-operated locking flaps.
Range—550–875yds (500–800m).
The G43 was extensively used on the Eastern Front, being first issued in 1943, and was found in much lesser numbers on other fronts. A large number of these rifles were issued for sniping, fitted with the Zundblickfernrohr 4 telescope.

2 StG44 assault rifle

Cal—7.92mm short.
Mag—detachable, 30 rounds.
Action—gas-operated tipping bolt.
Range—325–650yds (300–600m).
Of all infantry weapons, the Sturmgewehr was the only one which always worked in Russia's dirt, cold, and snow, had no misfires, and was resistant to stoppages.

3 FG42 automatic rifle

Cal—7.92mm.
Mag—detachable, 20 rounds.
Action—gas-operated turning bolt.
Range—650 (600m).
An outstanding weapon with an integral bayonet, its box magazine attached to the left-hand side rather than from below. Produced in smallish numbers for the Fallschirmjäger.

4 MP 40 machine pistol

Cal—9mm.
Mag—detachable, 32 rounds.
Action—straight blowback open bolt.
Range—110–275yds (100–250m).
The MP38 was redesigned to make the maximum use of stampings and welded assemblies. The new model was known as the MP40—often mistakenly called the Schmeisser—and was used on every front. The ammunition pouches for MP38 and 40 came in two sets of three, as did those for the Kar98k. The former (**left**) carried six magazines with a total of 192 rounds; the latter (**5 opposite**) had two clips of five in each pouch: 60 rounds in total.

1 and **2 Maschinengewehr 34 (MG34)** *This was an impressive and versatile weapon that could meet almost every possible requirement. Firing up to 900 7.92mm rounds/min it was the most advanced MG of its day. It could be fired from the hip, on the ground with its bipod, and from an MG-Lafette tripod in the sustained fire role (**Opposite, Top** with MG42 in place). A lightweight tripod was also available for AA use. The drawbacks were that it was a complex and expensive weapon to produce, prone to malfunction in poor weather/ground conditions. It was belt fed (**2**) or used single (**1**) or double drum magazines. Its effective range was 220–2,200 yd (200-2,000m).*

3 *The basic equipment of the German machine gunner—in this case an MG34. Note pistol and at **A** the equipment pouch for the gunner that included cleaning materials etc. The white mitt that was used to handle hot barrels was available to be used at a moment's notice. Barrel changes on German MGs were needed regularly because of the high rate of fire, and tubes containing spares were carried by the second man of the two-man team. The German infantry squad was based around the machine gun, so all of them carried extra ammunition. It was the main internal MG for armored vehicles because of the ease of barrel change.*

4, 5, *and* **6 Maschinengewehr 42 (MG42)** *The MG42 met the same requirements as the MG34 but was cheaper to produce because of the wide use of stamping, welding, and riveting during manufacture. There were also slacker machining tolerances allowing for mass production. The primary exterior MG for armored vehicles, it differed from the MG34 by having a rectangular barrel shroud vented on the left and opening on the right for ease of barrel change. It fired 1,050–1,350 7.92mm rounds/min with the same effective range as the MG34. Neither were particularly accurate when compared, for example, to the Bren gun, but their versatility made them the progenitor of the postwar GPMG. A heavier tripod converted it to the HMG mode (**6, Opposite top**).*

7 Panzerfaust 30 *The Bazooka and its German equivalent, the Panzerschreck, were excellent weapons but they needed a two-man team and gave off much position-revealing smoke. The Panzerfaust (pl Panzerfäuste) was one-meter long 6.8kg in weight. A one-man weapon, it was usually used used in 30m or 60m versions. Achtung! Feuerstrahl! (Warning! Fire spurt!)—these weapons had vicious backblasts.*

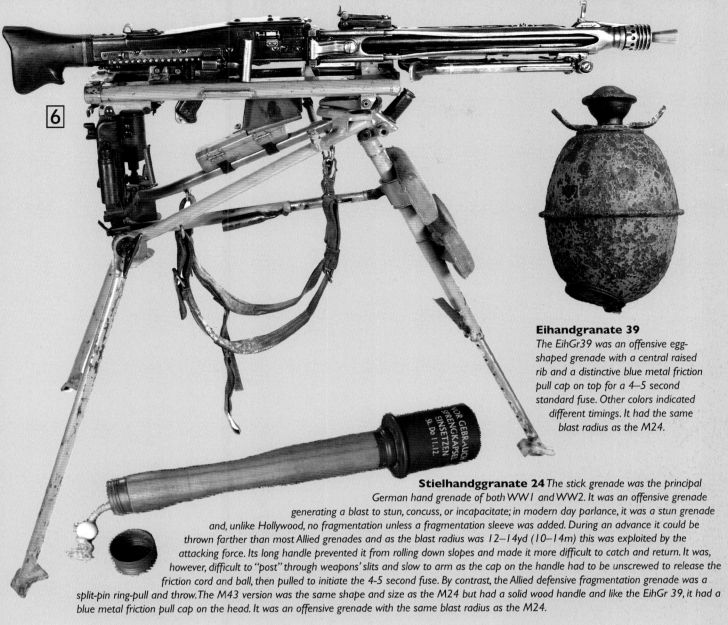

6

Eihandgranate 39

The EihGr39 was an offensive egg-shaped grenade with a central raised rib and a distinctive blue metal friction pull cap on top for a 4–5 second standard fuse. Other colors indicated different timings. It had the same blast radius as the M24.

Stielhandggranate 24 The stick grenade was the principal German hand grenade of both WW1 and WW2. It was an offensive grenade generating a blast to stun, concuss, or incapacitate; in modern day parlance, it was a stun grenade and, unlike Hollywood, no fragmentation unless a fragmentation sleeve was added. During an advance it could be thrown farther than most Allied grenades and as the blast radius was 12–14yd (10–14m) this was exploited by the attacking force. Its long handle prevented it from rolling down slopes and made it more difficult to catch and return. It was, however, difficult to "post" through weapons' slits and slow to arm as the cap on the handle had to be unscrewed to release the friction cord and ball, then pulled to initiate the 4-5 second fuse. By contrast, the Allied defensive fragmentation grenade was a split-pin ring-pull and throw. The M43 version was the same shape and size as the M24 but had a solid wood handle and like the EihGr 39, it had a blue metal friction pull cap on the head. It was an offensive grenade with the same blast radius as the M24.

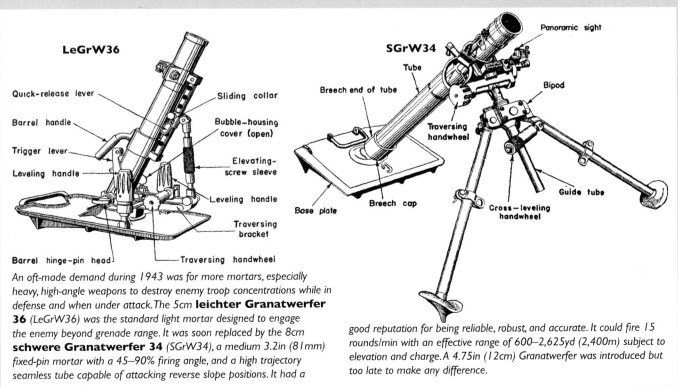

LeGrW36

- Quick-release lever
- Barrel handle
- Trigger lever
- Leveling handle
- Sliding collar
- Bubble-housing cover (open)
- Elevating-screw sleeve
- Leveling handle
- Traversing bracket
- Barrel hinge-pin head
- Traversing handwheel

SGrW34

- Panoramic sight
- Tube
- Breech end of tube
- Bipod
- Traversing handwheel
- Base plate
- Breech cap
- Cross-leveling handwheel
- Guide tube

An oft-made demand during 1943 was for more mortars, especially heavy, high-angle weapons to destroy enemy troop concentrations while in defense and when under attack. The 5cm **leichter Granatwerfer 36** (LeGrW36) was the standard light mortar designed to engage the enemy beyond grenade range. It was soon replaced by the 8cm **schwere Granatwerfer 34** (SGrW34), a medium 3.2in (81mm) fixed-pin mortar with a 45–90% firing angle, and a high trajectory seamless tube capable of attacking reverse slope positions. It had a good reputation for being reliable, robust, and accurate. It could fire 15 rounds/min with an effective range of 600–2,625yd (2,400m) subject to elevation and charge. A 4.75in (12cm) Granatwerfer was introduced but too late to make any difference.

German armor

There's no doubt that German armor played a significant role in bolstering the crumbling Nazi defenses in late 1944 and into early 1945. However, the problems associated with Germany's belated attempts to increase production—exacerbated by the Allied strategic bombing campaign—and the lack of the training standards that had made the Panzerwaffe so effective, meant that the quality of crews and vehicles fell. German armor would still play an important role, even if its effectiveness was reduced by Hitler's erratic command decisions that saw the best units sacrificed in the Ardennes and around Budapest. Increasingly, armor was used in penny packets, supporting infantry from fixed, dug-in positions rather than making use of its mobility and potential for spearheading counterattacks.

In the final battles around Berlin, a number of tanks without running gear were dug in at major road intersections so that only their turrets were visible (see pages 212–213). They gave a good account of themselves.

Jochen Peiper of *Leibstandarte* had this to say about German armor:

"In general it should be noted that we had too many different partly over-developed weapons. A Panzerdivision with 150 different kinds of ammunition is in the long run unbearable for the supply system. Since our war industries

1 *The Hetzer—the Jagdpanzer 38—was a late-war development based on the Czech Panzer 38(t) chassis. Small, low to the ground and armed with a 7.5cm PaK 39 L/48 gun it saw service on every front in the last months of the war as production reached 2,800.*

2 *Rushed into action at Kursk, the Panther had difficult teething problems. On July 10, four days after the start of* Unternehmen Zitadelle, *there were only 10 operational Panthers in the front line. Of the others, 125, 25 had been destroyed (23 in action; two having caught fire before reaching the start line). Fully 100 Panthers needed repairs—56 had either been mined or sustained damage in action; 44 had broken down. Mechanical reliability improved in the months after Kursk, but would still dog the Panther until the end of the war.*

3 *The Tiger II or Königstiger was a beast—but a rare one. Over the course of the entire war, only 1,347 Tiger Is and 492 Tiger IIs were produced. Most of them were abandoned by their crews following automotive problems. However, they worked often enough to gain a fearsome and justified reputation on every front they fought.*

4 *Jagdpanzer IV/70 at the Aberdeen Proving Grounds. Peiper rated this TD highly.*

5 *The dependable StuG III—this one an Ausf F/8 at Belgrade Military Museum. Over 10,000 were built. Its low silhouette and uprated gun meant that it became an excellent tank killer.*

6 *The Tiger saw extensive use on the Eastern Front, with eight independent heavy tank battalions (sPzAbt) and elements of three SS-Panzerdivisionen (*Leibstandarte, Das Reich, *and* Totenkopf) *and the army's* Großdeutschland *Division. Note the size of the tracks and the Zimmerit anti-magnetic paste applied over hull and mantlet. For all its automotive and mobility issues, the Tiger had high crew survivability and this meant old experienced crews.*

as well as the economic mobilization were still too much within the infant stages, this had a bearing particularly on the motor vehicles.

The multitude of types and the resulting difficulties of obtaining spare parts caused worries which could not be solved, even by the best improvisations.

Our Panzers were superior to all enemy tanks. But here too, the fancy of the German for complicating became apparent and overdeveloping them, which in turn had to have their effect on the output. ... The loss of a great number of Panzers due to faulty servicing had to be the result. Our demand, therefore, was continuously, the return to a certain degree of simplicity, The poor raw material and the many substitutes represented the greatest obstacles!

Of the great number of Panzers which I lost, 3/5ths of them had to be blown up. This is the fate of any mechanical failure in the course of a continuous withdrawal.

The Panzer Jaeger III [Sturmgeschütz III] was our most dependable assault gun. The Panzer Jaeger IV [Jagdpanzer IV/70] introduced in the last year was good and lived up to all demands. (I consider the American TD/M10 as superior.) I do reject Jagdpanther (Anti-tank Panther) and Jagdtiger. They did not prove themselves in my opinion."

Right: A StuG III waits for a target surrounded by sunflowers. By 1944 the StuG's original assault gun function had been superseded by the need for cheap, effective anti-tank weapons. The low profile and powerful 7.5cm gun were a lethal combination, particularly in the hands of an experienced crew. The armored side skirts protecting the chassis were, by this stage of the war, standard issue.

Center right: The PzKpfw IV was steadily upgunned through the war, starting off with a 7.5cm KwK 37 L/24 with a muzzle velocity of 385m/sec in the Ausf A to F, and ending with a long-barreled 7.5cm KwK 40 L/48 with an MV of 930m/sec and correspondingly better armor penetration figures. The gun was used on more than 6,000 later PzKpfw IVs, over 8,000 StuG IIIs, all 1,139 StuG IVs, and 780 Jagdpanzer IVs.

Below right: Two of the five-man crew of a Nashorn (rhinoceros) tank hunter of 655th Heavy Tank Hunter Battalion rest and relax. Before 1944 it known as the Hornisse (hornet). This cheap and efficient vehicle mated an 8.8cm gun with a PzKpfw IV chassis. The success of this crew is recorded by the kill rings on the gun barrel.

Opposite, Above: A platoon of StuG III assault guns waits behind one of a number that has driven into an undetected ditch. This type of unexpected event was just the sort of thing that held up even the best planned operations. Retrieving the ditched vehicle was not difficult in itself, but bridging the obstacle was a different matter. Many were recovered by their companions—as here—rather than by specialized equipment.

Opposite, Below: A field workshop team replaces the gun of a Marder III tank hunter. An open-topped, lightly armored vehicle, it gave good service on all fronts. It shared a chassis with its intended replacement, the fully enclosed Hetzer.

The Germans made significant use of what they called *Beutepanzer*—tanks and other vehicles they captured or acquired after they had successfully invaded other countries. Tucker-Jones (2007) puts the number of AFVs acquired 1938–45 as 16,651, including 6,571 from Czechoslovakia, 2,410 from France, and 5,326 from Italy.

Many of these vehicles were supplied from manufacturers who continued production—975 Marder IIIs and 2,584 Hetzer based on the Czech PzKpfw 38(t) chassis; 1,035 Renault 35/40s; 785 Italian M13/40s and 895 M14/41s. The production of

trucks and other vehicles was also important: 6,000 Chenilette d'infanterie Renault/AMX UE carriers; 11,400 STZ prime movers; 12,500 Austrian Steyr 270 4 x 4 trucks; 15,000 Citroën and 30,000 Peugeot 4 x 2 trucks.

While such allies as Hungary and Romania produced a small number of tanks (see p. 129), their armies needed up-to-date equipment. Hungary's armed forces received 100 Hetzers, 62 PzKpfw IVs, and even three Tiger Is—a total of 385 AFVs; Romania received 347; Bulgaria 264; and Finland 77, 59 of which were StuG IIIs.

The Luftwaffe

The Luftwaffe struggled to fulfill its commitments in 1944 and 1945. Attrition in the field and the Western Allies' bombing campaign were the main culprits, but the speed of the Russian advances didn't help as airfield after airfield succumbed to the Red Army. Assailed on so many fronts from the Baltic to the Black Sea, the Luftwaffe struggled because it hadn't been designed to cater for, or been equipped for, such defensive duties. There was no strategic bombing capability, which meant that the Russian production lines that had been spirited east were as safe as those in the United States. The half-hearted attempt to prepare a strategic arm in 1944 by the Luftwaffe Chief of Staff, Generaloberst Günther Korten, failed as the pilots in training and their aircraft kept being called to fight fires and assist the ground forces' attempt to stave off the Russian attacks. The attrition was sizable as it was during the Baby Blitz of London in early 1944 (when 329 bombers were lost).

Not all the news was bad. In 1944 aircraft production increased to 36,000 in spite of the dispersal of operations. On the Eastern Front in early 1945, taking advantage of their shorter lines of communication and the awful weather that grounded the Russian aircraft on their makeshift runways, the Germans pulled aircraft from the west in order to help defend the Reich. The fighting to relieve Budapest, for example, saw the Luftwaffe flying 300 sorties a day. And while the wonder weapons—such as the Messerschmitt Me262, and the V1 and V2—finally came into service, it was too little too late. In the end, losing the oilfields to the Russian advances, and the effects of the USAAF's bombing campaign irreparably impaired the Luftwaffe's viability.

Right: *A Messerschmitt Bf110 long-range fighter. By 1942 it was outclassed by the majority of Soviet fighters and was withdrawn from daylight operations. As a night fighter it gained a good reputation as a bomber interceptor. The majority of this type were withdrawn from the Eastern Front by late 1943 to defend the Reich against the aerial offensive.*

Below right: *Hungarian Focke-Wulf Fw190F-8. "Mica" was flown by Pilot Lajos Vargha of the 102nd Fighter-Bomber Group which was based December 1944–March 1945 at Várpalota. Nicknamed "Fóka" (Seal) by the Hungarians, the F-8 carried two 20mm MG 151/20 cannon in the wing roots and a range of bombs—an SC250 on an ETC 501 centerline rack and SC50 bombs on ETC 71 racks. The latter have been modified for the anti-personnel role by the extensions on the nose of the bomb which would detonate it fractionally earlier than a standard bomb causing it to spread shrapnel over a wider area. Here they are also sporting racy sharks' teeth.*

Left: The Ju88, pictured here receiving its bomb load, served the Luftwaffe from the first to last day of the war. It was modified to fulfill different roles such as anti-tank and bomber hunting. Numbers were also sold to Finland and Romania.

Center left: The tank-buster version of the Ju87 Stuka. By late 1944 less than 200 Stukas remained operational and were almost exclusively operated as anti-tank gun platforms. This machine carries two underwing BK 37mm anti-tank guns. Although inaccurate and heavy enough to affect the aircraft's flying capabilities in the hands of an expert such as Rudel, it was an extremely effective weapons' system.

Below left: An He111 showing a beautifully applied winter camouflage scheme. By late 1943 this mainstay of the Luftwaffe's bomber fleet was unable to operate during daylight over the Eastern Front due to Soviet air superiority. However, it was used extensively as a transport, particularly the He111H-20, the last major production variant. It could carry up to nine 550lb containers. Luftwaffe transport operations had to continue, and not just eastward. As the German armies left Greece and the Mediterranean, maneuvering their way through the bandit country of Yugoslavia, they needed supplies of everything including winter clothing that had been unnecessary in sunnier climes. Those who had stayed on the Mediterranean islands—as many as 22,000 on Rhodes and Crete—were supplied with food from Vienna's airfields, missions that continued to May 8, 1945. There were flights to the German groups in the Harz Mountains, Taunus, and Sauerland and to the forces in East Prussia and the Courland Pocket until late April. Some of the last operations undertaken were transport duties for the besieged garrison of Budapest and bombing Soviet bridges over the Oder River.

Rerik (Luftflotte Reich)
Gruppe Uhl—He111
LS-Kdo—DFS230

Hohenmauth (Luftflotte 6)
Gruppe Herzog—He111,
Do17, DFS230, Go242.

TERRITORY STILL UNDER
GERMAN CONTROL, APRIL 30, 1945

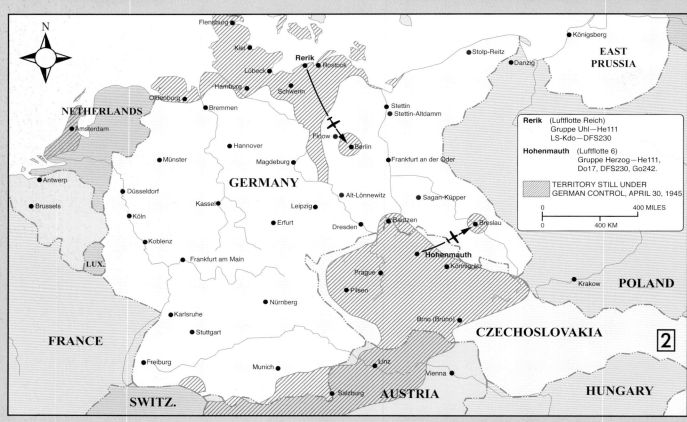

RESUPPLY BY AIR

1 An aerial shot of Gotha Go242 gliders being towed by either a Ju52 or He111. They could carry up to 4,000kg of cargo. Such was the desperate need for pilots that even members of the Hitlerjugend's flying section were recruited for these missions.

2 The last glider missions to Breslau and Berlin took place on April 30. Hohenmauth (today's Vysoké Mýto in the Czech Republic) was a prewar emergency landing ground that had been lengthened and used from August 1944. In the last months of the war various small units of Luftflotte 6 (under Generaloberst Otto Deßloch) flew from it, including Gruppe Herzog in April and May 1945. On April 25 the unit had 11 Do17, 15 He111, 3 Ju87, 13 DFS230 and 6 Go242 stationed at Hohenmauth and at Königgrätz. In **red** the airfields from which resupply missions flew to encircled Festungen in 1945: Stolp-Reitz to Elbing; Finow and Stettin-Altdamm to Arnswalde; Alt-Lönnewitz to Posen, Glogau, and Breslau. It was from Sagan-Küpper that resupply missions were flown to Gruppe Nehring (General Walther Nehring's XXIV. Panzerkorps) and Gruppe von Saucken (General Dietrich von Saucken of Panzerkorps Großdeutschland) as they and their "Wandernden Kessel" ("moving pocket") negotiated their way back to German lines January 19–31.

3 Resupply for the Budapest garrison was often carried by glider such as the Gotha Go242 shown here. The loss of the main airfield in the early days of the siege—it was lost on January 9—forced the garrison to use the Vérmezo meadow near the Royal Castle in Buda.

4 What would the Luftwaffe have done without the "Tante Ju"? This maid of all work, however, was obsolete by the end of 1940. With a top speed of 165mph, it was too small and too slow to move the amount of supplies German forces needed—as was well exemplified at Stalingrad. There were too few of them and with only 2,804 delivered to the Luftwaffe 1939–44, new builds didn't keep pace with attrition.

5 On February 5, 1945, the last glider resupply mission to Budapest took place. Six DFS230s landed but one crashed into the top story of 31 Attila Road. The gliders delivered "97 tonnes of ammo, 10 tonnes of fuel, 28 tonnes of food, and four engine-oil drums and spare parts crates" (Ungváry, 2006). After the loss of the airfield 36 DFS230s transported ammunition, fuel, food, medical supplies, and flour. The losses in the operation had been severe: 48 gliders had landed, but at a cost of 36 Ju52s, 7 He111s, a Ju87, and a Do17. After the breakout, the fleeing troops were airdropped supplies on February 14 (by nine He111s) and 15 (nine He111s and three Ju52s).

6 World War II aircraft don't get much bigger than this—the Messerschmitt Me323 Gigant. It was a motorized version of the Me321 glider and while it was easy meat for fighters, it provided heavy haulage and resupply options the Allies could only dream about.

Festungen (fortresses)

Vistula–Oder strongpoints, 1945

Festung	Date of surrender
Arnswalde (Choszczno)	23.02
Breslau (Wrocław)	06.05
Brünn (Brno)	26.04
Budapest	12.02
Cottbus	22.04
Danzig (Gdańsk)	30.03
Deutsch-Krone (Wałcz)	12.02
Elbing (Elbląg)	10.02
Frankfurt an der Oder	30.04
Glogau (Głogyw)	03.04
Gotenhafen (Gdynia)	28.03
Graudenz (Grudziądz)	06.03
Kolberg (Kołobrzeg)	18.03
Königsberg (Kaliningrad)	09.04
Küstrin (Kostrzyn nad Odrą)	30.03
Lötzen (Giżycko)	26.01
Memel (Klaipéda)	27.01
Olmütz (Olomouc)	06.05
Oppeln (Opole)	22.03
Pillau (Baltiysk)	22.03
Posen (Poznań)	23.02
Prag (Prague)	09.05
Schneidemühl (Piła)	14.02
Stettin (Szczecin)	26.04
Thorn (Toruń)	08.02

The concept of the fortresses didn't find favor with German Army commanders but they were forced to embrace it. Initially, the Führer Order set up fortresses in Russia and the Baltic States (see map **Opposite**), but they didn't last much longer than the first few days of Operation Bagration. However, when Guderian became Chief of the OKH, he started a building program to turn a number of cities in Germany and Poland into fortresses (map **Below**). Many of these locations had been besieged in earlier times and already had some defensive works. These fortresses proved to be difficult to take and many didn't fall until April, bolstered by retreating troops and as much aerial supply as was possible this late in the war. Indeed, Breslau held out until two days before the final surrender.

So was the strategy successful? It's easy to knock down: all those troops bottled up in Courland and the fortresses could have defended Berlin, and, ultimately, all the fortresses fell to the Red Army—but it took special efforts by the Soviets to take them and enabled citizen soldiers such as the Volkssturm to participate directly in the battles in a way they couldn't have done in open warfare. The Soviets paused in their surge toward Berlin and instead of fighting across the Oder, stopped to sort out the "Baltic Balcony" and the fortresses in its way. Although the reasons for Zhukov's pause at the Oder are much debated, there's no doubt that there was a strong military case for securing his flanks.

The fortress strategy also reinforced the nihilism of the Nazi regime in its final death throes: first, it enabled fortress commanders such as Karl Hanke to force Germans to fight to the bitter end and murder hundreds of citizens and soldiers who were seen as cowards or backsliders; second, it led to the complete destruction of some of Germany's most historic cities.

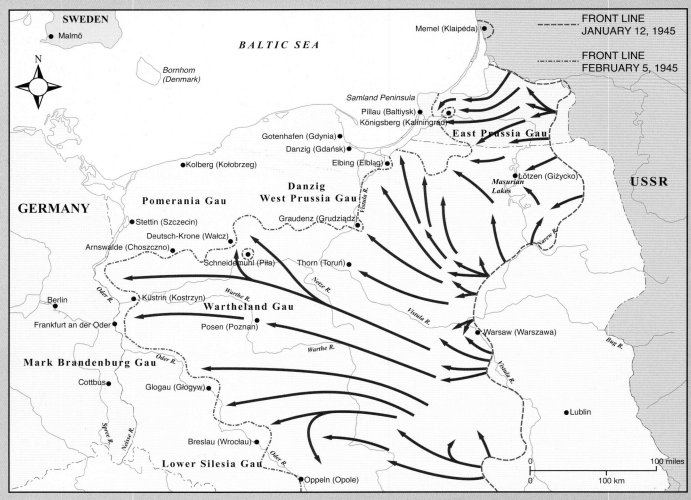

Führer Order No. 11 of March 8, 1944
(Commanders of the Fixed Strongpoints and Combat Commanders)

1. ... The "*fixed strongpoints*" are to serve the same purpose as formerly the fortresses. They are to prevent the enemy from seizing these operationally important spots. They must permit themselves to be surrounded, thereby tying up as strong enemy forces as possible. Thereby they will create favorable circumstances for successful counteroperations.

The "*local strongpoints*" are meant to be stubbornly defended strongpoints within the local combat zone. When they are included in the main line of battle they are to serve as the backbone of the defense, and in case of enemy penetrations they are the pivot points and cornerstones of the front and the initial points for counterattacks.

2. The "*commander of the fixed strongpoint*" should be an especially chosen, hardened soldier, if possible a general. He will be appointed by the Army Group involved. The commander of the fixed strongpoint is personally responsible to the Commanding General of the Army Group.

The commander of the fixed strongpoint is answerable with his honor as a soldier for fulfilling his tasks to the last.

Only the Commanding General of the Army Group in person with my permission can relieve the commander of the fixed strongpoint of his task, and possibly order that the fixed strongpoint be abandoned.

The commanders of the fixed strongpoint *are subordinate* to the Commanding General of the Army Group or of the army in the area where the strongpoint is located. They must not be subordinated to other commanding generals.

The commanders of fixed strongpoints *have authority over* not only the entire garrison but also all other persons stationed or assembling there, both military and civilian, regardless of their rank or position.

The commanders of the fixed strongpoint have the *command authority* and disciplinary powers of commanding generals. They are to be provided with mobile military tribunals to assist them in carrying out their tasks.

The *staffs of the commanders of the fixed strongpoints* are to be organized by the Army Group concerned. The chiefs of staff will be appointed by the Army High Command on request of the Army Group.

3. The *garrisons* of the fixed strongpoints will be divided into the security garrison (*Sicherheitsbesatzung*) and the regular garrison (*Gesamtbesatzung*).

The *security garrison* must permanently be stationed in the fixed strongpoint. The Commanding General of the Army Group will determine its strength. It will depend on the size of the strongpoint and the tasks to be carried out (preparation and construction of defenses, defense of the strongpoint against surprise attacks or local raids by the enemy).

The *regular garrison* must be brought up early enough to be able to take up defense positions and receive instructions before an expected systematic enemy attack. Its strength will be determined by the Commanding General of the Army Group in accordance with the size of the fixed strongpoint and the tasks to be carried out (main defense of the fixed strongpoint).

4. The "*combat commander*" is under the troop commander (*Truppenführer*), is appointed by him, and gets his assignment from him. His rank depends on the importance of the strongpoint in the combat area and the strength of the garrison. Especially energetic and proved officers are needed for such posts.

5. The *strength of the garrison* of the "local strongpoint" depends on the importance of the strongpoint and the forces available. The strength is determined by the superior of the combat commander.

6. The *tasks* of the "commanders of fixed strongpoints" and of the "combat commanders", as well as a list of the fixed strongpoints and of the reports to be submitted by the Army Groups are contained in the appendices.

7. All orders previously issued concerning combat commanders are hereby canceled.

A supplementary order said that: 1. Railroad personnel should be exempted from fighting to maintain railroad communications. 2. A number of antiaircraft batteries can be included in the regular garrison (*Gesamtbesatzung*) of a fixed strongpoint.

Strongpoints of March 8, 1944

1. Reval (Tallinn)
2. Wesenberg (Rakvere)
3. Jewi (Jõhvi)
4. Dorpat (Tartu)
5. Pleskau (Pskov)
6. Ostrov
7. Opochka
8. Rositten (Rezekne)
9. Polotsk
10. Witebsk (Vitebsk)
11. Orscha (Orsha)
12. Mogilew (Mogilev)
13. Borissoff (Barysaw)
14. Minsk
15. Bobruisk (Babruysk)
16. Sslusk (Slutsk)
17. Luniniec (Luninets)
18. Pinsk
19. Kowel (Kovel)
20. Brody
21. Tarnopol (Ternopil)
22. Proskuroff (Khmelnytskyi)
23. Shmerinka (Zhmerynka)
24. Winniza (Vinnytsia)
25. Uman (Uman')
26. Nowo Ukrainka (Novoukrainka)
27. Perwomaisk (Pervomaysk)
28. Wosnessensk (Voznesens'k)
29. Nikolajew (Nikolaev)

ТЫ

Д.МООР

ЗАПИСАЛСЯ
ДОБРОВОЛЬЦЕМ?

1-е Государственная типо-лит. (Шатурский под.) Москва, Пятницкая, 71.

№ 100.

Д-- Изд. Отдѣл Политическаго Управленія Реввоенсовѣта Республики.

Finland and the Baltic States 1

The end of the Continuation War—what the Finns call the period of World War II, when they were allied with the Germans and fought against the Red Army (see pp. 68–69)—came with a cease fire on September 5, 1944. Part of the resolution confirmed by the Moscow Armistice of September 19 was that German forces had to leave the country. This left 20. Gebirgsarmee, under Generaloberst Lothar Rendulic, in a perilous situation. Straddling the Arctic Circle, it was in serious danger of becoming isolated, and quickly began moving toward Norway, as did all the German forces in Finland, following carefully laid down plans. Their enemies were snapping at their heels.

The Soviet offensive aimed to push through harsh Arctic terrain in order to liberate Finnmark—the northernmost county of Norway—and began doing so on October 7. Undertaking such a major operation at the onset of the region's severe winter would be unthinkable to most western armies, however, the Soviet troops—most of whom were used to such conditions—were able to cope very well. The advance was a combined operation composed of units of the Fourteenth Army (Lt Gen Vladimir Shcherbakov) of the Karelian Front (Gen Kirill Meretskov) as well as soldiers of the Northern Fleet (Admiral Arseniy Golovko). The initial aim was to take the small town of Kirkenes as well as the air and naval bases sited there and at Petsamo, both of which are close to the Finnish and Soviet borders. The German defenders were XIX. Gebirgskorps.

By the middle of the month, after much fierce fighting, there was a desperate shortage of supplies and the Soviet troops also badly needed to rest. The Soviet capture of the port of Petsamo on October 15 significantly helped with the resupply situation but Shcherbakov still ordered that combat should be paused for three days during which period both sides resupplied, reorganized, and repositioned.

The second phase of the battle lasted for four days, and saw the Red Army advance some 20 miles (35km) and take the area's key nickel mine. More importantly from a military perspective, the previously strong German forces had also been split into two isolated groups, and a whole Soviet rifle corps had established itself on Norwegian territory.

Continued on p. 73.

Opposite: *"You—have you volunteered yet?" This propaganda poster by Dmitry Moor was produced in 1920 at the time of the Russian Civil War and is as iconic in the east as Kitchener's World War I recruiting poster is in Britain or Uncle Sam's in America.*

Above: *Hjalmar Siilasvuo (R) (1892–1947) was promoted general after the Winter War, led III Corps in the Continuation War, and commanded Finnish forces in the Lapland War.*

The end of the Continuation War

Attacked by Russia on November 30, 1939, the Finns had given a good account of themselves during the Winter War. In the middle of a freezing winter, they had held the Soviets, inflicted serious losses but had, in the end, been forced to concede to the Soviet Union, giving up 11 percent of their country.

Unsurprisingly, therefore, when "Barbarossa" took place, the Finns took the opportunity to regain their lost land. They fought on the German side from June 25, 1941 to September 19, 1944, regaining their territory and more. However, after the Germans lost Stalingrad, the Finns realized that the war was going to take a turn for the worst and began to make peace overtures. Gustav Mannerheim—the Finnish commander-in-chief and from September 1944 president—had warned the Germans that Finland would have to sue for peace with the Soviet Union, particularly if Estonia fell. After Leningrad's siege was lifted, the Soviet Union piled pressure onto the Finns, bombing Helsinki, and forcing the Finnish defense lines on the Karelian isthmus.

The crucial moments came in June and July 1944, when the Finns were able to hold and beat the Soviets at Tali-Ihantala (June 25–July 9) and Ilomantsi (July 26–August 13). These successes meant that Finland could negotiate if not from a position of strength, then certainly from a better position than if the Soviets had rolled up the whole of the isthmus.

The result was the Moscow Armistice, signed by new head of state, Mannerheim. This saw Finland cede the territories it had taken and return to the 1940 borders. They agreed to pay reparations and to expel the Germans, disarming them if they remained.

Who won? The departing Germans followed a scorched earth policy that damaged the country severely, and Moscow insisted on 1938 values for the reparations: but Finland remained free and if you're Finnish that was the crux of the matter.

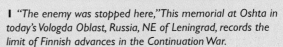

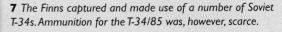

1 "The enemy was stopped here," This memorial at Oshta in today's Vologda Oblast, Russia, NE of Leningrad, records the limit of Finnish advances in the Continuation War.

2 Hitler meets Finnish commander-in-chief Field Marshal Gustav Mannerheim (L) and President Risto Ryti on June 4, 1942, Mannerheim's 75th birthday. Mannerheim became president in 1944 and negotiated the peace with the Soviet Union.

3 Peace with the Soviets saw PoWs exchanged. These are Russians at Lahti on October 20, 1944.

4 Finnish troops crossing the Simojoki on October 6, 1944, as they progressed toward Kemi during the Lapland War. The color image shows the color of the Finnish M/36 greatcoat and cap (nicknamed "verikauha"—blood scoop). For details of Finnish uniforms and equipment, you need look no further than the incomparable www.jaegerplatoon.net.

5 A Soviet captain of a Guards infantry unit (L) and a Finnish officer compare watches on September 4, 1944, at Vyborg— one of many such propaganda shots at the cease-fire marking the end of the Continuation War—a couple of weeks before the Moscow Armistice was signed.

6 Finnish soldiers carrying Panzerfäuste pass by the remains of a destroyed Soviet T-34 tank at the battle of Tali-Ihantala, the last and biggest of the battles between the Finns and the Red Army. Note that the lead man has a Suomi M/31 SJR submachine gun (the SJR from suujarru—muzzle brake). Drum and box magazines were available but the 72-round drum (usually only filled to 70) was the most used.

7 The Finns captured and made use of a number of Soviet T-34s. Ammunition for the T-34/85 was, however, scarce.

The Lapland War

The other price that Finland had to pay for peace with the Soviet Union was the Lapland War against Germany, hitherto their comrades with whom they enjoyed a "*Waffenbrüderschaft*"—brotherhood of arms. The Finns needed to show the Allies that they were prepared to fight, that they were expelling the Germans: that they actually had changed sides. This was made easier by the Germans themselves when, on September 15, before the official armistice had been ratified by the Finnish parliament, they tried to assault what the Finns called Suursaari island and the Germans called Hochland. It was a small island, but it had great strategic value—from there the minefields that kept the Soviet fleet cooped up in the eastern Gulf of Finland, in Leningrad, and Kronstadt were monitored.

Until this point, while there had been friction, both Finns and Germans had worked closely enough to facilitate the movement of troops and matériel from Finland. However, the German operation—codenamed *Unternehmen Tanne Ost* (Fir East)—tipped the balance and the Finnish reaction proved beyond doubt that Finland meant what it had agreed.

The Germans had assumed that the Finns would give up the island. They hadn't anticipated a military response that included attacks by motor torpedo boats. The naval threat prompted the Kriegsmarine to move its ships, leaving the ground forces without heavy support. Soviet air attacks finally led the naval units to leave the island, returning to Tallinn. The surviving Germans—153 had been killed, 175 wounded—1,231 in total, became PoWs.

The German evacuation of Finland—*Unternehmen Birke* (Operation Birch)—had been continuing relatively smoothly but was too leisurely for the Allies and, pressurized to do more with the threat of Soviet soldiers being sent, the Finns moved troops by sea to Röyttä behind the Germans. From there, they moved on Tornio on October 1. The German counterattack, with supporting armor—Hotchkiss H39s and Somua S35s—pushed the Finns back, but they lost four tanks. By the 6th, the Finns had been reinforced and the Germans were forced to retreat. They had, however, secured their route through Rovaniemi. On October 4, Hitler approved *Unternehmen Nordlicht*, that saw all German forces head to the prepared positions at the base of Lyngen Fjord in northern Norway.

Left: The battle of Tornio on October 1–8, 1944, was the first major engagement between the erstwhile "brothers-in-arms." The Germans, however, hadn't supported Finland out of altruism. Petsamo and Kolosjoki were important centers of nickel mining and Hitler didn't want to lose them. However, in August 1944, after increased production and in spite of Allied bombing raids, Albert Speer was able to tell Hitler that they had sufficient stocks of nickel to last until 1946 so the mines became less important. Lt Gen Siilasvuo planned an amphibious landing at Tornio and an overland attack toward Kemi. This photo of a knocked-out Hotchkiss H39 was taken on October 10 after the fighting.

Center left: Lightweight bicycles are loaded onto a ship bound for Röyttä, October 5, 1944.

Below left: The Germans had destroyed the Kaakamonjoki bridge but not sufficiently to stop Finnish troops from following them.

Below: Finnish T-26s on their way to clear the Germans from the outskirts of Tornio. The Soviets had lost many of this type in the Winter War, and the Finns still had 114 operational, some of which equipped 1st Tank Company of the Finnish Tank Brigade which had been carried by sea.

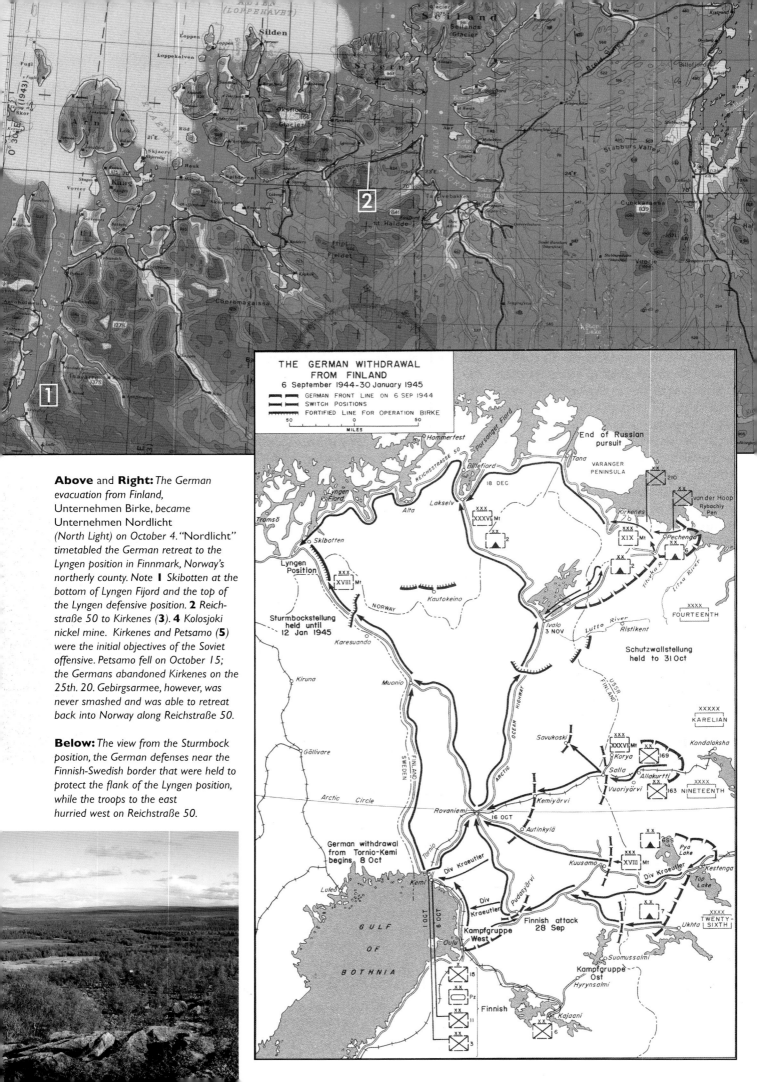

Above and **Right:** *The German evacuation from Finland,* Unternehmen Birke, *became* Unternehmen Nordlicht *(North Light) on October 4.* "Nordlicht" *timetabled the German retreat to the Lyngen position in Finnmark, Norway's northerly county. Note* **1** *Skibotten at the bottom of Lyngen Fijord and the top of the Lyngen defensive position.* **2** *Reichstraße 50 to Kirkenes (3).* **4** *Kolosjoki nickel mine. Kirkenes and Petsamo (5) were the initial objectives of the Soviet offensive. Petsamo fell on October 15; the Germans abandoned Kirkenes on the 25th. 20. Gebirgsarmee, however, was never smashed and was able to retreat back into Norway along Reichstraße 50.*

Below: *The view from the Sturmbock position, the German defenses near the Finnish-Swedish border that were held to protect the flank of the Lyngen position, while the troops to the east hurried west on Reichstraße 50.*

THE GERMAN WITHDRAWAL
FROM FINLAND
6 September 1944–30 January 1945

GERMAN FRONT LINE ON 6 SEP 1944
SWITCH POSITIONS
FORTIFIED LINE FOR OPERATION BIRKE

50   0   50   100

MILES

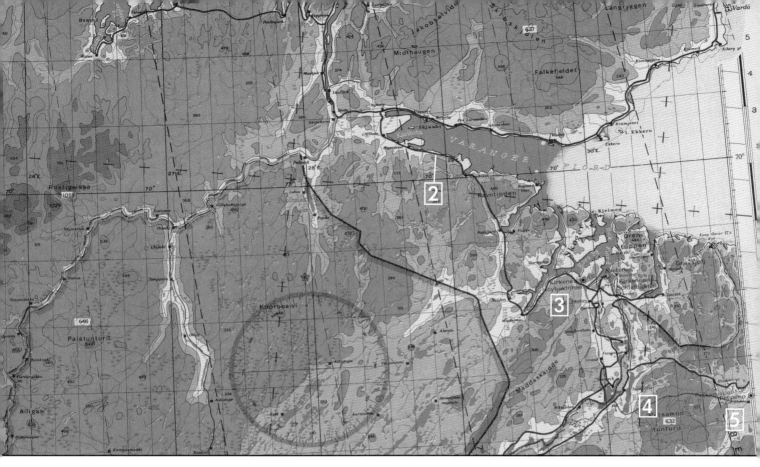

A third phase then developed with the Soviet forces were divided into two in order to pursue both groups of Germans, one component of which had moved north toward the town of Kirkenes, the other having gone south toward the village of Ivalo. The Germans withdrew from Kirkenes on October 26, and this part of the offensive ended on November 1, 1944, with the Soviet XXXI Rifle Corps having advanced approximately 100 miles (160km).

The next stage for the Soviets was to clear the rest of the enemy from the area—this action was spearheaded by the 10th Guards Division, under Maj Gen Khudalov. On the German side, under Hitler's direct orders, the Germans enacted a scorched-earth policy (although General Rendulic was cleared of this at Nuremberg) whereby all local infrastructure and any remaining buildings were destroyed as they withdrew. In order to deprive the Soviets from gaining any local support, much of the civilian population was also forcibly evacuated—somewhere between 43,000 and 45,000 Norwegians were moved out.

"But the price had been heavy: half of Lapland's reindeer (a vital food source and economic staple) had been killed, most towns and settlements had been burnt to the ground, and all forms of communication and infrastructure were crippled. Both sides had lost a large number of troops. Finnish losses amounted 2900 wounded and 1000 dead." (Mann & Jörgensen 2016)

On October 25, while the Soviet forces were still engaged in the last stages of the battle, Norwegian troops (whose commanders were still based in Great Britain), were sent to the area to assist. They were led by Colonel Dahl whose role was to liaise with the Soviets and then to re-establish Norwegian civil administration. Known as Force 138, they were shipped to Murmansk on HMS *Berwick*, arriving on November 6. From there they were taken

Above: *Shot up German column on the road from Tornio. 2cm Flak 30 in the foreground towed by the versatile Kfz 12 mittlere geländegängige Personenkraftwagen (middle weight cross-country passenger car). There's a 7.5cm PaK 40 anti-tank gun further up the road in the background. The Germans lost 22,000 of 200,000 men on their retreat; Rendulic would boast that only 200 people had escaped deportation. In fact, most of the Laps (some 8,500) and the Finns who survived the battle to take Kirkenes were able to avoid deportation.*

Right: *In the far north of Norway, up in the Arctic Circle, on the border with the Soviet Union, lies Vardø on the island of Vardøya. It's north of Kirkenes and less than 200km from Murmansk. (See top right of map on p. 73.) There were two German coastal batteries on Vardøya—1./448 Vardö-Renösund had four 10.5cm K331(f) guns, and 5./448 Vardö-Bussesund had three 21cm Mrs18s. Both were demolished and evacuated in October 1944. The island had a fort as early as 1306. Vardøhus Fortress was extensively renovated in the 18th century and was an active unit of the Norwegian Navy under the command of Naval District 3 in Tromsø at the start of the war. Occupied from July 17, 1940, Vardøhus became a German barracks. In 1944, retreating from the Soviets, the Germans burned the town leaving little standing.*

Right: *Murmansk welcomed 78 Allied Lend-Lease convoys. They braved the weather, the coastal guns, and German naval forces in the Barents Sea to maintain a lifeline to the USSR.*

Below right: *Finnish soldiers raise the flag at the three-country cairn between Norway, Sweden, and Finland on April 27, 1945, after the end of the Lapland War and thus, the end of World War II in Finland.*

Opposite: *Wartime shots of German batteries in Finnmark.*
1 and 2 Heavy Flak position of MKB 4./513 Vardö with 8.8cm Flak 37, later evacuated to MKB 3./516 Lödingen in October 1944 as the Soviets advanced.

3 Camouflaged 28cm SKL/45 gun "Scharnhorst" of MAB 3./513 Kiberg (south of Vardö). It saw combat with the advancing Soviets and was also destroyed in October 1944.

4 Leitstand of MAB 4./517 Mestersand just north of Kirkenes. This position had four 24cm SKL/40 guns and was also evacuated before the Soviets could take it in October 1944.

ARMS FOR RUSSIA . . . A great convoy of British ships escorted by Soviet fighter planes sails into Murmansk harbour with vital supplies for the Red Army.

part-way on a smaller vessel and then on to Finnmark itself by truck, arriving on November 10. Although the numbers were small, they soon recruited about 1,500 local volunteers. A few days later supplies and more men arrived from the UK.

One of the immediate tasks for the newly arrived troops was to rescue the remains of the civilian population, many of whom had little food or shelter. In January 1945, over 500 men, women, and children were successfully evacuated from the island of Sørøya. Skirmishing actions between local militias and German forces continued for some time, but on April 26, the county of Finnmark was declared to be finally free of enemy forces. The following day marked the complete withdrawal of German troops from Finland.

NORWEGIAN RESISTANCE

Norway had put up a real fight in 1940 and the resistance movement—both passive and active—continued throughout the war. The passive resistance included non-fraternization and ostracization. The active resistance included Norwegian Independent Company 1, a British Special Operations Executive group formed in March 1941 and led by Norwegian Capt Martin Linge whose name it used after his death early in the raid on Måløy (Operation Archery). Kompani Linge was involved in a number of sabotage raids, including the famous attack on the Germans' heavy water plant, linking up with the main Norwegian resistance organization, Milorg. Latterly, Sweden helped Norwegian resistance by allowing training camps and equipment storage along the Norwegian border under the subterfuge that they were police training camps. Upward of 7,000 men were trained secretly in Sweden. They were involved helping the Soviets and Free Norwegian Forces in the last months of the war.

The royal cipher of King Haakon VII (the H7 symbol **Below**) was used to signify resistance to the Germans and support for the monarchy in exile.

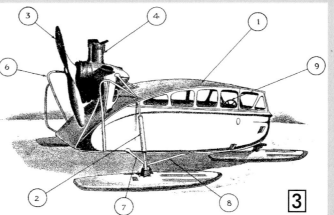

AERO-SLEDS

1 and **2** "The most satisfactory and efficient type of mechanized sled for winter transport has been found to be the aero-sled, powered by an airplane-type engine and mounted on either three or four skis." (Tactics and Trends 12 of 1942.) Both sides used them for reconnaissance, flank security, patrolling, communication, troop transport, and evacuation of wounded, towing heavy weapons and deploying smokescreens. These are Finnish aero-sleds.

3 Soviet NKL-16 with (**1**) enclosed streamlined cabin for 6–8 persons plus freight, depending on the horsepower of the motor and design of the sled. The cabin is mounted on shock absorbers (**2**), connected to three (or four) skis. The M11 motor (**4**) is mounted in the rear with a pusher-propeller (**3**) and a guard (**5**). The skis are connected to the body also by means of universal-joint semiaxles (**6**) and "unloading" connecting rods (**7**). Steered by wheel linked to front ski (**8**).

The Atlantic Wall

As the photographs on pp. 74–75 show, Hitler's Atlantic Wall fortifications spread up to the Arctic Circle. Wasteful of men and matériel, the organization seemed to be on autopilot in late 1944–45, with contractors still working on many batteries placed to stop Allied landings—something that Hitler continued to be worried about long after the Allied deception operation, Operation Tindall in late 1943, had helped reinforce his fears. Not all considerations in the north were to stop Allied invasions. As early as September 28, 1943, Hitler started making preparations for Finland collapsing. Führer Directive No. 50 ordered that:

"a. The routes needed [to withdraw the German forces from Finland] *should be built and kept open and resting places provided,*
b. Supplies for the withdrawing army should be prepared.
c. Preparations should be made to destroy installations in the area being evacuated which would be of importance to the enemy.
d. The supplies should be shifted,
e. Quarters should be prepared in the future operations areas of the withdrawing parts of the Army.
f. Communications should be prepared."

A year later, in September 1944, Hitler ordered that the Lyngen position should be expanded so it could be occupied by 120,000 men, as around 300,000 men from

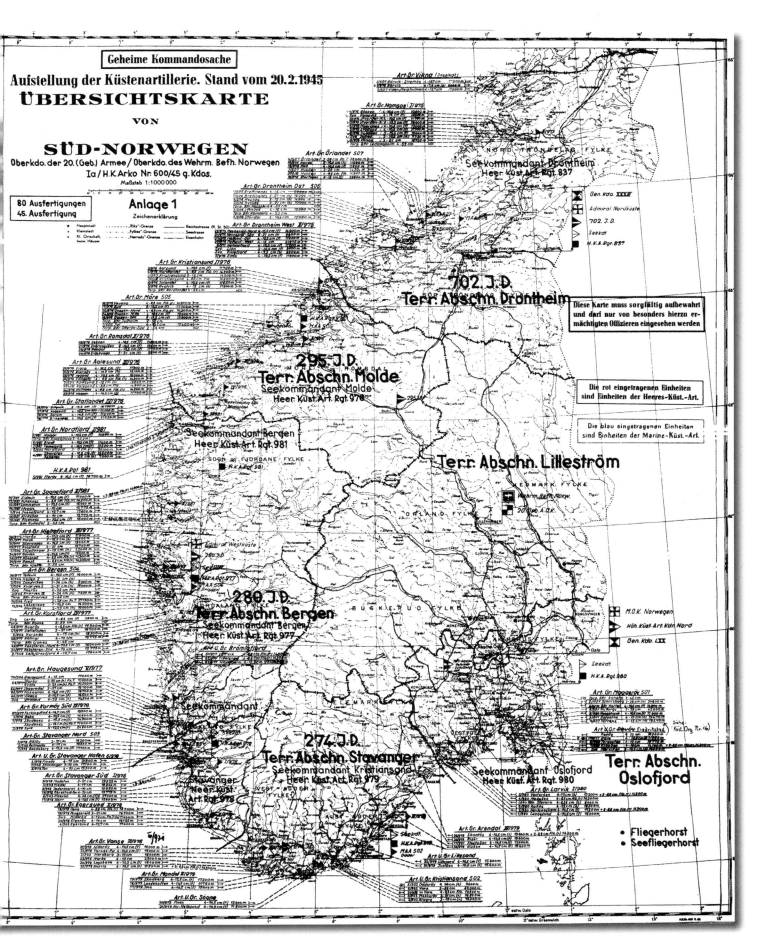

all parts of the Wehrmacht, including the OT, were expected to be repatriated via Reichsstraße 50—the coast road along the north of Norway, a major feat as the Arctic winter set in. With the Soviets close behind, the Germans retreated west and *"Nordlicht"* ended in January 1945.

Above: *This map shows the huge number of coastal batteries in Norway as part of the Atlantic Wall.*

The Courland Pocket

The area which became known as the Courland Pocket is a peninsula to the west of Riga, in Latvia, with the Gulf of Riga to the east, and the Baltic Sea to the north and west. As a result of the Soviet Baltic Offensive, around 200,000 German and Latvian troops from Heeresgruppe Nord had been surrounded by the 1st Baltic Front of the Red Army. Despite being cut off from Heeresgruppe Mitte when Soviet troops reached the Baltic coast near Memel (modern day Klaipeda) on October 9, 1944, and having no land communication or supply routes, they managed to hold out until the end of the war in May 1945.

Although Hitler's military advisors regularly attempted to get permission to evacuate the pocket, this was refused on the grounds that it was required to defend German submarine bases in the Baltic. At this stage, Hitler still believed that the Allies could be forced out of the war by his new secret weapons, and thus wanted to maintain the Courland position as a bridgehead to strike back on the Eastern Front. The 33 divisions—mostly from 16. and 18. Armeen, commanded first by GFM Ferdinand Schörner, then by Generaloberst Lothar Rendulic, and later Generaloberst Carl Hilpert, withstood six separate offensives by the Soviets between October 15, 1944, and April 4, 1945.

The first of the battles lasted from October 15 to 22, 1944. Although its original mission was to defeat the German forces, after failing to achieve its objective, its task became to prevent the troops from escaping. Despite this shift of emphasis, rather than simply masking the area as the Western Allies did to coastal locations such as Lorient, the attacks continued.

The second phase began on October 27 and lasted nearly a month, finally ending on November 25. Enormous numbers of troops were involved, at one stage 52 divisions attacked simultaneously; then a little later, 80 divisions were thrown against German defenses over a front that was 7.5 miles (12km) wide. Although some ground was taken, the offensive stalled.

Below: *The defense of the Courland Pocket involved a front line of 100 miles from just below Liepaja, on the Baltic coast, toward Tukums and the Gulf of Riga to the east. The pocket withstood six attritional attacks until it surrendered in May. The Courland Pocket typified Hitler's ideas of* Festungen *that were ordered to hold out to the last man. The sizable number of men and equipment that held out until war's end would certainly have been more useful elsewhere, although it wouldn't have altered the eventual outcome.*

Königsberg

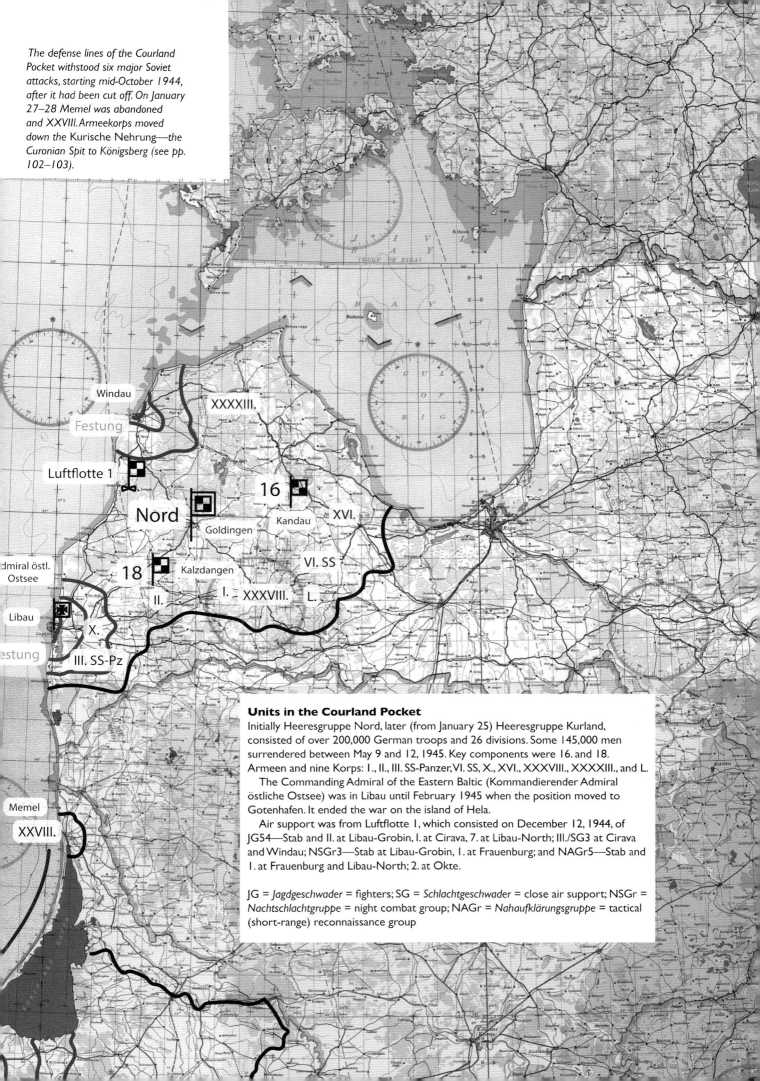

The defense lines of the Courland Pocket withstood six major Soviet attacks, starting mid-October 1944, after it had been cut off. On January 27–28 Memel was abandoned and XXVIII. Armeekorps moved down the Kurische Nehrung—the Curonian Spit to Königsberg (see pp. 102–103).

Windau

Festung

Luftflotte 1

XXXXIII.

Nord

16

Kandau

XVI.

Goldingen

VI. SS

18

Kalzdangen

dmiral östl.
Ostsee

II.

I. – XXXVIII.

L.

Libau

X.

estung

III. SS-Pz

Memel

XXVIII.

Units in the Courland Pocket

Initially Heeresgruppe Nord, later (from January 25) Heeresgruppe Kurland, consisted of over 200,000 German troops and 26 divisions. Some 145,000 men surrendered between May 9 and 12, 1945. Key components were 16. and 18. Armeen and nine Korps: I., II., III. SS-Panzer, VI. SS, X., XVI., XXXVIII., XXXXIII., and L.

The Commanding Admiral of the Eastern Baltic (Kommandierender Admiral östliche Ostsee) was in Libau until February 1945 when the position moved to Gotenhafen. It ended the war on the island of Hela.

Air support was from Luftflotte 1, which consisted on December 12, 1944, of JG54—Stab and II. at Libau-Grobin, I. at Cirava, 7. at Libau-North; III./SG3 at Cirava and Windau; NSGr3—Stab at Libau-Grobin, I. at Frauenburg; and NAGr5—Stab and 1. at Frauenburg and Libau-North; 2. at Okte.

JG = Jagdgeschwader = fighters; SG = Schlachtgeschwader = close air support; NSGr = Nachtschlachtgruppe = night combat group; NAGr = Nahaufklärungsgruppe = tactical (short-range) reconnaissance group

Right: *Barely recognizable under its passengers this SU-76M is noted as being, "somewhere in Pomerania" in early 1945. The open-topped self-propelled gun was thinly armored and unpopular with its crews due to its vulnerability to small-arms fire.*

Below right: *IS-2 near Tallinn in 1944. September 17–26 saw the Soviets attack into Estonia. The German retreat—Unternehmen Aster—included the evacuation by sea of over 50,000 military personnel and civilians. Estonia went on to face thirty years of hell as Sovietization included mass deportations The Baltic states—Estonia, Latvia, and Lithuania—became Soviet until the fall of the Soviet Union saw them gain independence in 1991, 1991, and 1993 respectively. The IS-2's only drawback was the fact that its D-25T 122mm gun took 20–30 seconds to reload (it used two-piece ammunition). The Panther, in comparison, could fire at least five rounds in that time.*

Opposite, Above: *Latvian Daugavpils—the Germans called it Dünaberg—on the banks of the Daugava river was lost to the Soviets on July 27, 1944, but the Germans were able to slow the advance. The Courland Pocket held out until May 1945. Some 7,000 of the Krupp Protze 6 x 4 trucks—were built. This one, Krupp L2H 143 Protze mit 20mm Flak 38, is being used in the ground role. In the background, on the left, a StuG III Ausf E.*

Opposite, Below: *A burning Soviet tank on the road at the front in Courland; in a roadside ditch, the culprits with Panzerfaüste.*

The third phase began on December 21 when the Soviet 1st and 2nd Baltic fronts launched an attack near Saldus (German: Frauenburg), on the pocket's southern boundary. Part of the overall strategy was to establish a robust blockade to prevent the Germans from being supplied or evacuated. The action ended on December 31 by which time the front lines were more or less fixed.

Heeresgruppe Nord became Heeresgruppe Kurland on January 25, 1945, under Gen Rendulic. Around the same time Generaloberst Heinz Guderian, the Chief of the German General Staff, managed at last to get permission from Hitler to evacuate some men from the pocket. Those to leave before the final surrender included elements 4. Panzerdivision, 31., 32., 93., 227., and 389. Divisionen; some units went to East Prussia to reorganize—11. SS-Freiwilligen Panzergrenadier-Division *Nordland* would end up fighting in Berlin. The fourth Soviet offensive started on January 23, 1945, when they attempted to force the lines in the general

direction of Liepaja and Saldus. Although they briefly managed to establish bridgeheads across two rivers, German counterattacks spearheaded by 14. Panzerdivision and the Tigers of sPzAbt 510 retook the ground.

Another attack, began on February 12, coming in from the direction of Riga and heading toward the small town of Džukste. While this was going on, 11 divisions assaulted slightly further north in an attempt to take the town of Tukums, and 21 divisions also attacked in the area to the south of Liepaja. Despite protracted and fierce fighting, none of the Soviet attacks succeeded. The sixth offensive began on February 16, and was directed toward the 19. Division, but this also petered out, by which time Soviet attention was more focused on the Vistula-Oder and Berlin offensives.

On May 8, Generaloberst Carl Hilpert—who had taken over command of the pocket on April 6, 1945—was ordered to surrender by Dönitz. Due to communication problems, however, he didn't receive the message for two days. One of the few German units to remain undefeated, Heeresgruppe Kurland's bits and pieces of 27 divisions—around 180,000 troops—then surrendered, and by May 23, they were all in Soviet captivity. As is usual at this stage of the war, it's difficult to be precise about the awful statistics but it would seem that casualty figures were 150,000 German and 160,000 Soviet.

The Baltic battleground

When asked about the war in the Baltic in 1945, most people's thoughts will turn to the enormous loss of life occasioned by the sinking of ships filled with refugees—civilian and military—as the Germans evacuated the Baltic states and German enclaves in the face of the Red Army. In a war that had been fought with few niceties, the sinking of *Wilhelm Gustloff* (9,400 dead), *General von Steuben* (4,000), and *Goya* (7,000) were dramatically awful events, as was the tragic sinking by RAF aircraft of the *Cap Ancona* in Lübeck Bay on May 3. It was carrying 5,000 concentration camp prisoners.

The speed of the advance of the Red Army—and Hitler's fortified places strategy—meant that the German Navy had little option but to deliver supplies to the beleaguered Festungen and bring out the refugees. *Unternehmen Hannibal* was the designation given to the refugee evacuation between January 23 and May 8, 1945. While there were large losses of life during "Hannibal," the remarkable operation was an evacuation that dwarfed even Dunkirk: in 15 weeks 800,000–900,000 civilians and 350,000 soldiers were taken from the east to Germany and Denmark in spite of fuel shortages, Soviet mines, and submarines. Up to 1,000 vessels were used and 160 were lost, and while many of the "*Goldfasan*" top brass ensured they themselves got away, the Kriegsmarine performed heroically to move civilians as well. This movement continued after the war ended.

An important part of the Soviet battle plan in the Baltic was the laying of mines. Soviet minelaying submarines accounted for eight German vessels in 1945. They themselves were able to avoid the German minefields laid in the Gulf of Finland by using Finnish bases.

The Germans had few capital ships in the Baltic, but the most successful was probably the heavy cruiser *Admiral Scheer* whose bombardment of Soviet positions attacking Samland allowed the re-establishment of the connection between Pillau and Königsberg which helped the city hold out until April 9.

Opposite, Above: *Soviet submarines of the Baltic Fleet sank 13 transports in 1945. Lembit—seen in Helsinki—was a minelayer and her mines sank M421 and Vs343 in 1945.*

Opposite, Below: *Captain-Lieutenant Suvorov in the combat cabin of his G-5 class torpedo boat—300 built, 73 lost. By the end of the war there were 24 in the Baltic and 124 in the Pacific.*

Above: *Taken from a German propaganda magazine, this graphic view of a sinking merchant ship highlights the role of the submarine during World War II—not just in the Atlantic, but in the Baltic as well.*

Left: *Refugees from Königsberg aboard Hans Albrecht Wedel in 1945. She was bombed and sank on April 8.*

Below: *The Wilhelm Gustloff was torpedoed on January 30, 1945, by Soviet submarine S-13 in the Baltic Sea while evacuating Germans—civilians and military—from Gotenhafen (Gdynia). As many as 9,400 people died.*

ВИКТОР ИВАНОВ, О. БУРОВА-45

ВРАГ КОВАРЕН
— БУДЬ НА-ЧЕКУ!

Poland 2

By January 1945, the Red Army had fought its way into a position where it could begin a final drive toward Berlin. The Germans didn't quite realize the depth of their predicament. The war in the east had always been far away in the east and the whole of Poland was between the communists and the Reich. The Vistula was 375 miles (600km) of German-held territory away from the Oder. Further south, the Carpathians protected Slovakia and Hungary. Anyway, there were more immediate things to worry about in August 1944—such as the collapse of their defenses in Normandy. But the huge defeat inflicted on them by Operation Bagration showed how things were going to go in the future and the final days of the offensive saw the Soviets gain bridgeheads over the Vistula at Sandomierz and near Warsaw. After beating off the inevitable counterattack, the Soviets dug in and prepared for their next offensive.

The Vistula–Oder Offensive

The next offensive would be a while coming. In order to be suitably manned and supplied, huge numbers of troops and enormous stockpiles of equipment were built up in the regions of the three jumping off points during the December 1944–January 1945 period.

One of the biggest factors in the Soviets' favor in January 1945 was that although German intelligence was aware of the intensive preparations, Hitler refused to believe the reports given to him by Guderian, dismissing them as fantasy. This directly led to his refusing permission to withdraw further troops from the besieged Courland Pocket, thus reducing the chance to bolster the defenses. To make matters worse, Hitler moved Heeresgruppe A's IV. SS-Panzerkorps from its position on the Vistula near Warsaw, along with 96. and 711. Infanterie-Divisionen, to Hungary to support *Unternehmen Konrad*—a vain attempt to break the encirclement of Budapest.

The brunt of the initial attack fell on Heeresgruppe A under Generaloberst Josef Harpe. A lack of equipment and manpower meant the German forces were far weaker than they should have been as well as badly overstretched,

Opposite: *"The enemy is crafty—be on your guard!," a 1945 poster by Viktor Ivanov, 1945.*

Above: *The border between Germany and Poland is reestablished in 1945. In fact, Russia would retain its 1940 appropriations and Poland would shift its borders west to the Oder–Neisse line, in the process losing 20 percent of its land area.*

ranging the best part of 250 miles (400km) from east of Warsaw down along the banks of the Vistula and as far as the Carpathian Mountains. Heeresgruppe A was made up of three armies: 9. (Gen Smilo von Lüttwitz) which was located in the Warsaw area, 4. Panzer (Gen Fritz-Hubert Gräser) which was based opposite the Soviet bridgehead—the Sandomierz or Baranów salient—and 17. (Gen Friedrich Schulz) which was positioned further to the south. Together these were made up of some 450,000 soldiers, 4,100 artillery pieces, and 1,150 tanks, although many were outside the zone of the current Soviet offensive (especially the armor reserves which had been sent to Hungary).

In stark contrast, the Soviets were able to field over 2.2 million soldiers who were spread between two fronts. One of these, under Marshal Georgy Zhukov, was the 1st Belorussian Front, which was distributed from the Warsaw area to the south around the Magnuszew and Puławy bridgeheads. The other—the 1st Ukrainian Front, commanded by Marshal Ivan Konev—was based at the Sandomierz bridgehead.

The numerical advantage was not just in troops though—the Red Army also had enormous quantities of heavy equipment. There were more than 7,042 tanks and self-propelled assault guns, as well as 13,763 artillery guns, 14,812 mortars, 4,936 anti-tank guns, 2,198 Katyusha multiple-rocket launchers, and 5,000 aircraft.

The Germans were not only at a massive disadvantage in terms of manpower—their problems were compounded by the fact that they did not know where the Soviets would choose to strike. This meant that they had to defend the entire length of the Vistula. They had been making use of whomsoever they could—1.5 million civilians, slave labor, etc—to dig antitank ditches and trenches. But instead of robust concentrations of defenders, they were spread far too thinly to have any significant chance of success. It also forced them to reduce reserves and fall-back positions to a minimum, going completely against German military doctrine, since the usual policy was to fall back and then make immediate counterattacks using mobile armor reserves whenever defenses had been overcome.

As if all this wasn't bad enough, Hitler had refused Guderian's recommendations to shorten and straighten the front lines. The Führer had ordered that the front line (*Hauptkampflinie*) and *Grosskampflinie* (main defense line) be placed closer together in an attempt to make up for

Continued on p. 91.

Below: *a Soviet 152mm M1935 Br-2 gun. Only 39 of these guns were made and production ended in 1940. They, along with other heavy, semi-mobile artillery pieces, were grouped together as part of the Supreme Command's Special Reserve. As such they were allocated to support offensives against fortified areas in what were known as Breakthrough Artillery Divisions. Crewed by 15 men, it fired HE and concrete piercing rounds up to a range of 25kms.*

Below right: *ISU-152 Moskva of the 1419th Heavy Self-propelled Gun Regiment, VII Guards Tank Corps in Poland, January 1945. As part of the 1st Ukrainian Front, VII Corps took part in the Sandomierz-Silesian Offensive advancing through Poland.*

Opposite, Below: *This Soviet 120mm mortar M1938 was issued 4–6 per infantry regiment throughout the war. Six crew men could fire up to 15 rounds per minute. It was mounted on a purpose-built chassis that could be motor or horse drawn. An improved version was available from 1943 onward.*

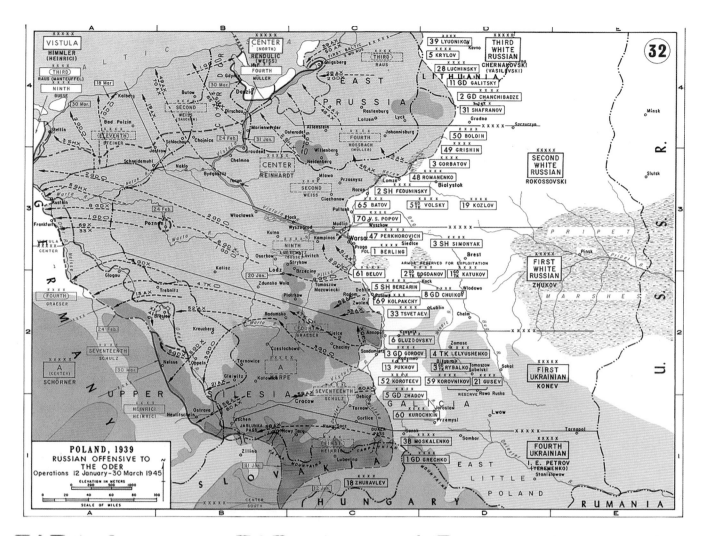

POLAND, 1939
RUSSIAN OFFENSIVE TO
THE ODER
Operations 12 January–30 March 1945

ELEVATION IN METERS
200   500   1000

0   20   40   60   80   100
SCALE OF MILES

Above: *The Soviet offensive that started in early January 1945 took the front from the Vistula to the Oder, an advance of 300 miles inside two weeks. The defense thickened as the Red Army neared Germany, but by the time they reached the Oder, they were less than 50 miles from Berlin.*

With so many men and so much armor lost in the Ardennes and the remnants then sent to Hungary, the Soviet attackers had a significant strength advantage—probably a numerical superiority of nearly four to one:

	Armored corps	Infantry divisions
Konev	9	66
Zhukov	13	53
Rokossovsky	7	59
Chernyakhovsky	2	60
Total	31	238

In mid-January German orders of battle show the following divisions (many understrength) between the Carpathians and Memel:

	Panzer divisions	Infantry divisions
Heeresgruppe A	5	32
Heeresgruppe Mitte	2	44
Total	7	74

Warsaw Rising

The Warsaw Rising by the Polish resistance which took place in the summer of 1944 lasted for 63 days before it was brutally suppressed by the Germans. It had been organized to break out just before the Soviets arrived, with the belief that the resistance would get significant help from the Red Army. The accepted view in the west is that Stalin, however, had other ideas, and halted his troops until the Nazis had done their work in wiping out the uprising. Whether this is true is debatable. There's no doubt the Red Army was fighting hard battles to the south of the city—but it's also true that Stalin's regime had itself committed atrocities against the Poles after taking its share of the country in 1939 and didn't want to relinquish the land it had annexed. Whatever the truth, when it was all over, the Germans rounded up the Polish Army soldiers who had joined the battle and sent them to PoW camps. The whole civilian population was then evicted from the city—some were sent to transit camps, while tens of thousands of others went to labor and concentration camps. The lucky ones were transported elsewhere and released. The city itself was then systematically destroyed through a mix of demolition and burning. The Red Army finally liberated Warsaw on January 17, 1945.

Opposite, Above: *"The city must completely disappear from the surface of the earth and serve only as a transport station for the Wehrmacht. No stone can remain standing. Every building must be razed to its foundation." — SS chief Heinrich Himmler, October 17, 1944, SS officers conference. This is the Warsaw Ghetto after the Germans had razed it.*

Opposite, Below: *The Polish Home Army troops leave the city after the capitulation.*

Right: *Maj Ivan Denisovich Frolov (center) with officers of the Russian National Liberation Army during the Warsaw Uprising. Frolov, along with other ROA members, was found guilty of treason by the USSR and hanged in 1946. Note the ROA badge on the arm of the man at right (see also p. 16).*

Below: *Panoramic view of the monument from the eastern corner. The rising was downplayed in postwar years and the Soviet-backed government was happy to condemn both the Home Army and the Polish government in exile. A memorial, designed by sculptor Wincenty Kućma and architect Jacek Budyn, was unveiled on 1989.*

Right: *Kraków survived most of the war unscathed but as the front line came closer it was at risk of becoming victim to the German scorched earth policy. Luckily, however, the city wasn't easily defended—and had no real strategic significance, so the Germans abandoned rather than destroyed it. They left on January 17, 1945, and the only demolitions were the bridges along the river Dunajec. Additionally, they closed one of the downstream dams raising the water level considerably. The extra time the Red Army took to cross the river allowed the Germans time to retreat with all their loot. The Soviets arrived two days later on January 19, 1945. This is Debnicki Bridge over the Vistula, with Wawel Castle in the background.*

Center right *Parade of the First Polish Army on Marszałkowska Street in captured Warsaw on January 19, 1945.*

Below right *Military Cemetery in Powazki—a ceremony unveiling the monument in honor of those who died in the fights for the liberation of Warsaw.*

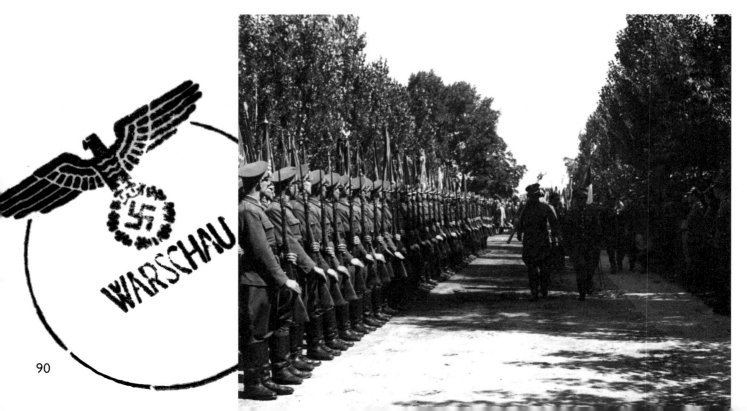

the low numbers of troops available. He hoped that by concentrating them they could be mutually supporting—but this meant that the front line was unable to fall back to the second line to save itself from any artillery bombardment because the Soviet artillery could reach both lines when the assault began.

Although the original planning had been for a start date of January 20, 1945, the actual offensive began at 04:35 on January 12 with a protracted artillery bombardment in the Sandomierz–Baranów bridgehead. The date had been brought forward due to reports that there might be an early thaw in the region. If this had happened during the battle, the transition from frozen ground to mud would have been disastrous as the Soviet armor would have been stranded.

The opening barrage by the guns of the 1st Ukrainian Front was brought to bear on the positions held by 4. Panzerarmee, particularly those of the XLVIII. Panzerkorps. It was so intense that several of the units more or less ceased to exist. After that had finished, several skirmishes took place which were then followed up by another intense artillery barrage at 10:00. When the Red Army's Third Guards and Fourth Tank armies advanced at 14:00, they found a badly damaged 4. Panzerarmee, which had lost two-thirds of its artillery and a quarter of its troops.

Within the first week of the Soviet's attack, Harpe had been replaced as commander of Heeresgruppe A by Generaloberst Ferdinand Schörner, and shortly after, Gen Smilo van Lüttwitz of 9. Armee was relieved by Gen Theodor Busse. The result of the offensive was more or less a foregone conclusion due to the overwhelming superiority of the Soviet forces. Once the defenses had been breached, the Soviet armor then poured through and headed west. This enabled them to cut off the city of Kielce before it could be further reinforced. Within five days of the beginning of the battle, they had penetrated over 80 miles (130km).

The German lines were also crossed in several other places, particularly from the Magnuszew and Puławy bridgeheads by the 1st Belorussian Front. They attacked the German 9. Armee at 08:30 with a similar protracted artillery barrage to that earlier fired by the 1st Ukrainian Front. The bombardment was followed up by the Soviet Thirty-third and Sixty-ninth armies which forced their way out of the Puławy bridgehead, making 19 miles (30 km), while the Fifth Shock and the Eighth Guards Armies also broke through from the Magnuszew bridgehead.

Above: *German PzKpfw V Panther from Panzer-Regiment 31 of 5. Panzerdivision in Goldap, one of the first cities in East Prussia captured by the Red Army. It fell on October 20, 1944, but a German counterattack returned the city to their control. This proved short-lived and it was retaken by the Red Army in January 1945 by which time 90 percent of the buildings had been destroyed.*

Below: *The award for taking part in the capture of Warsaw.*

Their roles completed, they then passed the reins for the follow-on attack to the Second and First Guards Tank armies. The German 9. Armee tried to mount several counterattacks, but they faced such superior forces that they all failed. Before long Warsaw was encircled, but the main focus of operations was to reach the line of the Oder river. The Germans were in such disarray though that once the Soviets had broken through into their rear areas, they were unable to put up much defense. Despite the logistical problems imposed by supplying the troops over such large distances, by January 25, the attackers had got beyond Posen (Poznań). Although the mileages they achieved daily then slowed down, they still reached the banks of the River Oder by the beginning of February—at this point, they were only 43 miles (70km) from Berlin. In just over two weeks, the Red Army had covered 300 miles (485km).

The speed of the offensive had practically destroyed Heeresgruppe Mitte and Heeresgruppe A. On January 25, Hitler renamed his broken armies. Heeresgruppe Nord trapped in the Courland Pocket became Heeresgruppe Kurland; what was left of Heeresgruppe Mitte around Königsberg became Nord and a new unit—Heeresgruppe Weichsel (Vistula)—was formed from what remained of Heeresgruppe A and other units. Instead of appointing a seasoned veteran to lead it, Hitler selected Reichsführer-SS Heinrich Himmler. Although he lacked a military background, he made up for this with a mix of fanatical loyalty and a total adherence to the imposition of harsh discipline, matters that Hitler felt were more relevant. Needless to say, he was useless.

Lower Silesian Offensive

Silesia runs either side of the Oder from Germany into Czechoslovakia. On the banks of the Oder the Red Army paused to regroup and began operations to protect its extended flanks. On February 8 Marshal Ivan Konev's 1st Ukrainian Front attacked. The aim was to broaden the gains made in the Vistula–Oder Offensive and to neutralize any threat from the south or from the fortress city of Breslau. Konev's men used the Steinau and Ohlau bridgeheads that had been established on the west bank of the Oder at the end of the previous offensive. The Soviets quickly broke through the German lines and pushed into the rear areas.

The Third Guards Tank Army then encircled Breslau and attacked from the rear (pp. 94–95) while the Fourth Tank Army moved directly westward from its jumping off point at Steinau. By February 15, the encirclement was complete with only the German 269. Infanterie-Division managing to escape being trapped. While the isolation of Breslau was under way, the Fourth Tank Army was fighting the 4. Panzerarmee and making its way toward the banks of the Neisse river.

The Germans certainly had not lost their resolve, and elements of the *Panzerkorps Großdeutschland* and XXIV. Panzerkorps made an unexpected and strong counterattack that almost encircled Lelyushenko's Fourth Tank Army. Before this could happen though, the Soviet Fifty-second Army and the Third Guards Tank Army were brought in, removing the threats to the Fourth Tank Army's flanks. The offensive left the Red Army on the banks of the Neisse river.

Upper Silesian Offensive

The second operation in Silesia was needed to remove the threat of German 17. Armee under General Friedrich Schulz, based in the Sudeten Mountains that range across parts of Poland, the Czech Republic, and Germany.

Heeresgruppe Mitte, under Generaloberst Ferdinand Schörner, planned to launch a major counterattack against Konev's 1st Ukrainian Front and maintain German control over a region that was not only an important part of the overall German defense strategy, but that also contained vital economic resources. To this end, the build-up of Schulz's forces was prioritized for military supply before the LVI. Panzerkorps and the XXXIX. Panzerkorps

Continued on p. 96.

FIRST POLISH ARMY

When Germany invaded Russia, the position of Poles taken as PoWs in 1939 and those deported from Soviet-occupied Poland in 1939–1941, changed. Freed, some ended up as Anders' Polish II Corps that fought in the Italian Campaign. Others finally became First Polish Army commanded until October 1944 by Lt Gen Zygmunt Berling, and then Maj Gen Stanislaw Poplawski. Its first action was in summer 1944 with 1st Belorussian Front. In September 1944 it took part in fighting around south Warsaw and, eventually, liberated the city in January 1945. Second Polish Army entered service in January 1945. First Army took part in the battle of Berlin and sustained 10,000 casualties. It was disbanded in August 1945. The "Berling Army" was seen as Soviet by the government-in-exile in Britain and its commander a traitor.

1 Soviet tanks enter Ścinawa. A T-34/85 memorial remembered the event.

2 Another T-34/85 memorial. This one in Gliwice remembers General Jozef Kimbar and the Polish I Armored Corps which fought northeast of Dresden, then in Berlin, and, finally, Prague

3 Polish IS-2. 4th Heavy Tank Regiment of First Army was equipped with 21 IS-2s. It crossed the Oder, fought on the Hohenzollern Canal and ended the war in Zuhlsdorf, north of Berlin.

4 Reenactors remember the 1st Tadeusz Kosciuszko Infantry Division that formed the basis of First Polish Army.

5 Monument in Sandau remembering First Polish Army.

Below: Polish Piast dynasty eagle used as a cap badge by the Polish 1st Tadeusz Kosciuszko Infantry Division which fought in Berlin.

Breslau

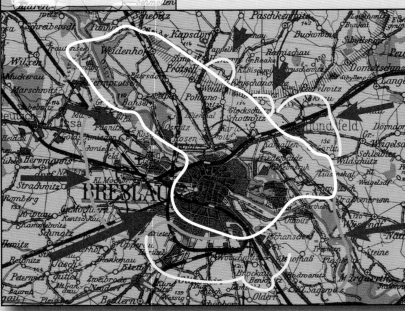

Attacks
January 1945
Middle of February
End of March
At capitulation

In the summer of 1944, Hitler made Breslau (present-day Wrocław) a fortress, under the command of Gauleiter Karl Hanke. Hanke had an interesting pedigree. He gave up his position of Secretary of State in the Ministry of Propaganda to fight in Poland and then with Rommel's 7. Panzerdivision in France. Trouble was that he was the lover of Magda Goebbels and the two wanted to marry. Refused permission by Hitler, Hanke took up a position in Silesia—probably lucky to have escaped execution. His loyalty, however, doesn't seem to have been affected because he conducted the siege with draconian strictness. Nicknamed the "hangman of Breslau," he and his regime killed over a thousand people accused of cowardice or backsliding, including the deputy mayor, who was shot in front of the city hall with the epitaph, "Whoever fears death in honor, dies in shame!" Of course, when push came to shove, Hanke himself fled the city in a specially prepared aircraft, only to die later in Czechoslovakia while attempting to evade capture.

Hanke refused to allow any evacuation of civilians until January 19. By this time the Soviet bombardments had destroyed more or less all the area's transport links, and so those who were able to leave had to do so on foot. It has been estimated that 100,000 died of the cold while trekking toward the west.

Any chance of escape was finally removed when the Soviets finally surrounded the city on February 15. The following day, the Red Army made its first serious attack on the city. The fortifications were so strong, however, that the attacks slowed almost to a halt and the fighting came down to an attritional street by street and house to house grind, with the casualties rising: over 70 Red Army tanks in the first three days alone.

Top: *A 1939 map of Breslau showing the main axes of attack and shrinking perimeter.*

Above: *A memorial in modern-day Wrocław.*

As things got more and more desperate, both civilian and slave laborers were forced into the fray, demolishing bridges and building defenses. The coercion was simple—if they didn't work, they didn't eat. The Soviets finally launched a much heavier operation on April 1—this saw the city put under a seemingly endless bombardment, destroying much of what was left. It failed to stop the fighting though, which carried on among the ruins and down in the sewers.

Breslau held out until May 6, by which time the death toll on both sides was immense—although sources vary, it has been estimated that 170,000 civilians, 6,000 German, and 13,000 Red Army troops died during the 80-day siege. The invaders wasted no time in finding any alcohol that was left, and went on a drunken rampage, looting and raping wherever the opportunity presented itself.

Left: Soviet ROKS-3 flamethrower unit in the city. Flamethrowers are horribly effective weapons in urban fighting and their operators were targeted wherever they were used. To make them more difficult to spot, the Soviets made the flame tube look like an ordinary rifle (see photo p. 119).

Center left: The wreck of an IS-2 of 87th Guards Heavy Tank Regiment.

Below left: Soviet troops pass a knocked-out 8.8cm flak.

Below: The Silesian Daily of January 26 leads with an announcement from Gauleiter Hanke. "Women of all ages as well as children under 16 and men over 60 must leave the city of Breslau.
   To aid the transport of the sick and frail, all who can should set off on foot."
   Resupply of the encircled city fell to the Luftwaffe which flew large numbers of missions. As an example, Morzik (2017) cites

Schlesische Tageszeitung
AMTLICHES BLATT DER NSDAP UND SÄMTLICHER BEHÖRDEN

16. Jahrgang / Nr. 22 **   Festung Breslau, Freitag, den 26. Januar 1945

Anordnung

Frauen jeden Alters sowie männliche Jugendliche unter 16 Jahren und Männer über 60 Jahre haben das Stadtgebiet von Breslau zu verlassen.

Um den Abtransport von Kranken und Gebrechlichen weiter zu ermöglichen, setzen sich alle Gehfähigen zu Fuß in Marsch.

Hanke
Gauleiter und Reichsverteidigungskommissar

operational reports for 2. Gruppe, Lufttransportgeschwader 3, which flew 566 missions from February 7 till April, delivered 657 tons of supplies, 3,770 troops (two battalions of Fallschirmjäger—II./FJR25 was delivered on February 28 by Go242 and DFS230 gliders towed by He111s and Do17s; III./FJR26 arrived a few days later, landed on Breslau-Gandau by Ju52), and evacuated 3,282 wounded. 2 Gruppe lost 52 Ju52s—out of 152 lost in the period—along with 21 KIA, 23 WIA, and 84 MIA. Two other Gruppen—1. and 3./Kampfgeschwader 4—flew similar sorties from Königgrätz (see also pp. 62–63).

Right: *Heavily loaded with infantrymen, a column of T-34 tanks drive past the wreck of a Marder (Marten) III into a German industrial area in Upper Silesia. On the pole to the left a Soviet engineer repairs telephone lines.*

Below right: *T-34/85 of IX Tank Corps in Poland, 1945. On January 14, 1945, the corps was part of the 1st Belorussian Front's attack from the Puławy bridgehead on the west bank of the Vistula. This had been created in August 1944 by Sixty-ninth Army. The corps would go on to take part in the battle of the Seelow Heights and the assault on Berlin.*

undertook a two-pronged attack on March 1—*Unternehmen Gemse* (Chamois). These were led by General Nehring and made up of the 17. Panzer and the Führergrenadier divisions in the north, and the 8. Panzerdivision in the south. (The Führergrenadierbrigade had been upgraded to divisional status on January 26, under Generalmajor Erich von Hassenstein, as had the Führerbegleitbrigade under Generalmajor Otto Remer.)

Although the strength of the attacks caught the Soviets by surprise, within two days they were building up their own counterattacks. This threat caused Nehring to rein in his plans, and instead of a wider sweep, he ordered the 6. Volksgrenadier Division to encircle the town of Lauban, where they cut off and massacred large numbers of Soviet troops. This was followed up by an offensive to the southeast on March 9 at Striegau where over the night of March 11–12 parts of the Fifth Guards Army were once again cut off and massacred.

The success at Lauban was one of the last real successes for the German Army and much was made of it for propaganda purposes. Goebbels visited the town and made a broadcast. More famously, Hitlerjugend messenger Willi Hübner was awarded the Iron Cross and visited Hitler at the Reichskanzlei (see p. 218).

The success spurred Schörner to push to the north to relieve encircled Breslau, but Konev anticipated the risk and redeployed his Fourth Tank Army

Left: *A Soviet column of IS-2 tanks of 1st Belorussian Front prepare to leave a relatively undamaged village in Pomerania. Passengers, such as those shown here, were always welcome as they could act as the tank's eyes to preempt ambushers wielding Panzerfaüste. Note the cable on the last tank: for use hauling broken down vehicles off or back on to the road.*

The IS-2 proved its worth in August 1944 when sPzAbt 501 counterattacked the Sandomierz bridgehead over the Vistula. The battle lasted from August 11–13. Sledgehammers (2004) identifies the Russian defenders as being nine T-34/76s of 53rd Guards Tank Brigade, eleven IS-2s and a IS-85 of 71st Independent Heavy Tank Regiment. "Throughout three days of fighting, Soviet forces destroyed or captured 14 King Tigers out of a total strength of around 30 or 31 King Tigers in two companies of Heavy Tank Battalion 501." Of the eleven IS-2s, three were destroyed and seven damaged.

Below left: *T-34/85 of 1st Guards Tank Brigade in Poland. The brigade was part of VIII Guards Mechanized Corps, an element of Col Gen of Tank Troops Mikhail Katukov's 1st Guards Tank Army. VIII Corps was made up of four brigades—1st Guards, 19th, 20th, and 21st Guards Mechanized—and, attached in 1945, 64th Guards Tank Regiment. Included on its inventory for the fighting around Warsaw, in Pomerania, and Berlin were 185 Lend-Lease M4A2 tanks.*

to prevent any such threat from developing. They moved forward and attacked on March 15, breaking through the German lines to the west of Oppeln and then heading south toward the town of Neustadt. While this was going on, the IV Guards Tank Corps struck out toward the Neisse and the Fifty-ninth and Sixtieth armies broke through the lines to the southeast of Oppeln. Once through, they then pushed west to join up with the Fourth Tank Army. This placed 1. Panzerarmee's XI. Armeekorps at serious risk of being encircled.

Further south, the Soviet Thirty-eighth Army attacked troops of LIX. Armeekorps, which then withdrew with minimal losses. The LVI. Panzerkorps was not so fortunate though—the Estonians of 20. Waffen-Grenadier-Division der SS (estnische Nr.1) and the 168. Infanterie-Division were caught by the Fourth Tank and Fifty-ninth armies. Some 15,000 Germans were captured and another 15,000 killed as a consequence. The Red Army launched further attacks on March 24, and within a week the towns of Ratibor and Katscher fell. This marked the end of major offensives in the region.

Slowly, the Red Army forced its way through the area, pushing the Germans back to the Czech border—they were still fighting right up until the war ended, when Schörner's men finally surrendered. The Soviet Silesian offensives may have cost them many men and tanks, but it had removed Heeresgruppe Mitte's threat to the southern flanks of the 1st Ukrainian Front as it advanced on Berlin.

Posen

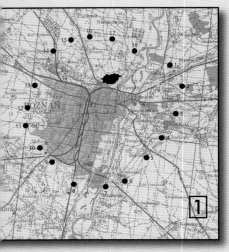

In January 1945, Posen (Poznań in Polish) was designated a *Festung*. The fact that it had already been heavily fortified during the era of Prussian rule in the 1800s made it much easier to build further defenses at short notice. Around the city's circumference there were 18 enormous forts, each about 1.5 miles (2km) apart. These were largely underground and built with multiple stories. The forts were surrounded by ditches that were about 25ft (8m) deep and 30ft (10m) wide, and within the fort itself there were numerous bunkers with walls at least 3ft (1m) thick.

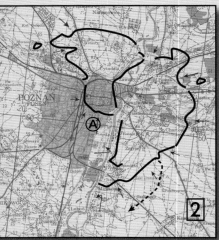

The problem facing the Red Army was that Posen was too much of a threat to simply go around. A communications hub, it lay between Warsaw and Berlin, and so had to be taken to remove the risk of counterattacks being launched from it. It had a sizable garrison, with a mishmash of other units, including Volkssturm, Luftwaffe ground forces, ex-policemen, as well as students from the area's officer training academies. They were opposed by the battle-hardened Soviet Eighth Guards Army under General Vasily Ivanovich Chuikov. Among many other offensives, these tough soldiers had fought with distinction at places like Stalingrad and Odessa.

The offensive against the area around Posen began on January 21, when the Soviet First Guards Tank Army crossed the Warthe (Warta) River. They and other tank units wrought havoc with German forces in the region, capturing large amounts of equipment and much infrastructure, including several airfields. They bypassed the city itself, however, leaving that task for others as they carried on moving to the west.

Chuikov's Eighth Guards Army began assaulting Posen's outer defenses on January 25, and a lightning attack by the 27th and 74th Guards Rifle Divisions saw two of the perimeter forts fall. From then on, there was little doubt as to the final outcome. In desperation, the Germans removed Generalmajor Ernst Mattern as the commander and replaced him with Oberst Ernst Gonell, a hardline Nazi, who was told of his promotion to Generalmajor in a telegram from Himmler dated February 9. He imposed a regime of harsh discipline, where any sign of defeatism was met with the death penalty.

Gradually, the overwhelming might of the Red Army saw the Soviet troops inch their way toward the center of the city, fighting block to block, and house to house. Gonell was under the illusion that help from other German forces was on the way, but by February 15 he realized that, despite what he'd been told by higher command, this was not going to happen. In order to save some of his men, he ordered those who were on the east side of the Warta river to try to break through Soviet lines—and around 2,000 managed to do so. By that stage, the only part of Posen still under Gonell's control was the citadel, but disposed around it were the 29th Guards Rifle Corps, the 27th, 82nd, and 74th Guards Rifle divisions. The concluding attack began on February 18, starting with the troops crossing the ditches and scaling the ramparts using ladders—a throwback to an earlier age. A terrible price was paid though, as the redoubts to either side were able to enfilade machine gun fire on the soldiers throughout their assault. It took three days to clear them using everything from demolition charges to flamethrowers.

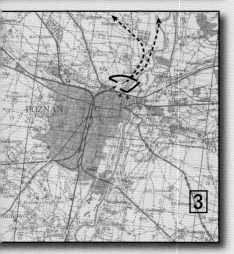

With the redoubts out of the way, on February 22 the Soviets built temporary bridges to get their tanks and self-propelled guns up and into the citadel's main area. Realizing that all was lost, Gonell allowed his troops to try to escape. He then shot himself in the head, rather than suffer the indignity of being taken prisoner. Command returned to Generalmajor Mattern, who surrendered the surviving 12,000 German troops.

1–3 The siege of Festung Posen took place between January 24 and February 23, 1945. The city had a large garrison of 15,700 men and additional forces including 8,000 Volkssturm, a battalion from the Hungarian Army, SS and Polizei troops, plus a number of Luftwaffe units. The precise figures are difficult to ascertain. Russian postwar documents supply the figure of 40,000, but that's almost certainly inflated. Günther Baumann (Posen 1945: Bastion on the Warthe) offers 15,000 German and Latvian troops, supported by a few Sturmgeschütze, one Tiger I, two Panthers, one Hetzer, and a few SPWs. Ranged against them were units of Sixty-ninth and Eighth Guards armies. The battle saw around 6,000 on each side killed. The three maps show the defenses shrinking from January 21 where the defense was based on a ring of forts (1), through February 7 (2), to February 23 (3) when only the citadel was left.

4 Established on August 1, 1940, Stalag Luft XXID took about 3,000 PoWs. Note the Polish caps.

5 Reichsführer-SS Heinrich Himmler with the Gauleiter of Reichsgau Wartheland, Arthur Greiser (left), and Chief of the General Staff Heinz Guderian (right) salute a parade of the Posen Volkssturm from the back of an SdKfz 7. Posen was a significant location for Himmler. It was in this city in early October 1943 that he gave two speeches discussing the progress of the extermination of the Jews.

6 IS-2s of the 34th Independent Heavy Tank Regiment in Wilda, southern Posen (around A in map 2). The regiment was supporting the 74th and 27th Guards Rifle divisions whose attack started on January 26.

7 and 8: Posen Town Hall then and in today's Poznań.

East Prussian Offensive

The first Soviet attack on East Prussia took place in October 1944 but wasn't powerful enough to achieve its aims. On January 13, 1945, alongside the Vistula–Oder Offensive, the 3rd Belorussian Front commanded by General Ivan Chernyakhovsky took center stage in a new offensive. The 3rd Belorussian Front's role was to drive against the German 3. Panzerarmee (Generaloberst Erhard Raus) and 4. Armee (General der Infanterie Friedrich Hossbach until January 29; thereafter General der Infanterie Friedrich-Wilhelm Müller) of Heeresgruppe Mitte (Generaloberst Georg-Hans Reinhardt). Simultaneously, the 1st Baltic Front under General Bagramyan aimed to tackle the elements of 3. Panzerarmee which were dug in along the Neman river (aka, the Memel) and in a bridgehead at Memel (present-day Klaipeda). This attack was in its turn supported on its left by the 2nd Belorussian Front led by Marshal Konstantin Rokossovsky.

The offensive started with an intense artillery bombardment, and then the troops attempted to push forward. The defense they faced—backed up by substantially built lines of defenses and field fortifications—was extremely strong and after five days of severe fighting little progress had been made: only some 12 miles (20km) of ground captured. Eventually, however, the weight of Soviet power began to tell, and what was left of 3. Panzerarmee retreated into Königsberg.

**HEINRICH HIMMLER
(1900–45)**

The second most powerful man in Nazi Germany, head of the SS, architect of the Holocaust, and planner of the Nazi's Plan for the East that would have involved genocide on an even larger scale than the Nazis perpetuated in the short time they had.

Himmler was a soldier in World War I but didn't reach the front line or see action. He certainly hoped for military honors but when the opportunity arose, he was found wanting, first on the Rhine in Alsace and then as commander of Heeresgruppe Weichsel—Army Group Vistula. Himmler's involvement lasted from January 25 to March 20, 1945, during which time he did very little except sit in his special command train. The strain of this busy life obviously got to him and he fled to the SS hospital at Hohenlychen north of Berlin, visiting Hitler to say "Happy Birthday" en route. Himmler ended his own life after being caught by former Soviet PoWs while posing as Feldwebel Heinrich Hizinger. While undergoing a medical examination by the British in Lüneberg, the Reichsführer-SS took poison. By that time he had been dismissed from all his posts by Hitler's successor, Admiral Dönitz. The Führer had pronounced him traitor and stripped him of his party membership and titles on April 29. The banality of his image brings to mind the words of Leonard Cohen's poem "All There is to Know About Adolph Eichmann":

*What did you expect?
Talons?*

Meanwhile Rokossovsky launched his push west on January 14 across the Narew river—this was also fiercely contested, but six days later, he was ordered at short notice to turn north and attack Elbing (present-day Elblag). This movement posed a serious threat to the positions of the two German armies—2. (Generaloberst Walter Weiß) and 4. (Gen Friedrich-Wilhelm Müller)—to the west of Königsberg, that risked being isolated if the Soviets were able to reach the coast. The situation was made worse for them by the capture of Allenstein (present-day Olsztyn) by the Red Army's III Guards Cavalry Corps on January 22. Although Weiß asked for permission to withdraw his troops in the face of such immediate danger, Hitler refused it. Two days later, Rokossovsky's forward tank units succeeded in making it to the beaches of the Vistula Lagoon.

Friedrich Hossbach had commanded 4. Armee since July 18, 1944. He had been Hitler's adjutant and was author of the Hossbach Memorandum, the minutes of a 1937 meeting that laid out Hitler's intention to use military action to gain his territorial aims. It was used at the Nuremberg trials in 1945. Around January 23, it became clear that the Soviet offensive threatened to encircle his army. In the east, Rokossovsky had reached the sea; in the west the Soviet Forty-eighth Army was between him and Elbing. What became the Heiligenbeil Pocket was forming with his army squeezed into a *Kessel* with his back to the sea. Hossbach decided to withdraw, fearing another Stalingrad. His personal opinion of the area and the fortresses within it was that they were all militarily useless, so he intended to relocate his men to the west of the Vistula where they stood a chance of holding their ground. Unfortunately for Gen Hossbach, however, he was acting in direct conflict with Hitler's orders, and he was summarily dismissed from his position and the withdrawal was canceled. He was replaced by the "butcher of Crete," Friedrich-Wilhelm Müller.

The situation deteriorated quickly and soon German forces in East Prussia— from January 25 retitled Heeresgruppe Nord—were isolated in pockets: in the east around Memel and Samland; in Königsberg; in the Heiligenbeil Pocket; and further west around Danzig. The pocket was finally defeated in the Soviet Braunsberg Offensive Operation (March 13–29), during which 3rd Belorussian Front commander, General Ivan Chernyakhovsky, was killed. The Russians claimed 80,000 killed and 50,000 captured. The survivors escaped across the Vistula Lagoon to the Nehrung— the Vistula Spit, that linked with Danzig (which fell on March 30) to the west and Pillau to the east, although some units such as the Fallschirm-Panzergrenadier-Division 2 Hermann Göring and 24. Panzerdivision were evacuated by sea.

Opposite, Above: *Polish troops running through a town. The men seem to be wearing tank crew coveralls. The man with the container on his back may be in similar dress with a telogreika (padded winter jacket) on top. Whatever is in the container is of value, as the carrier is clearly being protected.*

Opposite, Below: *Soviet troops in Poland. The artillery piece is an ML-20 152mm gun-howitzer. A successful design that saw service into the 1950s with the Red Army, some 6,900 were produced 1937–47 along with 4,000 ML-20S barrels that were used in the SU/ISU-152s.*

Left: *Men of the Polish People's Army in urban combat. They are wearing the traditional Polish cap, the rogatywka, a permissible symbol of their nationality. This group would appear to be artillery spotters. The majority of the Polish forces on the Eastern Front served with First Polish Army under the 1st Belorussian Front's command.*

Königsberg

Above: Medal awarded by the Soviets for taking part in the capture of Königsberg. It was established on June 9, 1945, at the same time as those for Budapest, Vienna, and Berlin.

Opposite: (G)RC = (Guards) Rifle Corps; (G) TC = (Guards) Tank Corps The battle for Königsberg was bloody and saw a large number of civilians killed both during and after the siege. Taking East Prussia was a costly business for the Red Army, with over 580,000 casualties and the loss of over 3,500 tanks and some 1,500 aircraft. The photos show an ISU-152 in the city after the battle with the shell of the castle behind, and a prewar view. The tower was demolished postwar. The ancient Prussian city—the Albertini was 400 years old in 1944 (**Below**)—was handed to the Soviet Union by the Potsdam Agreement of 1945 and today's Kaliningrad is a Russian exclave.

General der Infanterie Otto Lasch, an experienced and battle-hardened soldier, was appointed Fortress Commander of Königsberg on January 27, 1945. The city's defenses were based on a circle of forts, a good stock of artillery, plus troops retreating back toward the city swelled its defenders to over 100,000 men. On January 27–28 Memel was abandoned and the remaining units of XXVIII. Armeekorps retreated down the spit to Samland. Fighting continued as the Germans attempted to keep a corridor open between Königsberg and Pillau (present-day Baltiysk) which is located on a narrow spit of land on the seaward side of the Vistula Lagoon and was the port from which the civilian population, swelled by refugees from the fighting to over 200,000, attempted to escape back to Germany.

On February 19 elements of 3. Panzerarmee and 4. Armee opened up a corridor which allowed them to re-establish communications with Pillau. The breakout proved possible partly because of the length of the Red Army's supply chains—they struggled to cope with the combination of immense distances, poor roads, and the severe weather conditions experienced at that time of year. Another reason was that the Soviet generals in charge of storming the city were simply not in a hurry. They were determined to put carefully considered plans in place before acting, as they considered it to be a first class fortress which would be a tough nut to crack. Of particular concern were the city's heavy artillery batteries.

As part of the meticulous planning process for the pending assault on Königsberg, the Soviet High Command had a 390sq ft (36sq m) model made of the city at a scale of 1:3000. Its accuracy was kept up to date by a series of aerial reconnaissance photographic sorties, and by interrogating prisoners who were specially taken for the purpose. Hundreds of Red Army officers studied it intensely over the six-week build-up. During this time long-range artillery was brought in so that any troublesome strongpoints or Kriegsmarine vessels could be dealt with promptly. Since the fortifications were so substantial, it was decided that more manpower was needed, and so the Fiftieth Army was added to the roster.

It was quite clear to the defenders that the Soviets were in no hurry to attack—for a considerable time they appeared to be just standing back and observing. They didn't know it at the time, but the Red Army's officers were very well informed in the run-up, among other things attending multiple lectures detailing both the political and the military importance of Königsberg.

The destruction of the Heiligenbeil Pocket at the end of March opened the way for a direct assault on the city. Bad weather caused the organizers to consider postponing the attack, but with the advance on Berlin looming, Stalin was anxious to see Königsberg fall. As a result, the Soviet artillery began a softening up phase of bombardments on April 3—this was followed up three days later when four of their armies assaulted. Their efforts were considerably helped by air attacks. The first defense line was blown away by the bombardment. The second, predicated on the circle of forts, put up much tougher opposition, especially fort 5 in the northwest and 8 in the south. However, the ferocity and determination of the Eleventh Guards Army saw the Pregel crossed and the city center attacked. General Lasch capitulated on April 9 after three days of continuous fighting.

The forces which were trapped on the Samland peninsula—led by General der Panzertruppe Dietrich von Saucken and officially entitled AOK Ostpreußen from April 7—were ranged around the port of Pillau and they lasted a bit longer, but on April 25 their pocket also fell as the result of the Samland Offensive. This marked the end of the East Prussian Offensive, although a smaller group held out until the end of the war on the sandbar of the Vistula Spit.

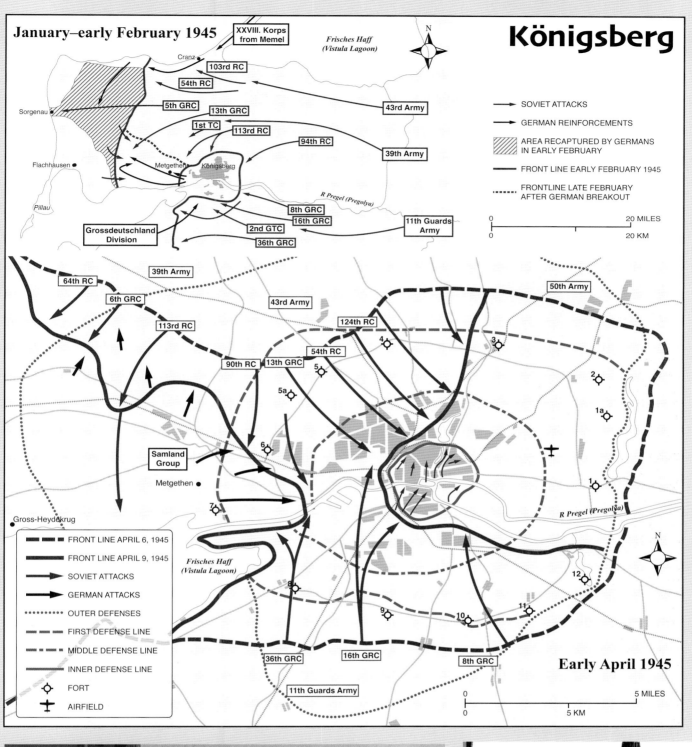

Königsberg

January–early February 1945

XXVIII. Korps from Memel

Frisches Haff (Vistula Lagoon)

N

Cranz
103rd RC
54th RC
43rd Army
5th GRC
13th GRC
1st TC
113rd RC
94th RC
39th Army
Sorgenau
Metgethen
Königsberg
Flachhausen
R Pregel (Pregolya)
Pillau
Grossdeutschland Division
8th GRC
16th GRC
2nd GTC
36th GRC
11th Guards Army

SOVIET ATTACKS
GERMAN REINFORCEMENTS
AREA RECAPTURED BY GERMANS IN EARLY FEBRUARY
FRONT LINE EARLY FEBRUARY 1945
FRONTLINE LATE FEBRUARY AFTER GERMAN BREAKOUT

0   20 MILES
0   20 KM

Early April 1945

39th Army
64th RC
6th GRC
113rd RC
43rd Army
124th RC
50th Army
54th RC
90th RC
13th GRC
Samland Group
Metgethen
Gross-Heydekrug
Frisches Haff (Vistula Lagoon)
R Pregel (Pregolya)
N
36th GRC
16th GRC
8th GRC
11th Guards Army

FRONT LINE APRIL 6, 1945
FRONT LINE APRIL 9, 1945
SOVIET ATTACKS
GERMAN ATTACKS
OUTER DEFENSES
FIRST DEFENSE LINE
MIDDLE DEFENSE LINE
INNER DEFENSE LINE
FORT
AIRFIELD

0   5 MILES
0   5 KM

Right: *A battle-hardened group of Waffen-SS infantry listen with grim resolution to new orders. They are dressed in their signature camouflage smocks and some have mosquito nets wrapped around their helmets. The central figure appears to be armed with a Soviet PPSh-41 submachine gun.*

Below right: *Both the Wehrmacht and the Red Army made use of armored trains as mobile defensive positions, railroad security, and fire support. This appears to be a German type BP-42. The flat car was used to transport a dismountable PzKpfw 38(t), the gun turret mounts a Soviet 76mm field gun and the flak unit is a quadruple 20mm gun equally effective against ground targets.*

Below: *A "brewed up" PzKpfw IV somewhere in Poland during January 1945. Interestingly, the smoke appears to be coming from the top of the turret not from the open hatch, suggesting a posed image. To the right, just visible through the smoke is what appears to be a Tiger I. The hull machine gun of the PzKpfw IV has been removed.*

Left: *German refugees in early 1945. On show at the Capitol cinema is the 1943 production of, A Colleague Comes, a reminder of happier times. The symbol on the wall indicates that this is a collection/ meeting point for the wounded.*

Center left: *A Wehrmacht engineer lays a mine. It appears to be a Tellermine 42 that the engineer is just fusing. This anti-tank mine incorporated a large central pressure plate and had the facility for two anti-handling devices. It contained 5.5kg of explosive and detonated at weights over 100kg.*

Below left and **Below:** *The memorial to the German 1914 victory over Russia at Tannenberg in East Prussia. When he died in 1934, the German commander during the battle and latterly German president—Generalfeldmarschall Paul von Hindenburg—was himself interred there (**Below**). In January 1945 German engineers, under the oversight of Hindenburg's son Oskar, removed the field marshal's coffin and blew up the memorial to prevent it falling into Soviet hands.*

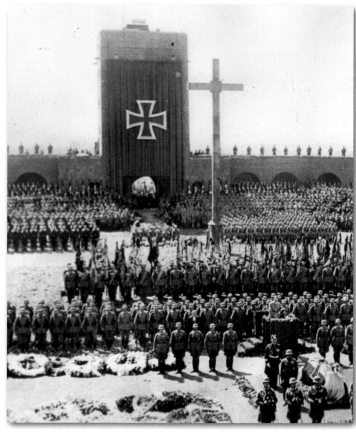

East Pomeranian Offensive

As we have seen, the Soviet offensive slowed in late January and did not continue to strike directly at Berlin. The Stavka decided that the exposed flanks had to be protected. One of the reasons for this decision was the weather: on January 27–28 heavy snow fell and then, on February 1, temperatures soared and a thaw set in. The mud hampered the Soviets' extended supply lines and made movement difficult. Then, the Germans launched a sudden counterattack southward from the town of Stargard on February 15. Codenamed *Unternehmen Sonnenwende* (Solstice), the brainchild of Heinz Guderian, its aim was to relieve encircled Küstrin, but it proved not to be the major assault he had intended, partly because Hitler decided not to commit 6. SS-Panzerarmee but mainly because the Germans found it impossible to concentrate the ten divisions (including seven Panzer divisions) at the starting point—Allied attacks on the German rail network made movement by train extremely slow. Then General der Panzertruppe Walter Wenck who was given the job of "assisting" Himmler was injured in a car crash—a phrase that well describes the abortive counterattack.

Right: An SdKfz7 heavy halftrack towing an 8.8cm Flak AA gun in Stettin—today it's called Szczecin and it's in Poland. It was captured on April 26, 1945 by soldiers of the 2nd Belorussian Front of the Red Army.

Below: The defenders of Pyritz in Pomerania—HJ volunteers, Waffen-SS, Volkssturm, and the Wehrmacht—discuss the city's defense plan against the advancing Red Army. Heavy artillery fire destroyed the old town. It held out for a month, but fell on March 2.

Although the German operation had failed, it was clear to Stalin and his advisors that the remaining forces in the so-called "Baltic Balcony" still posed a serious threat, and that future counterattacks could not be ruled out until they had all been dealt with. This helped delay the advance on Berlin, prolonging the war by some weeks and causing a debate that lasts to this day: should Zhukov have waited and by doing so, allowed the Germans to construct a coherent defense west of the Oder or just gone for broke?

We'll never know the answer. Instead, the first actions were on Konev's front in Silesia. In the north, the German forces ranged across Pomerania were neutralized primarily by Rokossovsky's 2nd Belorussian Front—which had been heading in that direction before being pushed northward toward Ebling on January 20. The forces involved were Rokossovsky's Second Shock, Nineteenth, Forty-ninth, Fiftieth, Sixty-fifth, Seventieth, and Fifth Guards Tank armies, along with Zhukov's Third Shock and First and Third Tank armies. Against them was Heeresgruppe Weichsel, since January 24 under the command of Reichsführer-SS Heinrich Himmler, and consisting of the mauled 2. Armee (Gen Weiß) and reconstituted 3. Panzerarmee (the shattered original being cooped up in Königsberg).

The operation had four elements, the first being the Konitz–Köslin Offensive, which began on February 24 and lasted until March 6, 1945. As the 2nd Belorussian probed the German defenses, Nineteenth Army—which had recently arrived from Finland—found a weak spot on the boundary between the two German armies. Quickly it advanced half the way to the Baltic. German counterattacks slowed the Soviets, but on March 1, Zhukov's right wing struck north, heading toward Kolberg. The First Guards Tank Army reaching the coast on March 4, the same day the 2nd Belorussian Front took Köslin. This effectively cut off both 2. Armee that retreated to Danzig and the communications corridor along the Baltic coast.

The Danzig Offensive Operation began on March 7. The port city was of prime importance to the Germans, not only for military reasons but because it was also one of the few places left where refugees could escape from East Prussia. It was part of a larger zone known as the Danzig–Gotenhafen (Gdingen) Fortified Area, the northern sector of which was based on a series of prewar Polish forts built on the Hel Peninsula.

Rokossovsky launched his main attack on March 15, with the Seventieth and Forty-ninth armies moving forward side by side toward Zoppot (present-day Sopot), on the coast. They reached the outskirts on March 19. Three days later, Seventieth Army severed the German lines by making it to the coast; this made the defense of the city untenable, and on March 30 it fell.

Before this happened though most of Danzig's surviving troops and civilians managed to retreat to the Oxhöft Heights (present-day Oksywie), from where around 265,000 were transported to the relative safety of the Hel Peninsula. Meanwhile, Danzig and its port had been more or less destroyed both by Soviet bombardments and deliberate demolitions by the withdrawing German troops. Maritime access to the harbor was also blocked by the hulk of the battleship *Gneisenau* which had originally been brought to Gotenhafen for extensive repairs after being bombed by the British while moored in Kiel. As part of the German retreat it was deliberately scuttled to prevent the Soviets using the facility.

Many of those who had made it to the Hel Peninsula were then embarked for safer destinations while being protected by the remaining troops who managed to hold off a series of attacks by the Red Army. Indeed, so concerned were they about preventing the Soviets from committing atrocities on the civilians that they did not actually surrender until six days after the war had ended. Soviet figures suggest that the Germans had 39,000 soldiers killed

The Free City of Danzig existed for around 40 years after World War I. With 98 percent of its population identifying as German, it's not surprising that there was considerable agitation for the area to become linked to the Reich. Nazification and antisemitism was rife and when the time came, the Polish defenders were beaten within a few days. Thereafter Poles and Jews were treated with unimaginable cruelty. The city was devastated by the fighting in 1944 and 1945, and fell to the Red Army on March 30, 1945.

At the end of the war the German population was evicted and Polish settlers were brought in—many expelled from their homes in the areas of Poland that became Soviet. Today, Gdansk is a thriving town, Poland's major port, and home to the Trade Union movement that was so instrumental in freeing Poland from communist rule.

Kolberg

Right: *The evacuation of Kolberg as part of Unternehmen Hannibal saw some 70,000 civilians and a large number of military personnel leave the area. A rearguard kept the Red Army at bay while this was going on. Fortress Kolberg held out between March 4 and 18 by which time there were only 2,000 German soldiers left. Ironically, Kolberg, a propaganda movie about the Napoleonic siege of the city in 1807 was released on January 30, 1945, to encourage the defiance of German defenders in all the fortress cities. A U-boat took a copy to the naval base at La Rochelle, itself a Festung.*

Center right: *IS-2s in Märkisch-Friedland. Mainly used for training from 1939, the airfield here was used for fighter and ground-attack aircraft in 1945.*

Below right: *The defensive perimeter contracted between March 6 and 17. The defenders were helped by naval gunfire carefully coordinated by the "Arko"—the Festung artillery commander—Maj Erich Schleiff.*

The fortress commander, Oberst Fritz Fullriede, said, "It was also particularly thanks to him [Schleiff] that the cooperation with the supporting ship artillery of destroyers 43 and 34 worked smoothly. Without this support, holding Kolberg for a fortnight would undoubtedly not have been possible." For his work, Schleiff was awarded the Ehrenblattspange, the Army Honor Roll Clasp. Fullriede was awarded the Oakleaves to his Knight's Cross.

Later in his report Fullriede identifies the heavy equipment:

"Heavy weapons available at the beginning of the siege: 8 leFH 18, 7 Flak 10.5cm, 7 Flak 3.7cm, 1 Flak 2cm, 820 heavy rockets in 16 prepared firing positions, as well as the Fortress MG Battalion (Festungs-Maschinengewehrbataillon) 91(M) and armored train Panzerzug 72a [blown up on Fullriede's orders]. On March 17 in the evening: 3 leFH 18s, 1 Flak 3.7, 2 Flak 2cm, and 6 launchers were left. The following were taken away during the transport: 6 launchers. The remaining heavy weapons were made unusable, as were ammunition, fuel and food supplies."

Postwar, the Germans still in the town were expelled and Polish settlers moved into today's Kołobrzeg.

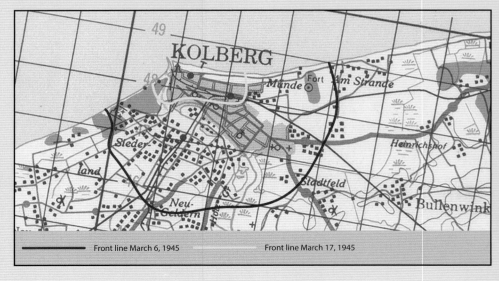

━━━━━ Front line March 6, 1945	───── Front line March 17, 1945

during the battle for Danzig with a further 10,000 taken prisoner. The Red Army also captured 45 submarines which had been abandoned in the port.

The third element of the campaign was the Arnswalde–Kolberg Offensive Operation which was launched on March 1 and included a major battle to take Festung Kolberg (today's Kołobrzeg) which lies on the coast. Kolberg was a vital part of the German military supply chain for the whole Pomeranian battlefront, and was thus heavily defended—by both the official garrison and those encircled in the pocket. Some were troops from 3. Panzerarmee including *33. Waffen-Grenadier-Division der SS "Charlemagne" (französische Nr. 1)* and *15. Waffen-Grenadier-Division der SS (lettische Nr. 1)*—French and Latvian Ostlegionen. Overall, they numbered somewhere between 8,000 and 15,000 men including Volkssturm.

To back these troops up, there were fewer than 20 tanks, a range of artillery pieces (see opposite) and very welcome sea support from the heavy cruisers *Lützow* and *Admiral Scheer*.

Command of the city was passed by General Paul Hermann, who fell ill during February, to Oberst Gerhard Troschel, and then from the beginning of March, Oberst Fritz Fullriede. The garrison fought off the initial attacks, and on March 6 the siege was passed to First Polish Army under General Stanislaw Poplawski, which included the Polish 3rd, 4th, and 6th Infantry divisions. They were introduced in stages as reinforcements arrived—by the end of the assault they numbered more than 28,000 men.

Desperate to protect those being evacuated, relying on the immense firepower from the nearby battleships, the garrison beat off two attacks with heavy casualties on both sides. Although the Germans were offered the chance to surrender, they refused.

The Poles launched a third assault on March 15, and although the Germans had been reinforced by extra troops brought in by sea, the Poles succeeded in taking some of the outer part of the city. It was clear to the defenders that they would be unable to hold out much longer, so the next day, they pulled back to consolidate their positions around the port. This was followed up the day after when they began evacuating their remaining forces to Swinemünde (present-day Świnoujście), on the coast around 60 miles (100km) to the west.

Around 70,000 refugees and some 40,000 German troops were successfully shipped out from the city as part of *Unternehmen Hannibal* that ferried over a million troops and civilians (see pp84–85). About 2,000 troops were left behind to defend the last stages of the evacuation. The city finally fell on March 18—it and those in it had paid a heavy price for the actions of the two weeks of fighting, however. More than 80 percent of the buildings were destroyed. Polish casualties were around 1,206 dead and missing, with a further 3,000 being wounded.

The fourth element of the East Pomeranian Offensive, the Altdamm Offensive Operation, opened on March 18. It began with an assault by parts of the 1st Belorussian Front on the heavily defended German lines at Altdamm, a suburb of Festung Stettin (present-day Szczecin) which lies on the River Oder. Two days later, Stalin announced to the world that his troops had captured the area and that they had also destroyed a strong German bridgehead on the east bank. As a result of this, there were no longer any enemy forces east of the river, and they were close to taking the city as well.

What Stalin did not mention was that taking Altdamm had cost vast numbers of casualties, with the Red Army sending seemingly endless quantities of men against the implacable German machine gun positions, which took an enormous toll. Amongst those driven into Stettin from the nearby bridgehead had been 11. SS-Freiwilligen Panzergrenadier-Division *Nordland*, which was mostly made up of volunteer Scandinavians. They had fought more or less non-stop since the beginning of the Red Army's Vistula-Oder Offensive, and were completely worn out, but still fought doggedly from street to street and house to house. A combination of firepower from Soviet tanks and artillery

The business end of a Soviet Stalinets-class submarine. On February 9, 1945, as part of Unternehmen Hannibal, the 14,660-ton General Steuben *sailed from Pillau for Swinemünde with around 5,200 souls on board. Just before midnight, the S13 fired two torpedoes, both of which hit the ship. Some 20 minutes later the vessel was at the bottom, taking 4,500 souls with it. T196, a torpedo boat, was able to save 300 from the deck before the sinking. They went to Kolberg where they were subsequently evacuated. A further 350 also survived.*

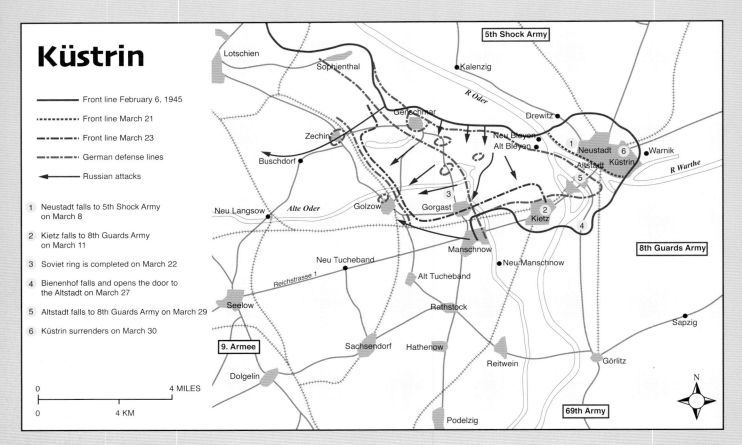

Küstrin

———	Front line February 6, 1945
········	Front line March 21
—·—·—	Front line March 23
—··—··—	German defense lines
←———	Russian attacks

1 Neustadt falls to 5th Shock Army on March 8

2 Kietz falls to 8th Guards Army on March 11

3 Soviet ring is completed on March 22

4 Bienenhof falls and opens the door to the Altstadt on March 27

5 Altstadt falls to 8th Guards Army on March 29

6 Küstrin surrenders on March 30

Above: The Soviet advance might have been held on the Oder until April but that didn't stop their encirclement of Festung Küstrin and its slow strangulation. The defense was commanded by SS-Gruppenführer Heinz Reinefarth, who had made his name murdering everyone in sight in Warsaw. (The Americans vetoed his extradition to Poland to answer for these crimes and he enjoyed a postwar political career.) Rather than fighting to the last bullet, Reinefarth and his men broke out. Tony Le Tissier (2008): "The breakout battle had cost the lives of 637 soldiers, with a further 2,459 wounded and 6,994 reported missing."

Above right: Today's Kostrzyn nad Odrą—Küstrin on the Oder—has little of the ancient still on show. Flattened by bombing and the battle that surged around it, the famous citadel—save for the Berlin Gate as seen here—and the city weren't rebuilt after the war. The bricks were instead sent to rebuild other places in Poland.

Right: Motorcyclists of the Second Polish Army, April 1945. The unit is equipped with American Harley-Davidson motorcycles, delivered to the USSR under the Lend-Lease agreement.

together with a total disregard for losses eventually overcame the desperate defenders who fought to the last. They held on until March 20 when they were ordered to fall back over the last bridge. The German authorities issued an evacuation order for the city's inhabitants, most of whom were also able to leave before Altdamm finally fell to the Soviets on April 26.

The Camps

One of the knock-on effects of the Germans withdrawing from the regions of Poland, East Prussia, Silesia, and Pomerania was that they had to work out what to do about all the area's concentration and PoW camps. Frightened of the world finding out about the scale of their atrocities, they wanted to obliterate as much evidence as possible. They had been let off lightly when the Soviets had discovered the Majdanek concentration camp after liberating Lublin the previous summer, but that was only because the momentous events going on elsewhere in the world meant that the news was overshadowed.

As the Germans knew that they wouldn't get away with it again, they began forcing all the prisoners to walk to the west. These were horrific undertakings—partly because of the complete lack of preparation, and partly because of the brutal treatment by many of the guards. There was little food, almost no shelter, virtually no medical treatment, and so on. Anyone who lagged behind risked being shot on the spot. Thousands of the quarter of a million or so died en route. The men and women involved had to cover hundreds of miles in frightful conditions—many relying on eating things like raw potatoes dug from frozen ground with their fingers.

When the columns first left for the west, the Germans had the guns, but by the time they got close to the Allied fronts, in some groups at least, the situation was reversed—the prisoners had the guns and protected their guards from vengeful civilians. When those from the Stalag Luft III PoW camp met the American vanguard coming the other way, the liberators ordered the guards to be lined up as though for inspection. They then went along asking about each man. Those who the prisoners considered to have been good to them were put to one side; the others were summarily executed. Needless to say, this was not documented at the time.

Due to the scale of their crimes, the hurried nature of the evacuation, and the state of utter disarray in the region much evidence was left behind. Not the least of these was the Auschwitz concentration camp which was discovered on January 27 by men from Konev's 322nd Rifle Division—part of the 1st Ukrainian Front. SS troops on the site had tried to obliterate it, but lacked the time and facilities to do so.

AUSCHWITZ

Reading about the camps, even after all the information that has been disseminated in the past 75 years, it is still surprising that such evil could be inflicted by humans on other humans. It's difficult to be precise about the numbers. The Nazis kept meticulous records, but even they realized that they had to hide the evidence. The accepted figure is around a million: postwar, Rudolf Höss, the camp commandant in two spells, thought that figure could be doubled.

There were three major elements to the camp: Auschwitz 1 was the administration; 2 Birkenau was extermination; 3 Monowitz was linked to the industrial production of Buna-N, a synthesized rubber, by IG-Farben who used the camp for slave labor.

At the end of the war, many of the survivors were sent away from the front in death marches during which thousands more died.

Postwar, less than 15 percent of those involved in running the camp were prosecuted. Among those who were found guilty was Rudolf Höss, who was hanged.

In total, 23 IG-Farben directors were tried for war crimes and 13 convicted. Remarkably, none served more than three years before being released by American high commissioner for Germany, John J. McCloy, who obviously didn't believe that the punishment should fit the crime!

Below left: *Arbeit Macht Frei—the lie that freedom could be gained through hard work.*

Below: *Railroads brought the cattle cars full of victims into the camp.*

The Holocaust

The depravities of Nazi rule became clearer as the Allies began to overrun the camps. The first to be freed was by the Red Army at Majdanek near Lublin in Poland in July 1944. Horrifying as it was, it would not be the last nor the largest. As the fronts moved, so the Nazi regime did what they could to obscure the facts: concentration camp victims, along with Allied prisoners, were force-marched away and many, many thousands died en route. The camps and their records were destroyed—but there was just too much evidence to hide the grisly details.

When the horrific facts were uncovered, it became clear that the deaths were in the millions—the U.S. Holocaust Memorial Museum supplies the following numbers: over six million Jews, seven million Soviet citizens, three million Soviet PoWs, nearly two million Poles, up to half a million Roma, 312,000 Serbs, and over 300,000 others—Jehovah's Witnesses, criminals, people with disabilities.

The systematic killings, the use of slave labor—most of the laborers being worked to death—and the barbarity of the methodology led to trials of the guilty (although the number tried, the number found guilty, and the number punished was laughably small), reparations, and many memorials set up to try to ensure that the Holocaust is never forgotten—in spite of the insidious lies of the Holocaust deniers—and never repeated.

Opposite, Above: *The infrastructure of the Final Solution—German concentration and extermination camps.*

Opposite, Below left: *Shoes at Auschwitz—representing one day's collection at the peak of the gassings, about 25,000 pairs.*

Opposite, Below right: *The Stolpersteine—stumbling stones—was a project started by the German artist Gunter Demnig in 1992. They record where Nazi victims lived or worked. There are now over 75,000 throughout Europe.*

Right: *As the front lines advanced, so the SS Einsatzgruppen moved in and began the deportations, enslavement, and murders.*

Below: *The Memorial to the Murdered Jews of Europe designed by architect Peter Eisenman and engineer Buro Happold.*

The Holocaust

- ☠ Extermination camp
- ■ Concentration camp*
- ✦ City with ghetto
- ○ Transit city
- ☠ Major massacre
- ➤ Major deportation route

Regions:
German name (PRESENT COUNTRY)

- Axis country/annexed by Axis
- Occupied by Axis
- Italy (Axis) at height of occupation
- Allied country
- Neutral

* includes labor, prison, & transit camps
Note: Not all camps and ghettos are shown
Borders are at the height of Axis domination (1942)
— Dotted borders are present (2007) borders

Hungary 3

When the war started, Hungary was already on the side of the Axis powers as a result of its economic and political policies during the 1930s. Consequently, it was fighting with the Germans when the Soviet forces pushed back against the Nazi invasion. By 1944, however, the country was more or less on its last legs and was considering leaving the alliance for its own survival. In order to prevent this from happening, Germany occupied Hungary on March 19, 1944. As time went on though, it became increasingly clear who was going to win, so the governor-regent, Admiral Miklós Horthy, tried to do a peace deal with the west.

Infuriated by this, Hitler ordered *Unternehmen Panzerfaust* to be launched in October 1944, in which Horthy was forced to abdicate power. The leader of the fascist National Socialist Arrow Cross Party, Ferenc Szálasi, took his place and immediately began work on fortifying Budapest against the advancing Red Army. Hitler provided two Waffen-SS divisions to help bolster the defenses. Under the command of SS-Obergruppenführer und General der Waffen-SS Karl Pfeffer-Wildenbruch they, along with various forces as well as men from the Hungarian Army, stood ready to be besieged.

The first stages of the city's isolation were begun on October 29, 1944, by the Soviet 2nd Ukrainian Front under Marshal Rodion Malinovsky. He had around a million men including several Romanian units under his command for the attack. The troops were split into two groups so that they could encircle the city and cut it off from any further outside assistance. By November 7, they had fought their way into the eastern suburbs, and then—after a pause to resupply—they began a second phase on December 19.

Since Budapest was one of Hitler's fortress cities, he refused point-blank to consider any evacuation, and declared that it was to be defended to the last man. The final part of the encirclement was completed on December 26, 1944, when Soviet soldiers cut the road linking Budapest to Vienna. By that point the puppet leader, Ferenc Szálasi, had already fled. The siege of Budapest then began in earnest, with around 33,000 German and 37,000 Hungarian troops as well as over 800,000 civilians trapped inside. Resupply missions were flown by the Luftwaffe, but not many supplies reached the city.

Opposite: *"Our land is strong in heroes." A poster by Viktor Ivanovich Govorkov from 1941.*

Above: *Rear Admiral Miklós Horthy had been Hungary's head of state since 1920 with the title of Regent. By early 1944 his government had been secretly in touch with the Allies seeking peace. However, Horthy was betrayed and removed from power, and the new Hungarian regime tied its fate to that of Germany.*

Budapest was more significant to the Soviets than merely as an immediate military objective. This was because Stalin was about to go to the Yalta Conference where he wanted to use its capture as a negotiation lever against Churchill and Roosevelt. Since the meeting of the world's predominant leaders was to sort out what postwar Europe would look like, he knew that demonstrating how powerful his armies were would allow him to wrest a more favorable settlement. As a result, his orders to Malinovsky were unequivocal—take the city as soon as possible.

The fastest way to meet his orders would have been to persuade the defenders to surrender, and so genuine attempts were made to achieve this via negotiations. The first was late on December 28, but the conditions were refused and the Germans opened fire on the Soviet emissaries as they returned to their lines, killing one of them. A second attempt began shortly after, but once again the Germans shot up the would-be negotiators before they even reached the site, killing all three.

As the Red Army continued to push in from the east of the city, the defenders gradually withdrew to keep their lines intact. Then, on January 1, 1945, a combination of German and Hungarian forces launched a counterattack from outside the city—*Unternehmen Konrad*. Intending to break the siege, it had three phases. The first saw IV. SS-Panzerkorps push in from the northwest. Two days later in answer to the threat, the Soviets introduced another four divisions— they successfully stopped the German advance before it got to within 12 miles (20km) of the city. After severe fighting, this part of the counterattack was canceled and the men withdrew on January 12. Meanwhile the second phase had already begun—on January 7—also undertaken by the IV. SS-Panzerkorps, who advanced from Esztergom heading toward Budapest Airport. As with the previous attempt, however, the attack failed although it did get relatively close to its destination.

While all this was going on, the fighting continued right around the city, with the defenders' supplies running low: the main airport had been overrun by the Red Army. A few transport planes and gliders were able to land on the city's open spaces, but in a repeat of the fiasco at Stalingrad, the Luftwaffe was unable to meet more than a tiny fraction of the army's need for fuel, ammunition, and food. Some supplies made it along the Danube on barges either at night or in fog, but when the river froze, this ended.

Continued on p. 120.

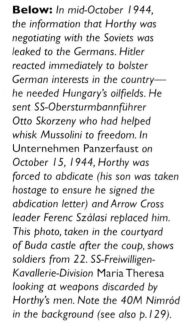

Below: *In mid-October 1944, the information that Horthy was negotiating with the Soviets was leaked to the Germans. Hitler reacted immediately to bolster German interests in the country— he needed Hungary's oilfields. He sent SS-Obersturmbannführer Otto Skorzeny who had helped whisk Mussolini to freedom. In Unternehmen Panzerfaust on October 15, 1944, Horthy was forced to abdicate (his son was taken hostage to ensure he signed the abdication letter) and Arrow Cross leader Ferenc Szálasi replaced him. This photo, taken in the courtyard of Buda castle after the coup, shows soldiers from 22. SS-Freiwilligen-Kavallerie-Division Maria Theresa looking at weapons discarded by Horthy's men. Note the 40M Nimród in the background (see also p.129).*

Left: *The Nazis genocide of the Jews had already claimed 64,000 Hungarians before the Germans took over control of the country by Unternehmen Margarethe on March 19, 1944. Thereafter they were either used as slave labor or went to the camps— just over 564,000 Hungarian Jews died between 1941 and 1945. Postwar revisionists have tried to hide the fact that, as Randolph L. Braham (2001) put it, this was done with "the active and often enthusiastic involvement of Hungary's wartime governmental and law enforcement authorities." This is the headquarters of the Arrow Cross Party in Budapest, 1944, today the House of Terror Museum (a museum created in memory of the victims of 20th century dictatorships). A far right party banned by Horthy, it came to power after he abdicated. During its tenure in office thousands of Hungarians— mainly Jews—were deported to their deaths. Over 10,000 others were killed by Arrow Cross gangs. Its leader, Ferenc Szálasi, fled before the siege of Budapest and was captured in Austria on May 6, 1945. Postwar he was executed for his crimes. Fortepan/Fortepan*

Above left: *Unternehmen Panzerfaust—Tiger II of sPzAbt 503 and Arrow Cross men in Szent György ter (St. George's Square) heading for Buda Castle.*

Left and Below: *"Shoes on the Danube Bank" is a memorial in Budapest, to the many thousands who were forced to remove their shoes, before being shot by Arrow Cross militiamen. Their bodies fell into the river. It was created by Can Togay and sculptor Gyula Pauer.*

TO THE MEMORY OF THE VICTIMS SHOT INTO THE DANUBE BY ARROW CROSS MILITIAMEN IN 1944-45

ERECTED 16TH APRIL, 2005

Right: *Budapest 1945, the Soviet and Romanian advance, and the breakout attempt by what was left of the garrison—primarily IX. SS-Gebirgskorps. Formed in June 1944 to coordinate two Croatian Waffen-SS divisions, in October in Hungary the corps had under command what was left of 13. Panzerdivision, Panzergrenadier-division Feldherrnhalle, 8. SS-Kavallerie-Division Florian Geyer and the 22. SS-Kavallerie-Division Maria Theresa after fighting in Debrecen. By the time of the breakout, February 11, this had dwindled substantially. Ungváry (2006) puts the figures at: 23,000 Germans including 9,000 wounded; 20,000 Hungarians including 2,000 wounded, 80–100,000 civilians. The breakout was a slaughter and very few Axis troops made their way through the Soviet cordon to friendly lines.*

Center right: *A Red Army gun crew on József körút (boulevard) near Pál utca (street) loads an 85mm air defense gun M1939 (52K), January 1945.*

Below right: *Here, SS-Sturmbannführer Karl-Heinz Keitel (in a cap and a leather coat), son of Generalfeldmarschall Wilhelm Keitel head of the OKW, meets the Hungarian Minister of War, General Károly Beregfy (third on the right) at a Waffen-SS command post on the Attila line belonging to the 8. SS-Kavallerie-Division Florian Geyer on the outskirts of Budapest. Note the Honvédség (the Hungarian armed forces) sidecaps, on the side of which is braid that identifies rank. Florian Geyer are best known for their brutal operations against guerrillas in Russia and being destroyed in the fighting around Budapest.*

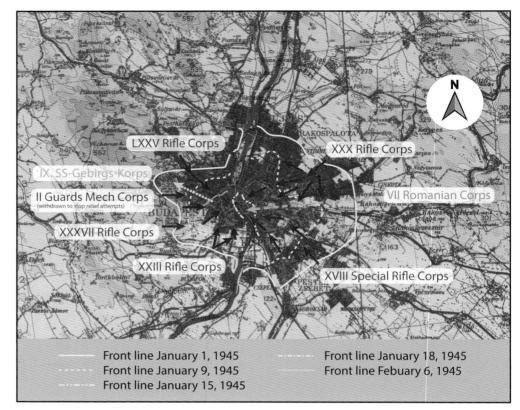

LXXV Rifle Corps

XXX Rifle Corps

IX. SS-Gebirgs-Korps

II Guards Mech Corps
(withdrawn to stop relief attempts)

VII Romanian Corps

XXXVII Rifle Corps

XXIII Rifle Corps

XVIII Special Rifle Corps

	Front line January 1, 1945		Front line January 18, 1945
	Front line January 9, 1945		Front line Febuary 6, 1945
	Front line January 15, 1945		

Above: A Ya-12 tractor towing a Soviet 152mm howitzer-cannon model 1937 (ML-20) passes under the watchful gun of a SU-76 tank destroyer.

Left: A Soviet hero of the fighting in Budapest, Sergeant Manakov of the 145th Rifle Regiment. As the original caption reads, "The sergeant killed 50 Germans and destroyed seven gun emplacements." Manakov was a flamethrower operator and his ROKS-3 is clearly visible here. To avoid drawing attention to flamethrower operators the design made the weapon look like a rifle and the fuel pack resembled an infantry pack.

Below left: Stretcher crew passing by a pair of T-34/85s. Russian medical care was patchier than that of the western allies with fewer drugs and less sophisticated equipment in the field. However, there was one field in which the Soviets were leaders and that was frostbite, which accounted for 2.0–4.0% of the combat surgical trauma in the Red Army. As the war progressed so the analysis of the stages and treatment of frostbite improved.

As the noose tightened, the fighting got more intense—taking place everywhere from down in the sewers up to the tops of the remaining buildings where snipers took their inevitable toll. The extreme cold and shortage of food made life even more difficult, with some of the defenders killing and eating their own horses. The Axis troops were struggling to cope with defending what was effectively two cities—Buda and Pest, separated by a large river.

Finally, on January 17, Hitler allowed them to abandon Pest and concentrate on holding Buda. As a result, a chaotic evacuation was hurriedly organized and the following day all five bridges were blown up. At more or less the same time as this was happening, a third phase of *Unternehmen Konrad* began as IV. SS-Panzerkorps was once again launched on a rescue attempt. Their massed firepower initially allowed them to make good progress against the Transdanubian front—they even managed to reach the Danube at the city of Dunapentele (present-day Dunaújváros) in just two days.

Over the next eight days and much fierce fighting, the SS tanks managed to get to within 12 miles (20km) of the city's outer defenses, but by then a lack of supplies and sheer exhaustion saw the advance grind to a halt and then reverse. When it became clear that the rescue had failed, permission was sought to evacuate the city. Hitler refused to countenance such a move and again demanded a last stand. The desperate defenders did their best and in places like Margaret Island particularly vicious streetfighting against the 25th Guards Rifle Division took place.

Elsewhere the defenders did whatever they could, such as exploiting Buda's hilly terrain to site artillery positions wherever the ground was beneficial. These guns took a huge toll on the attacking Soviets. Several assaults on the citadel of Gellért Hill by the Red Army, for instance, were driven off by defending Waffen-SS troops. Eventually, however, the strongpoint fell on February 11 after three simultaneous attacks managed to overrun it. The previous day the Red Army had also taken Castle Hill which left the German and Hungarian troops at risk of being cut in two. As they were squeezed into an ever-shrinking area, the massed Soviet artillery was able to shell them at will.

The Axis defenders still refused to contemplate surrender though, in spite of severe shortages of food and rampant disease. By this stage the fighting had developed into a house to house affair, and it was clear that the garrison could not hold out much longer. Hitler would still not listen to any suggestion

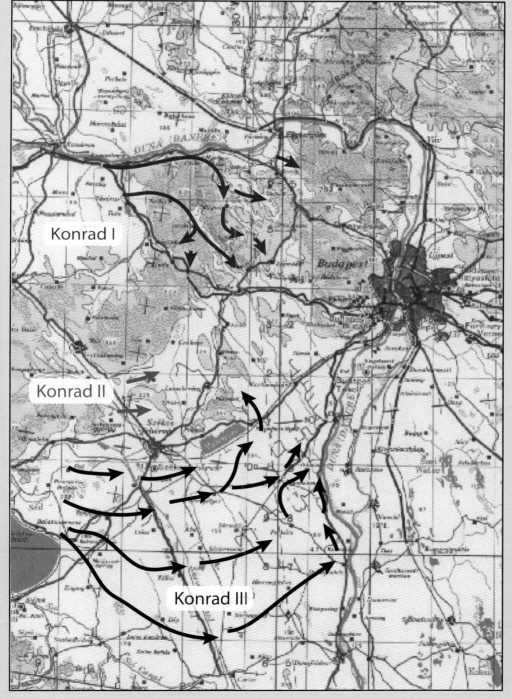

Konrad I

Konrad II

Konrad III

UNTERNEHMEN KONRAD

In January 1945, there were three attempts to break through to Budapest— Hitler saw them as a means to restore the front rather than allowing the garrison to escape. The first—Konrad (January 1–12)—was from the north. Although Guderian preferred the projected Unternehmen Paula from the south, Konrad used less fuel—by that time a critical consideration.

The Soviet response was ordered by the Stavka on January 6 as Konrad faltered. The 2nd Ukrainian Front was to advance with at least two rifle corps of the Seventh Guards and Sixth Guards Tank armies from the Esztergom area along the northern side of Danube in the general direction of Komarno (Komárom on map). They were to seize crossings to allow an attack on the flank of Konrad. While this part of the attack didn't materialize as intended, the Soviets succeeded in creating the so-called Hron bridgehead (red) which ended up extending some 10–15km from Esztergom on the northern side of the Danube.

While this was going on, Konrad II (January 7–12) was launched from the south (near Székesfehérvár), as was Konrad III (January 17–26). The latter was the most successful of the three, advancing to the Danube before being beaten back.

All were spearheaded by IV. SS-Panzerkorps with elements of 3. SS-Panzerdivision Totenkopf and 5. SS-Panzerdivision Wiking.

The Germans would try again to relieve Budapest in March (see pp. 126–127) but would need to clear the Hron bridgehead first (Unternehmen Südwind).

of surrender, and the German commander decided instead to attempt a breakout. On February 11 around 28,000 Axis troops began streaming through the frozen streets to the northwest in three waves, each of which was joined by thousands of civilians.

Many of those in the first group were able to use the thick fog to make an escape, but the people who followed on behind were decimated by persistent Soviet artillery and rocket fire. It is thought that only 600–700 troops made it all the way to the German front lines. The rest were killed or taken prisoner, including Pfeffer-Wildenbruch. Those who were left behind unconditionally surrendered on February 13. The enormous cost to the Axis of the futile defense of Budapest soon became clear. Germans units that were more or less wiped out included the 13. Panzerdivision, 60. Panzergrenadier-Division *Feldherrnhalle*, the 8. SS-Kavallerie-Division *Florian Geyer* and the 22. SS-Freiwilligen-Kavallerie-Division *Maria Theresa*. The Hungarians lost heavily too, including the I Corps, the 10th and 12th Infantry Divisions, and the 1st Armored Division.

Overall, the siege had lasted fifty days, and Budapest was taken by troops of the 2nd and 3rd Ukrainian Fronts. It is believed that on top of the massive troop losses—the Soviets lost untold numbers, somewhere between 100,000 and 160,000—around 38,000 civilians also died in the city. About 80 percent of the buildings were destroyed, along with all seven of the bridges across the Danube.

Unfortunately for them, the problems for Hungary's remaining inhabitants did not end there. Over half a million were transported to the Soviet Union as slave laborers, many of whom died while captive. These included a large proportion of Hungarian ethnic Germans. Meanwhile, many of the occupying Red Army troops went on extended rampages, raping and looting whenever the opportunity presented itself. All the males of working age were also used as forced labor to help build a series of pontoon bridges across the Danube as temporary replacements for those which had been destroyed. On a more positive note, the fall of Budapest meant that the Soviets were able to begin the Vienna Offensive.

Below: *The attempt to break out of the city, when it came, was a bloodbath. At many other stages of the siege the garrison would have stood a better chance, but on February 11 all that it did was send as many as 20,000 to their deaths. Krisztián Ungváry's graphic account of this makes uncomfortable reading. Led by the garrison troops, many civilians followed into withering crossfire. If they did get clear of the inner city, the hinterland was also full of Soviet troops. In the end around only 700 of the c. 44,000 escaped; a further 700 were able to hide in the countryside. Around 24,000 were captured and many of them were either killed or died in captivity.*

For the Soviet troops, the fall of Budapest was a cause for celebration and looting. The Red Army had suffered some 280,000 casualties between November 3, 1944 and February 11, 1945, with around 70,000 dead so it's not a surprise that the survivors look happy! **1** and **2** Fisherman's Bastion, Buda Castle—note the 8.8cm gun. **3** Russian troops seen from the Grand Boulevard, opposite the Museum of Applied Arts. **4** Elizabeth Boulevard as seen from the top of the New York Palace hotel as the Soviet flag is raised. **5** Soviet medal for those who besieged Budapest.

Opposite: *Budapest restored—postwar the city had to undergo the heavy hand of Soviet control that led to a crushed rebellion in 1956 before the fall of the Iron Curtain in 1989–90. Today, it's a vibrant city and most of the depredations of war have been rebuilt or restored. This is a good example: Deák Ferenc tér (square) is today the starting point of the glittering Fashion Street (**A**—note the same buildings).*

Left: *The bridges over the Danube were casualties of the fighting. This is Margaret Bridge.*

Below left: *Halász Street, the main street toward Clark Ádám Square is lined with AFVs. Note the SdKfz 251/21 mittlerer Schützenpanzerwagen Drilling with three MG-151 20mm AA guns.*

RAPE

Armies after sieges have rarely behaved well toward the citizens when the town falls. The Red Army gained a reputation for indiscriminate looting, and raping women, young and old. That it happened is indisputable and cannot be excused by citing revenge for the obscenities wreaked on the Russian people by the invading German armies. Too often a subject that is swept under the carpet, it does need to be contextualized. First, especially in those countries that fought alongside the Nazis, the depravities foisted on its civilians has been used to take away attention from—and to whitewash their own culpability for—involvement in the Final Solution. Second, in the west it is noticeable that rape and looting is always tagged to the Red Army or the mainly black French African Army and the many rapes and atrocities—and there are plenty of examples—committed by U.S., Canadian, and British troops are glossed over.

Right: *Soviet tanks had a hard time in Hungary 1944–45. On the first day of Unternehmen Konrad III, for example, 122 were KO'd. In the 108 days that Budapest was besieged, Krisztián Ungváry estimates (based on Krivosheev, 1997) 1,766 were lost.*

Center right: *An unidentified Waffen-SS armored unit bogs down. The Tiger Is, with their wide tracks, are moving cautiously around the truck as its crew off-load the fuel drums. The Tigers are the early version with the taller cupola on the turret.*

Below right: *A Soviet Ford G8T, passes a PzKpfw IV Ausf H. Note the extra bolted armor plate on the front superstructure and the welded one on the front hull. The tank was from 10. Kompanie, III./Panzer-Regiment 24 (of 24. Panzerdivision).*

Opposite, Top: *Unternehmen Südwind (1) was undertaken as a preparatory to "Frühlingserwachen." It accomplished its mission—to clear the Soviet bridgehead over the Hron River (Gran in German). This had been formed in early January 1945 and Peiper remembered Operation Südwind. "The fight against the PaK was much more difficult for us Panzer people than against the tanks. It constituted our 'daily bread' and as a rule was fought without any assistance. If we would have had the necessary help of artillery and especially of airplanes, PaK-Fronts would not have been any problem. In order to give to the reader a conception about the number in which the enemy employed this weapon, two examples from practical experience are cited: In winter 1943 we destroyed a PaK nest east of Shitomir which served as security for the main road Kiev–Shitomir. In a sector of 600 x 400m, thirty-two heavy PaKs were dug in. In the spring of 1945 I started with the mopping up of the Gran bridgehead [top map, opposite] with about 70 vehicles, mostly Panthers. Within six days we destroyed about 400 heavy PaKs. Simultaneously the engineers cleared about 20,000 mines and the fields were marked. With 8 total losses, I had 12 usable vehicles left."*

Note
1 = Drávaszabolcs
2 = Drávapalkonya
3 = Drávacsehi

Unternehmen *Frühlingserwachen*
(Operation Spring Awakening)

Germany's last major offensive of the war, its major objectives were twofold—first, to stop the Red Army's march on Vienna, and second to secure the last available oil reserves. The operation took place in Western Hungary, and was mounted in great secrecy using several units that had been pulled out of the abortive Ardennes Offensive, including men and equipment from the 6. Panzerarmee. *Frühlingserwachen* was launched on March 6 in three different directions.

The main (*Frühlingserwachen*—see **map 2**) was intended to be the northern part of a pincer movement. The plan was to advance to the southeast, past Lake Balaton and Lake Velence, and head toward the Danube river before dividing into two. One group would advance on Budapest and liberate it; the other would drive south to link up with units from Heeresgruppe E which were pushing north as the southern part of the pincer. This was the second part of the offensive ("*Waldteufel*"). If the link-up could be achieved successfully—a doubtful matter given the terrain (made worse by the recent spring thaw)—they would have managed to encircle the Soviet Twenty-sixth and Fifty-seventh armies.

The third element was codenamed *Unternehmen Eisbrecher*. It would see 2. Panzerarmee move up from the southwest of Lake Balaton and head to Kaposvár to attack the Soviet Fifty-seventh Army.

Despite being made up of many elite units, by March 14 all three parts of the offensive were in serious trouble. They were slowed by the lack of proper roads and vast areas of mud that eventually brought more or less everything to a standstill. On top of this, the Red Army fought back furiously, and their weight of numbers and superior resupply situation proved to be too strong for the attackers.

"*Eisbrecher*" failed to achieve its goals—Heeresgruppe E encountered much stronger opposition than it was expecting from the First Bulgarian Army, as well as from Tito's Yugoslavian Partisans. As a result, it was unable to make the desired "*Waldteufel*" link up. By the next day—March 15—the entire offensive had completely stalled, and then on March 16 the Soviet strike-back began with the first stages of their Vienna Offensive. The Red Army's absolute superiority in men and equipment gave them total battlefield dominance, and the Germans had no option but to be driven back before their Soviet opponents (see **map 3**); "*Frühlingserwachen*" was well and truly over.

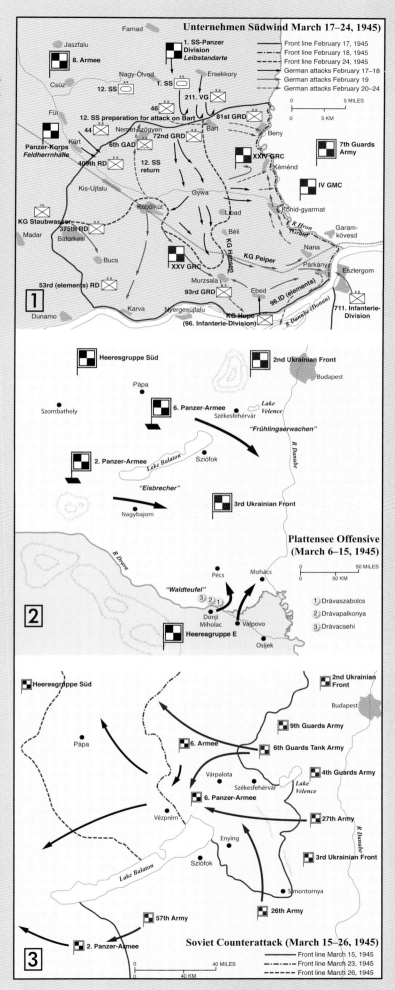

Right: *Hungarian troops manning a 40mm Bofors M36 anti-aircraft gun. These were license-built in Budapest and mounted on the Toldi tank chassis to create the Nimród SPAAG (see* **Opposite, Below**). *Hungary paid a high price for its involvement in the war on Germany's side—and continued to pay that price until the fall of Soviet communist control in 1989. The economy was ruined by German depredations and the fighting: war reparations set at $300 million in 1947 were to be implemented by the occupying Red Army. The number of Hungarians killed by the Holocaust, the fighting, and deportations was over a million. The Honvédség grew in size during the war, as did the casualties. In 1942–43, of the c. 260,000 men who served in the Second Hungarian Army in Russia, 177,000 became casualties of whom c. 10,000 were known to have been killed (Niehorster). In early 1944, the army strength was around 450,000 of which 90,000 were in the Soviet Union. This figure grew to a million during the year. As well as soldiers, the Hungarian Army used slave labor—usually Jews or Roma: at least 40,000 died. Hungarian military casualties—killed or missing— during the war were 300,000. At the end of the war, most of the Hungarian PoWs and many civilians went into the Soviet gulags. Up to 1948, 251,000 (about half the known total) were returned; many were in such bad condition that they died after their return. The rest almost certainly perished in the gulags.*

Center right: *Székesfehérvár Zichy Grove, opposite the Main (Nádor) street. The defensive operation around Lake Balaton was the last major defensive battle the Red Army fought during the war. Székesfehérvár changed hands during* Unternehmen Konrad III *but was recaptured by Soviet troops in March. These German tanks and SP guns were abandoned due to lack of fuel. In the foreground are two medium PzKpfw IVs.*

Below right: *Covered in infantrymen this SU-152 self-propelled gun crosses a river in Hungary. Nicknamed the "animal hunter" due to its ability to destroy Tigers and Panthers, it was originally designed to destroy fortifications—a role at which it excelled.*

HUNGARIAN-BUILT ARMOR

Germany's allies had their own well-established industries—and made use of them to make weapons. Hungary is a good example, building nearly 1,000 armored vehicles and 500 artillery pieces, as well as infantry weapons, and around 900 aircraft (mainly German and Italian types). After the German takeover in 1944, one of the first items on the agenda was to ensure that Hungarian armaments production—most of which was destined for Germany—continued.

Left: Hungary had little prewar experience in building AFVs as this early-war Toldi I 38M tank shows. The main armament was a 20mm heavy anti-tank rifle. Its thin armor, no more than 20mm on the upgraded series 2, was useless against any Soviet tank or anti-tank guns. The Hungarian green, red, and white cross is displayed prominently on the front plate and turret.

Center left: The Hungarian arms industry continued to develop new projects during the war, such as the 40/43M Zrínyi II assault gun. This one has been heavily uparmored with a large number of track sections welded to its hull. The 105mm gun was useful in urban combat but lacked any anti-tank capability. The Hungarian cross can be seen on the Zimmerit, anti-magnetic mine paste, coated, armored side skirts.

Below left: Mátyásföld, Budapest—Újszász street 41–43 was the Hungarian Royal Army car workshop. This shows it full of 40M Nimróds, probably the world's first specialized elf-propelled anti-aircraft gun (SPAAG). It was intended as a dual purpose anti-tank/AA gun but struggled against Soviet armor. It was, however, effective as a mobile AA gun.

Hungarian AFV production 1939–44

Vehicle	Armament	Built
39M Csaba	20mm	143
39/40M Csaba	MG	12
38M Toldi I	20mm	80
38M Toldi II	20mm	110
38M Toldi III	40mm	12
40M Turán I	40mm	285
41M Turán II	75mm	139
44M Zrínyi I	75mm	4
43M Zrínyi II	105mm	66
36/40M Nimród	40mm	135
(source Niehorster)		

Nagykanizsa–Körmend Offensive

By March 1945, Germany and its allies had lost most of their sources of oil—most recently the Romanian oilfields. They were now almost completely reliant on those of western Hungary which, following the failure of *Unternehmen Frühlingserwachen* and the Plattensee (Lake Balaton) offensive, were now threatened. The Red Army's Nagykanizsa–Körmend Offensive—part of its greater drive on Vienna—started on March 26, 1945, and pushed directly into the oilfields. It was undertaken by the 3rd Ukrainian Front under Marshal Fyodor Tolbukhin.

The Soviets were ranged against the forces of the German Heeresgruppe Süd (until September 23, 1944, known as Heeresgruppe Südukraine) which at that stage was commanded by General der Infanterie Otto Wöhler. His troops were attempting to defend a line which ran through an area of small settlements west of Lake Balaton and north of the Drava river. In typical German fashion, these men had established their defenses in depth—three lines sited behind the Mur river for extra protection.

Opposing them, the Red Army's forces consisted mostly of First Bulgarian Army which fielded some 100,000 troops. To its east was the Soviet Fifty-seventh Army and to its southwest were the Yugoslav Partisans under Tito. Before much action took place, however, it was quite clear to the German defenders that the war was lost, and they began retreating back toward their homelands. On April 2 the German army group was renamed Heeresgruppe Ostmark, and its commander was replaced by Generaloberst Dr. Lothar Rendulic who had spent 14 days commanding the Courland Pocket, 44 commanding Heeresgruppe Nord and now was charged with defending his native Austria.

The Bulgarians successfully crossed the Mur, but stalled with supply problems. On May 7, 1945, they resumed the advance, capturing many of the German and Hungarian troops who had not already managed to escape.

Below: *Grave of a German soldier near Lake Balaton. The Axis lost heavily in Hungary as they struggled to maintain their grip on the oilfields. Reich Minister of Armaments and War Production, Albert Speer knew the end was up when the oil ran dry. In January 1944, total synthetic petroleum output was approximately 3.6 million barrels; by the end of 1944 it had dropped another third, to 1.2 million barrels. The oilfields of Hungary and Romania were uppermost on Hitler's mind. He withdrew men from Warsaw to help in Hungary. On March 15, 1945—with Berlin immediately under threat—Army Group South had on strength the remnants of 29 divisions (including 12 Panzer), 772 tanks and assault guns and a further 1,000 under repair.*

Below right: *Hungarian infantry pause during a route march east of Budapest. They are wearing their camouflage shelter quarters. The stacked weapons appear to be 8mm Mannlicher M1895 rifles, their helmets are the German M1935 type.*

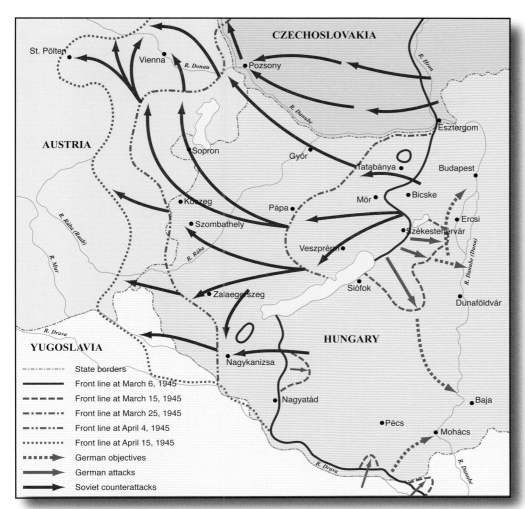

Left: *After the German "Konrad" attacks, the Nagykanizsa–Körmend Offensive drove the Soviet front line deep into Austria.*

Below: Panzerwerfer 42 *(43 in German references)* auf Maultier, SdKfz 4/1—to give this weapons system its full title (Maultier means mule)—*was a mobile rocket launcher introduced in 1943. The 10-barreled, 150mm launcher carried 20 missiles as the weight of shot reduced the ground clearance and mobility. Consequently, extra munitions were carried in a separate resupply vehicle. Not an accurate weapon, it also had a relatively short range, a maximum of 7,100yd (6,500m).*

Map labels:

CZECHOSLOVAKIA

St. Pölten

Vienna

R. Donau

Pozsony

R. Hron

Esztergom

AUSTRIA

Sopron

Győr

Tatabánya

Budapest

Köszeg

Mör

Bicske

Pápa

Ercsi

Szombathely

Székesfehérvár

R. Rába (Raab)

Veszprém

R. Rába

R. Danube (Duna)

R. Mur

Zalaegerszeg

Siófok

Dunaföldvár

R. Drava

HUNGARY

YUGOSLAVIA

Nagykanizsa

Nagyatád

Baja

Pécs

Mohács

R. Drava

R. Danube

Legend:

- State borders
- Front line at March 6, 1945
- Front line at March 15, 1945
- Front line at March 25, 1945
- Front line at April 4, 1945
- Front line at April 15, 1945
- German objectives
- German attacks
- Soviet counterattacks

The Balkans 4

The Balkan peninsula has always been a disputed land. From Roman times it was on the path of nomadic tribes from Asia who swept through with their eyes set on the wealth of the Classical western Mediterranean world; more recently, it was the fall of the Byzantine Empire in 1453 that doomed the Balkans to 300 years of Turkish rule. Christendom may have been saved outside the gates of Vienna by Polish King Jan Sobieski III in 1683, but the Turks weren't pushed out of the bulk of the peninsula until the 19th century. The result is a simmering mixture of ethnicity, nationality, and religion that has kept coming to the boil. Each time someone gets on top, they simply lay the foundations for future conflict—exactly what happened in the aftermath of World War I, when the Austro-Hungarian Empire was dismembered, and after World War II when Tito's Yugoslavia put the lid on a pressure cooker that would explode in 1991–2001.

During World War II, Italian aspirations in Albania and Greece led to the German invasion that saw Yugoslavia (April 6–17, 1941), Greece (April 6–23), and Crete (May 20–June 1) fall to the Nazis. Hungary, Romania, and Bulgaria, smarting from the territorial reorganizations at the end of World War I, all eventually sided with Germany to receive slices of their neighbor's possessions (map p. 139). Hungary gained territory from Czechoslovakia, Romania, and Yugoslavia; Bulgaria, forced into the Tripartite Pact, received chunks of Greece; Romania (which had lost territory to the Soviet Union), Hungary, and Bulgaria, got some back and some conquered Soviet lands to administer. All three sent forces into Russia alongside the Germans, and all persecuted the Jews to a greater or lesser extent.

Yugoslavia was dismembered. The initial occupation duties fell to the Italians and Bulgarians, with puppet regimes in Croatia and Serbia. The Banat was governed separately by Josef Lapp, an ethnic German. The Nazis did little to prepare for the problems that were to come. Preoccupied with the invasion of Russia, they seem to have spent too little time considering the difficulties that would be caused by insurrection. They were just interested in the economic exploitation of the area and keeping the lines of communication open with their forces in Greece.

Opposite: *"Will not give up what we won in October!" Mikhail Nikolayevich Avvakumov and V. Scheglov's 1941 poster shows the Axis recoiling from the counterattack.*

Above: *Josip Broz—Tito—whose Partisans were a thorn in the German side throughout the war.*

133

Right: *Užice, Yugoslavia (Serbia), September 1941, showing both Chetniks and Partisans escorting German prisoners. Initially, the resistance to the invaders of Yugoslavia came from both the communist Partisans and the nationalist Chetniks together. The first area to be freed, the so-called Republic of Užice, didn't last for long in the face of the first major German anti-guerrilla operation, September 27–November 29, 1941. Ideology ended up being a major problem, with Tito's communism being unworkable with the royalist Chetniks. By the end of November 1941 the Chetnik leader, Draža Mihailović, had already met the Germans, and increasingly the Chetniks cooperated with the Axis forces against the Partisans.*

Below: *The colors of the flag of the Partisans and Democratic Federal Yugoslavia were, as this tinted photo shows, those of the Kingdom of Yugoslavia but with a red star in the middle.*

Below center: *By the end of the war there were 800,000 partisans in the National Liberation Army and Partisan Detachments of Yugoslavia, organized militarily. These are soldiers of the 4th Montenegrin Proletarian Brigade in Jajce in September 1942.*

Below right: *Balkan justice was served on the members of 7. SS-Freiwilligen Gebirgs-Division Prinz Eugen (seen here in Dalmatia) who surrendered in 1945. They were executed and many of their families were also killed.*

It proved to be a major mistake: "1 in 7 soldiers in German uniform, whether German or not, became a casualty by the close of operations." The peoples of the Balkans had a history of guerrilla warfare in their centuries-old conflict with the Turks. A number of elements fanned the flames: the atrocities of the occupying troops and puppet regimes (which even surprised the Germans); massive reprisals for guerrilla actions on innocent, unconnected civilians; and the Reich's usual economic banditry that left the population on subsistence levels of existence. Then the Allies started bombing the Reich's puppets and collaborators. When the war against the Soviets started to go badly, one by one the countries that had sided with the Germans became part of the Allied fold: first Italy (October 1943); then Romania (August 1944), followed by Bulgaria (September 1944). Hungary tried (October 1944) but failed, and ended up on the losing side.

The battles were not just between Allies and Axis. The Greek communists (ELAS) and EDES—originally republican but latterly monarchist—fought a civil war in 1943–44 while still under German rule. In Yugoslavia, the rivalry between the anti-communist Chetniks and the communist Partisans also saw a layer of fighting on top of the guerrilla war. Indeed, weapons delivered to fight the Germans were often stored for use in the anticipated postwar struggle. The trouble for the Chetniks was that Tito picked up the popular vote by ensuring his troops were seen as anti-German and recruiting from every nationality. Tito's communists were able to win over their own people; then the Western Allies, who could see who was more powerfully placed, transferred their support from the Chetniks. With assistance from both west and east, the Partisans made the transition from guerrilla bands to organized army (the Germans started referring to Partisan units from mid-1944) and were the victors in 1945.

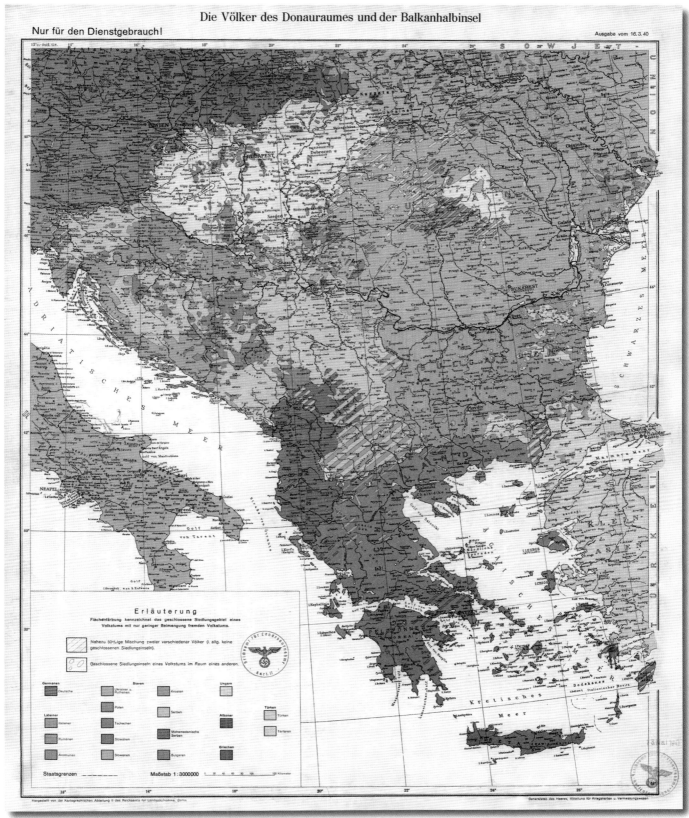

Die Völker des Donauraumes und der Balkanhalbinsel

Ausgabe vom 16. 3. 40

Erläuterung

Flächenfärbung kennzeichnet das geschlossene Siedlungsgebiet eines Volkstums mit nur geringer Beimengung fremden Volkstums.

Nahezu 50%ige Mischung zweier verschiedener Völker (i. allg. keine geschlossenen Siedlungsinseln).

Geschlossene Siedlungsinseln eines Volkstums im Raum eines anderen.

Staatsgrenzen   Maßstab 1:3000000

Balkan Jews and gypsies started to go to the death camps in the summer of 1941. The surprise was Bulgaria where the deportations that started in the territories they acquired—Macedonia and Thrace —didn't extend to Bulgaria itself, thanks to the protestations of the Orthodox Church, the Bulgarian parliament, and others. There was antisemitism and the Jews were sent to penal battalions but escaped the death camps—unlike Serbia, about which SS commander Harald Turner said in 1942, "Serbia is the only country in which the Jewish question and the Gypsy question has been solved."

Above: *A German map showing the Peoples of the Danube area and Balkan Peninsula. What it doesn't show is the peoples they would deport and murder —11,370 from Macedonia, 60,000 from Greece, 66,000 from Yugoslavia, 100,000 from Slovakia.*

Above: *1st Battalion, 32nd Serbian Brigade enters Obrenovac, 40km from central Belgrade.*

Above right: *Partisans enter Belgrade in October 1944.*

Below: 1 *Tito's monument next to his birthplace in Kumrovec, Croatia.*

2 *Tito (R) after having been wounded in a German air attack during the battle of the Sutjeska (the nearby river) in 1943. Tito's life was saved, it was said, by his first German Shepherd, Luks, who shielded him from the explosion. At left, Ivan Ribar who lost his entire family during the war: his two sons, Jurica and Ivo, were killed in action in 1943 fighting for the partisans, while his wife was executed by the Germans in 1944.*

3 *Tito and his second German Shepherd, Tiger, in June 1944.*

Tito and the Partisans

Josip Broz (1892–1980)—known as "Tito" from the 1920s when the Communist Party was outlawed in Yugoslavia—was a Croat who ended up becoming President for Life of his nation. After his death the centuries-old animosities reared their multiple ugly heads and the territory previously known as Yugoslavia quickly subsided into fragmentation and violence. It proved just how difficult Tito's role had been. On June 27, 1941, the Central Committee of the Communist Party of Yugoslavia appointed him commander of all national liberation military forces and his Partisans fought off both the royalist Chetniks and the Axis forces that controlled the Balkans. The size of the Partisan force and its involvement in the liberation meant that, postwar, the Soviet Union had less direct control over Tito and Yugoslavia, something that became apparent when he refused to follow Stalin's economic lead in 1948 and was expelled from Cominform in 1949. In the resulting standoff, Stalin blinked first. The anticipated Soviet invasion didn't happen, Tito consolidated his position and his regime remained unaligned.

1

2

3

Above: *Men of SS-Fallschirmjägerbataillon 500 dug in near Drvar. Note the para helmets, MG42, and Model 39 Eihandgranaten among a mass of equipment.*

Left: *Photo by SS-Untersturmführer Peter Renold showing Fallschirmjäger pulling a supply container. German paras carried very few weapons with them when they jumped and had to retrieve them from containers. These containers had wheels to allow them to be used to transport their contents—weapons, ammunition, rations, radios, etc.*

TARGET TITO: *UNTERNEHMEN RÖSSELSPRUNG* (KNIGHT'S MOVE)

In an attempt to rid themselves of the partisan threat, the Germans launched an operation to kidnap or kill Tito. SS-Fallschirmjägerbataillon 500 landed around the Bosnian town of Drvar where Tito had his HQ on May 25, 1944—they thought that date was Tito's birthday (in fact it was the 7th) and hoped to catch him off guard. In fact, the partisans had become aware of the Fallschirmjäger and had begun to vary Tito's HQ location and his living quarters, although he and his staff were at the location on the 25th. The British mission had also spotted a Fiesler Storch reconnaissance aircraft and had tipped off the Partisans that there might be a bomb attack.

The force the Germans put together involved around 900 SS paras who had to be delivered in three waves because of the paucity of aircraft and gliders. The first wave—the largest because, crucially, they thought Tito's HQ was in Drvar rather than the Citadel cave complex—was a para drop (c. 300 men); the second, simultaneous, a glider-borne attack on the caves (c. 100 men) and other targets including the British, Soviet, and U.S. military missions (c. 250 men); the third, a reinforcement mission (c. 200 men).

The land element that would hurry to linkup with the Fallschirmjäger was a significant force—some 16,000 men—

made up of elements of General der Infanterie Ernst von Leyser's XV. Gebirgskorps, reinforced by a number of other units including Panzerabteilung 202.

However, not much went according to plan. When the attack went in, the Partisan reaction was faster and more purposeful than had been expected. It took the ground forces two days to get to Drvar, by which time Tito, his mistress, and dog had been able to escape the attack, as had the foreign missions. The British had been able to keep in radio contact with their HQ and call in air support as needed. Tito's HQ was destroyed and he moved to the island of Vis where he reorganized under British protection. His HQ stayed there until it moved to Belgrade in late 1944.

The SS paras had attacked bravely but were badly mauled, especially the gliders at the caves where Partisan defense proved strong enough to let Tito escape. When finally relieved, only 200 paras were fit, with 576 dead, and 48 wounded. XV. Gebirgskorps losses were reported as 213 KIA, 881 WIA, and 51 MIA. Partisan losses during the operation are difficult to identify precisely: the Germans claimed 1,916 confirmed, plus a further 1,400 estimated killed, and 161 taken prisoner. Partisan sources said 399 KIA, 479 WIA, and around 100 MIA.

13.Waffen-Gebirgs-Division der SS *Handschar* (kroatische Nr.1)

The first non-Germanic Waffen-SS division, it was made up of Bosnian Muslims, some Croats, and had mainly German and Yugoslav Volksdeutsche officers and NCOs. The fact that they were Muslims was like a red rag to a bull as far as the Serb Orthodox adherents of Draža Mihailović were concerned. Involved in anti-guerrilla operations, they proved ruthlessly brutal, although as 1944 wore on there were numerous desertions. As Yugoslavia was freed by the Partisans and Red Army, the division was sent to fight in Hungary, retreating west as the Soviets advanced. Many ended up as prisoners of the British Army and a number of the officers were later tried for war crimes. Ten were executed.

1 Note collar titles (**2**) and fez headgear. The "Handschar" was the Turkish sword that was part of their collar insignia.

3 A Muslim soldier in the Balkans.

4 Albanian volunteers.

Serbia

For anyone who wants to understand Balkan politics today, first stop should be the genocidal anti-Serb regime in Croatia and the violence against its own people in Serbia. Over 200,000 Serbs, 35,000 Jews and the same number of Roma were murdered in concentration camps, as reprisals for guerrilla attacks, and other atrocities. In Croatia, the regime of Ante Pavelić was violently anti-Serb. In Serbia, the appalling truth, however, is that much of the dirty work was taken on by the German puppet regime—the so-called Government of National Salvation—under Serbian Milan Nedić (previously the Royal Yugoslav Army's chief of staff). The murders were undertaken or abetted by the Serbian State Guard or the fascist militia, the Serbian Volunteer Corps. Memories are long in the Balkans, as events since the fall of Yugoslavia have shown.

Below left: *The breakup of Yugoslavia after the German invasion saw the creation of the Independent State of Croatia, ruled by the Ustaše under Ante Pavelić. Serbia was occupied by the Nazis, with the Bulgarian Army used to control an ever-increasing portion of it. I Occupation Corps of three divisions was formed in 1941 and had 22,632 men; in 1943 this was expanded with a fourth division taking the manpower up to 31,484. The Banat was administered by Josef Lapp, an "ethnic German." The Banat was the area that produced the 7. SS-Freiwilligen Gebirgs-Division Prinz Eugen—a mixture of volunteers and conscripts. While the original invasion of the Yugoslavia and Greece cost the Germans few casualties, the four years of fighting saw huge numbers die. In Yugoslavia 1.2 million of a population of fourteen million; in Greece the figures were 300,000 out of a population of seven million. The Bulgarian Army's II Occupation Corps was set up in November 1943 with three divisions and 58,573 men. Bulgarian forces in Greece had increased to nearly 70,000 by September 1944.*

Below: *Members of the White Russian émigré unit known as the Russian Guard Corps. These men were veterans of the Russian Civil War who had settled in Yugoslavia and fought against the communist partisans. They surrendered to the British in 1945.*

LIBERATION

In the closing months of 1944 the military picture in southeast Europe turned irrevocably against the Nazis. With Bulgaria and Romania changing sides, German forces in the eastern Mediterranean (Heeresgruppe E) were in danger of being cut off. Suddenly, Serbia was threatened by the Soviet 2nd and 3rd Ukrainian fronts in the east, the Bulgarians in the southeast, and the People's Liberation Army of Yugoslavia (NOVJ)—Tito's Partisans—in the west. The failure of German anti-guerrilla operations in summer 1944 had allowed Tito to move large contingents into Serbia. This and Operation Ratweek—air and land attacks by the Western Allies on the German lines of communication—preceded the offensive against the Serb capital.

Above: The body of a collaborator hangs from a lamppost in newly liberated Belgrade. Such examples of summary justice were common throughout the Balkans as Partisan groups caught up with their former oppressors.

Right: Riverine operations took place on the great rivers of Europe and the Danube was large enough to support a flotilla that played an important role in the offensives against Belgrade, Budapest, and Vienna (see p. 193). At Pinsk on the Dnieper—where another flotilla was based—there's a memorial to the Soviet river flotillas, a BK (for bronekater, armored gunboat).

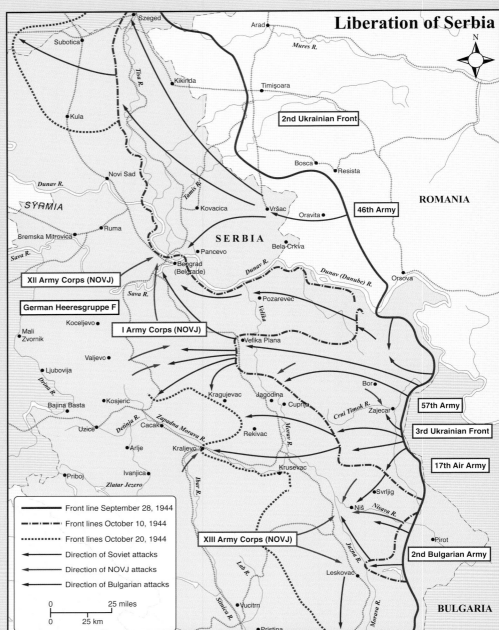

Liberation of Serbia

N

2nd Ukrainian Front

ROMANIA

46th Army

SERBIA

SYRMIA

German Heeresgruppe F

XII Army Corps (NOVJ)

I Army Corps (NOVJ)

57th Army

3rd Ukrainian Front

17th Air Army

XIII Army Corps (NOVJ)

2nd Bulgarian Army

BULGARIA

— Front line September 28, 1944
—·— Front lines October 10, 1944
····· Front lines October 20, 1944
← Direction of Soviet attacks
← Direction of NOVJ attacks
← Direction of Bulgarian attacks

0 — 25 miles
0 — 25 km

BELGRADE

The battle of Belgrade (**Below**) started on October 12 and was all over by the 20th. There were two major German elements—the garrison inside the fortified city (**Left**—German signal position on the outskirts of Belgrade. Note the Yugoslav auxiliaries wearing an Adrian helmet and field caps, and the ZB vz26 LMG), and outside: what was left of Armeeabteilung Serbien (commanded by Generalleutnant Walter Stettner, CG of 1. Gebirgs-Division) attempting to link up with the defenders from the east. On the 14th the Russians and partisans moved into Belgrade, and the city fell on the 15th. The same day, Armeeabteilung Serbien reached Grocka, some 15 miles down the Danube from Belgrade. On the 16th, Stettner was 10 miles closer; on the 17th he tried again. On the 18th they lost radio contact. Pushed south and west sustaining casualties as they went, on the 21st they finally crossed the River Sava to safety. The Russian losses in the fighting in Belgrade were 1,000. Those of the NOVJ were 2,953.

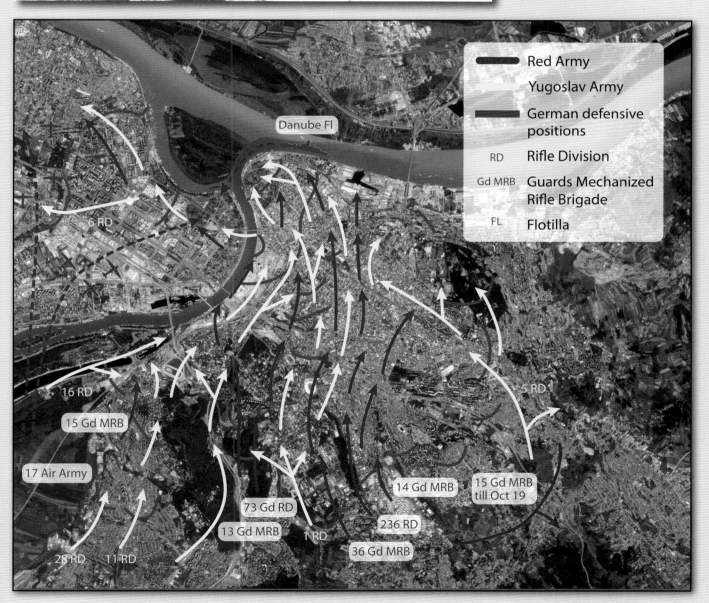

Red Army

Yugoslav Army

German defensive positions

RD — Rifle Division

Gd MRB — Guards Mechanized Rifle Brigade

FL — Flotilla

Danube Fl

6 RD

16 RD

15 Gd MRB

17 Air Army

28 RD   11 RD

73 Gd RD

13 Gd MRB   1 RD

36 Gd MRB

236 RD

14 Gd MRB

15 Gd MRB till Oct 19

5 RD

While the Germans tried their best to let their clients and collaborationists take the strain, the continued problems of getting to grips with irregular forces, partisans, and nationalists—all aided by British SOE and American OSS operations—forced them to introduce front-line troops. It's difficult to be precise about German losses in the Balkans. Rüdiger Overmans puts it at over 100,000. There were certainly seven major anti-guerrilla operations in Yugoslavia known to the Partisans as the Seven Enemy Offensives. They weren't able to quell the resistance, and by March 1945, Tito commanded 800,000 men. German strength in late 1944 was over 300,000 in Yugoslavia and over 300,000 in Greece

Above: SdKfz 8 12-ton halftrack towing an 8.8cm Flak 36 gun on the Balkan front in Serbia.

Above right: German soldiers push cars over rough terrain on the Balkan front. Corduroy roads were the only way to move vehicles in the mountains during winter.

Right: A skirmish between German troops and Yugoslav guerrillas over a village on the Balkan front.

Croatia

The German invasion of Yugoslavia led to the creation of the Independent State of Croatia under the Ustaša, the Croatian Revolutionary Movement. The regime was headed by the so-called *Poglavnik* (head or chief) Ante Pavelić, who had been living in Italian exile because of his involvement in the assassination of King Alexander of Yugoslavia at Marseilles in 1934. Pavelić's original 100 men soon became an army that was bent on one main objective: the genocide of the Serbs. To achieve this they planned to kill a third, expel a third, and forcibly convert a third to Catholicism.

They were as good as their word. By the end of the war the regime had murdered 300,000–350,000 Serbs, as well as tens of thousands of Jews and Roma, often with the silence of, if not the complicity of, the Catholic church, which to this day tries to downplay the horrific events. Even the Nazis were shocked at the brutality and court-martialed the infamous Franciscan monk and chief guard of the Jasenovac concentration camp.

Croatia, however, was a cornerstone in the Germans' arrangements for Greece and the Balkans, essential to the maintenance of lines of communication. In the end, a lot of men that could have been usefully fighting elsewhere ended up trying to keep the escape route north open for Heeresgruppen E and F.

1 *Soldier of the 4. SS-Polizei-Panzergrenadier-Division during the fighting in Dalmatia, September 1944. The division was responsible for widespread atrocities, such as that at Distomo in Greece on June 10, 1944, where over 200—some say many more—civilians were butchered in reprisal for partisan attacks.*

2 *Cossacks cross the Sava River in Croatia. Late in the war, the Waffen-SS took over the Cossack units and formed the XV. SS-Kosaken-Kavallerie-Korps.*

3 *and* 4 *The fascist head of the Nezavisna Država Hrvatska, (NDH—Independent State of Croatia), Ante Pavelić. Note his standard.*

Right: When the Italians changed sides, much of their equipment was taken up by the Germans. This tank is an Italian M14/41 and is carrying SS grenadiers in pursuit of partisans in the mountains of Bosnia. In combat with Allied AFVs the M14/41 would have been ineffective—its 40mm frontal armor and 47mm main gun would have struggled against a T-34—but against the guerrillas, it was more than adequate.

Center and **Below right:** The Sturmgeschütz L6 47/32 530(i) StuG L6 is the German designation for the Semovente L40 da 47/32 in Wehrmacht service. The original L6/40 version had not proved to be able to withstand British tanks in the desert, but the license-produced Böhler 47/32 gun mounted on the L.40 da 47/32 proved useful against lighter British and U.S. armor. About 280 were produced, many of which were exported to Croatia. Note the shield for the MG (**Below right**).

Opposite, Below: 17th Muslim Brigade Maxim gunners. By 1945 Tito commanded around 800,000 Partisans of which roughly 2.5–3.5% were Muslim, mainly Croats, although this figure was area-dependent (so, in Bosnia and Herzegovina the percentage was 25–30%).

Left and **Below left:** Northwest of Belgrade, the Syrmian Front—the area between the Danube and the Sava—was the arena for a six-month battle, starting in October 1944 and ending April 1945, as Tito's Partisan army, with some help from the Red Army, tried to destroy the retreating remnants of Heeresgruppe E. The German forces were still a functioning fighting unit and knew they had to reach a location that would enable them to surrender to the British or Americans rather than endure the reprisals of the Yugoslavs. This is Vinkovci, 100 miles NW of Belgrade, at the end of the campaign. Gaj Trifković (2016) summed up the capture of the town and the final days of the campaign: "With the taking of Vinkovci, the Syrmian Front ceased to exist. In operational terms, the 1st Yugoslav Army had won a bloody, but clear-cut victory: at the cost of some 606 killed, 2,200 wounded, and four missing, as well as four destroyed and seven damaged tanks, it had successfully stormed the strongly fortified German line in Syrmia and advanced 30–40km in two days, netting an estimated 2,000 prisoners and large quantities of equipment."

It hadn't destroyed Heeresgruppe E but, realistically, that was unlikely. The Partisans were transitioning from guerrillas into a fully functioning army and having to cope with such things as inexperienced new recruits, minefields, tanks, and trenches. They found that officer and NCO casualties were too high because they were used to leading from the front. Most of the men weren't used to wearing helmets. They didn't have sufficient bridging equipment or ammunition for significant artillery bombardments. The learning curve was steep, but "In the end, it turned out that the 1st Army needed respite more than anything else. During the quiet period on the Syrmian Front between late January and early April 1945, the units were brought up to strength, rested and trained in the use of their new equipment."

BATTLE OF ODŽAK

The final battle of World War II began on April 19, 1945, and continued until May 25, more than two weeks after the end of the war in Europe. It was a bitter, no-quarter battle, fought between the Croatian Ustaše and the Partisans. It ended—once the Partisans used airpower—in defeat for the Ustaše. Exact figures of both sides' strength and losses are matters of debate and considerably distorted postwar for political ends. The story was suppressed after the war as the new Yugoslav government, built around Tito, attempted to reconcile all sides to a new, inclusive state.

Romania

When World War II started, things went badly for Romania, and the loss of the province of Bessarabia to the Soviets as well as other parts of the country to Hungary and Bulgaria led to King Carol II—under German pressure—abdicating. His place as leader was then taken by the extreme right-winger General Ion Antonescu, who soon allied Romania with the Axis powers. (The official date was November 23, 1940.) The immediate consequence of this was that Romania had to supply troops to assist with the German invasion of Russia.

The upside of the arrangement was that a month later, at a cost of 4,112 KIA, 12,120 WIA, and 5,506 MIA, the Romanians had regained the territories they had lost. The downside became apparent over the next three years. The Stalingrad debacle saw serious losses—158,854 casualties between November 19, 1942, and January 7, 1943. With their economy in tatters—the Germans paid for none of the oil, grain, and equipment Romania supplied—they were forced to retreat before the Soviet Dnieper–Carpathian Offensive.

As the Red Army crossed into Romania, the country was in turmoil. King Michael I—who had become monarch after his father's abdication—took the

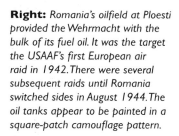

Above: *Commander of the Großdeutschland Division, Hasso von Manteuffel, in Romania in July 1944. The division had helped the Romanians halt a thrust by General Konev's 2nd Ukrainian Front. Großdeutschland was sent north in August to break through to the Courland Pocket. Von Manteuffel was chosen by Hitler to lead the attack in the Ardennes, commanding 5. Panzerarmee and promoted to General der Panzertruppe.*

Right: *Romania's oilfield at Ploesti provided the Wehrmacht with the bulk of its fuel oil. It was the target the USAAF's first European air raid in 1942. There were several subsequent raids until Romania switched sides in August 1944. The oil tanks appear to be painted in a square-patch camouflage pattern.*

Below right: *The figure standing in the foreground (**A**) is the de facto ruler of Romania until August 1944, Marshal Ion Antonescu. In the center (**B**) is GFM Walther von Brauchitsch. Arrested on August 23, 1944, Antonescu was imprisoned in the Lubyanka prison in Moscow and returned to Romania in 1946. He was found guilty of war crimes and shot on June 1, 1946.*

opportunity to stage a coup, deposing Antonescu from power. His actions were supported by opposition politicians, much of the army, and by anti-Fascist civilians. Romania declared war on Germany on August 23, 1944, and from this point on—together with her sizable army—she was once more on the Allies' side.

The switch in allegiance was not without its own problems though—there were still some 60,000 German and Yugoslav troops in the country, and there was the further risk of invasion from Bulgaria and Hungary. After protracted and heavy fighting, however, Romanian troops managed to overcome these Axis forces and they were then able to join with the Red Army in pushing the Germans back across their borders.

Top: *The King of Romania, Michael I (foreground, center) in conversation with the head of the Romanian labor service, Gen Emil Palangeanu (right), in August 1942.*

Above: *Soviet ISU-122 assault gun and IS-2 heavy tank on one of the roads in Transylvania (Romania). They belong to the 2nd Ukrainian Front of the Red Army, September 1944.*

The Romanian Army in Hungary, Czechoslovakia, and Austria

The Romanian Army was involved in much of the heavy fighting through southeastern Europe into the Reich from late 1944 up until the end of the war. The front line between the Black Sea and the Carpathians had been blown away in the summer as the 2nd and 3rd Ukrainian Fronts burst into Romania. Between August 20 and 31, 1944, the Second Jassy–Kishinev Operation—which had significant air support from the USAAF—resulted in a massive defeat for the Germans who were once again badly hampered by Hitler's refusal to permit any strategic withdrawals. They suffered enormous casualties, more than 115,000 were taken prisoner, and huge quantities of equipment were lost. More importantly, perhaps, so were the Ploesti oilfields.

When the attack started, Romania was still on the Axis side, but midway through the operation it switched sides and joined the Allies. Soon after, Romanian troops were involved in clearing the Germans from their country and by the start of September, the new front line ran along the Danube from the Black Sea into Serbia, and along the Carpathians in Hungary.

September 6 saw First and Fourth Romanian armies pass to Malinovsky's command as part of the 2nd Ukrainian Front. Malinovsky, who had

Above: *Advancing slowly through wooded terrain without infantry cover was a dangerous undertaking due to the possibility of ambush. The need to flush out Axis troops armed with Panzerfaust hand-held anti-tank weapons was a vital task. Here, Romanian infantry is accompanied by Soviet armor. The battle of Turda resulted in heavy infantry casualties on both sides, with as many as 30–40 percent of 23. Panzerdivision's infantry lost. Hungarian 25th Infantry Division losses between September 8 and 22, amounted to some 2,250, including 750 dead. Of the casualties, 85 percent were infantry.*

Left: *Another view of Red Army troops in Bucharest, August 31, 1944. Note the classic lines of the Maxim PM1910/30 7.62mm MMG. The Soviets built around 176,000 between 1910 and 1945.*

masterminded the summer assault, was made Marshal of the Soviet Union and told to roll up the Axis forces between him and Vienna. And that, in spite of all the Germans could throw at him—including 6. SS-Panzerarmee in Hungary—is exactly what he did, although he didn't have it all his own way and at no stage did the German retreat become a rout. Between September 1944 through to May 1945, Malinovsky's front, including the Romanian armies, advanced over 600 miles (1,000km) from Brasov to Brno in Czechoslovakia.

However, September didn't start as well as could have been hoped as the Hungarian Second Army pushed the recently reconstituted Fourth Romanian Army back, assisting German 6. Armee extract itself through the Carpathian passes. The fighting was particularly intense around Turda, where the Fourth Romanian and Russian Twenty-seventh fought it out against German 8. Armee and the Second Hungarian Army. This was one of the biggest and bloodiest engagements fought in Transylvania, with both sides losing many men—so much so that the Hungarians were merged into Armeegruppe Fretter-Pico (CG 6. Armee) who reported on the 17th "that Second Army was in a 'catastrophic' state" (Ziemcke).

These mobile units were often used where terrain or weather limited the use of heavier armored forces. The cavalry on horseback were particularly useful in Russia where forests and swamps were no-go areas for tanks. The CMGs were named after their commander, for example Cavalry-Mechanized Group Gorshkov (Lt Gen Sergey Gorshkov) or Pliyev (General Issa Pliyev).

Typically, a mobile unit would have a combination of mechanized and cavalry corps, with motorized rifle brigades, cavalry divisions, a number of tanks units—regiments or brigades—and SP artillery regiments.

Intelligence Bulletin noted: "Red Army doctrine stresses that cavalry should be used as an independent striking force; that cavalry is not a substitute for mechanized forces, but is a powerful force for operations where motorized units are handicapped ... Russian cavalry has great power in supporting weapons. The organization is so designed as to provide a small and mobile striking force with adequate support of artillery, mortars, and automatic weapons. Cavalry and tanks have been combined into a smooth working and effective organization."

Top right: A Soviet mountain artillery unit carrying a Model 1938 76mm mountain gun. It broke down into nine parts for transport by horse, with a further 14 for the limber and roughly 100 shells.

Above right: The Axis used cavalry, too. Thousands of Cossacks enrolled in the Wehrmacht from 1941 onward. In mid-1943 all Cossack troops were united in 1. Kosaken-Kavallerie-Division. A second division was created as both were taken over by the Waffen-SS as the XV. SS-Kosaken-Kavallerie-Korps, but did not wear SS insignia. The corps took part in the southern section of Unternehmen Frühlingserwachen along the Drava River.

While the battle of Turda was still raging, further west at Păuliș, south of Arad, there was another engagement, on September 14, between Second Hungarian Army's 1st Armored Division and elements of the Romanian Army who were reinforced by the Soviet Fifty-third Army. When the Soviets arrived, the tables were turned and the aggressors were beaten back to their starting points. At this time Hungary was teetering on the edge of panic and was seriously considering swapping sides as Romania and Bulgaria had done. The German *Unternehmen Panzerfaust* (see p. 116) in mid-October put paid to that and German units were sent to the area to stiffen Hungarian resolve.

October saw the Romanians involved in the complicated engagements around Debrecen, about 100 miles (160km) east of Budapest. Both sides were planning attacks: Hitler wanted, in his usually unrealistic way, to use four Panzer divisions to attack through Oradea and then west along the Transylvanian Alps to trap Malinovsky's forces. The Soviets were hoping 4th Ukrainian Front would thrust through the Dukla Pass and meet an attack northward by Sixth Guards Tank Army, while to the southwest Forty-sixth and Fifty-third armies, along with Cavalry-Mechanized Group Pliyev, would aim for Budapest—a similarly over-ambitious plan.

Left: *Romanian PoWs, summer 1944. Their berets indicate they are mountain troops. Having spearheaded the Axis advance into the Caucasus in 1942, in 1944 they fought in a similar role in the Tatra Mountains alongside the Red Army.*

Below: *The Red Army advance into central Europe once Romania had come over to the Allies. Over 500,000 Romanians served during this period, with casualties of nearly 170,000. Soviet troops didn't leave Romania until 1958.*

The Allied advance through Romania, Hungary and Czechoslovakia, August 1944–May 1945

⟵ Soviet troop movements	
⟵ Romanian	
⟵ Czech Corps	
⟵ German and Hungarian	
—— Front line April 15, 1945	
–·–· Front line March 5, 1945	
– – – Front line October 29, 1944	
–··–·· Front line September 6	
········ Front line September 26	

1st UF = 1st Ukrainian Front
2nd UF = 2nd Ukrainian Front
3rd UF = 3rd Ukrainian Front
4th UF = 4th Ukrainian Front
4th GA = 4th Guards Army
6th GTA = 6th Guards Tank Army
7th GA = 7th Guards Army
40th A = 40th Army
27th A = 27th Army

53rd A = 53rd Army
Gorshkov = Cav–Mech Gp Gorshkov
Pliyev = Cav–Mech Gp Pliyev
1st G Cav = 1st Guards Cav-Mech Gp
ICC = I Czech Corps

0 ——— 100 MILES
0 ——— 100 KM

N

The Soviet southern group made good progress after overcoming the Third Hungarian Army, and the Dukla Pass fell on October 6, but the northern group stalled when they ran into heavy opposition in the form of 1. and 23. Panzerdivisionen of the III. Panzerkorps. On October 10, as Ziemcke (1968) puts it: "the divisions attacked east and west below Debrecen into the flanks of the Soviet spearhead. Late that night their points met. They had cut off three corps. The army group envisioned 'another Cannae' ... The next day, when Sixth Guards Tank Army put up a violent fight to get the corps out, who had trapped whom began to become unclear." Much fighting took place and there were many convoluted battlefield maneuvers particularly around the town of Nyíregyháza which the Germans lost and then retook, again trapping three Soviet corps. This time there was no escape and the survivors abandoned their heavy weapons on October 29 and fled south leaving the Axis with an unbroken front line. The battle left 15,000 German and 20,000 Hungarian casualties, and 18,000 Axis troops were taken PoW. Armored losses are estimated as 200, and artillery losses are given as 490 Axis pieces. The Red Army had 117,360 casualties—33,500 of them Romanian.

The next major military action for the Romanian Army was the battle of Carei, which was fought to retake the last part of the country that had been handed over to Hungary in 1940 under the terms of the Second Vienna Award. This final phase of re-establishing the country's borders ended on October 25. Although the campaign was fought over very harsh terrain in terrible weather with most of the roads mined and the bridges destroyed, the mixed Romanian forces eventually overcame their Hungarian adversaries and once more raised the national flag in Carei.

As covered in the preceding chapter on Hungary, the First and Fourth Romanian armies also took part in the Budapest Offensive (October 29, 1944—February 13, 1945), and the Siege of Budapest (December 29, 1944—February 13, 1945). Romanian troops also took part in the Bratislava–Brno Offensive (March 25–May 5, 1945). It saw the First and Fourth Romanian armies as part of the 2nd Ukrainian Front take Bratislava, the capital of Slovakia, and then Brno, the capital of Moravia. The operation began when the Soviet Seventh Guards Army mounted a surprise night attack on the German front line, breaking through the River Hron line across an area that was over 11 miles (17km) wide.

This bridgehead was rapidly exploited and the Red Army pushed toward Bratislava as fast as it could. Where the terrain allowed, this made for rapid progress, but much of the country was mountainous and caused considerable

delays. Meanwhile, the day after the offensive first started, the Fourth Romanian Army liberated the city of Banská Bystrica, where the Slovak National Uprising had been defeated on October 27, 1944.

The Red Army reached the outskirts of Bratislava on April 2 and the following night the defending Axis forces—consisting of the German 6. Armee and the Third Hungarian Army—blew all the bridges across the Danube, (which bisects the city), to strengthen their positions. After fierce fighting, however, they had little option but to withdraw. The parts of the city on the north bank fell late on April 4, 1945. The next day the southern areas were also captured.

Other Soviet forces pushing toward Vienna from the northwest had to face the barrier of the River Morava which ran through a mix of dense woodland and marshes—at that time of year, normally considered impassable. The troops of the VI Guards Cavalry Corps, however, overcame the problems and managed to cross the river. They were able to reach the railroad embankment that was above water. This left them in a position to begin mounting an assault on the town of Lanžhot which was strongly defended by German armor, including more than sixty tanks, some of which were Tiger IIs of sPzAbt 503 *Feldherrnhalle*. The attack on the town took four days to complete, by which time most of it had been destroyed by the severity of the fighting. (sPzAbt 503 knocked out ten enemy tanks and lost one of its Tigers during the fight on April 11. Just over two weeks later, fighting 25 miles to the northeast, the tank of its

leading ace, Unteroffizier Kurt Knispel, who claimed 168 kills, was knocked out. Knispel died in a nearby field hospital.)

Also pushing from slightly different directions toward Brno, the Soviet Fortieth Army took the city of Trencín on April 10 and the Fifty-third Army assaulted the city of Hodonín, liberating it on April 13. Having crossed the River Morava the Red Army kept moving forward until they were stopped by Panzerkorps *Feldherrnhalle* at the town of Rajhrad. This lies 9 miles (15 km) south of Brno, so rather than allowing themselves to be held up, the main units went around the blockage to the west, finally coming to a stop at the village of Ořechov.

German counterattacks then encircled some of the forward Soviet units and recaptured Ořechov, but they did not have the strength to finish the job. The battle—predominantly an armored slugfest—raged for seven days. Matters were complicated for the Germans when Czech partisans captured the commander of 16. Panzerdivision, and in the end the Red Army retook the whole area. By comparison with other actions in the theater, the casualty

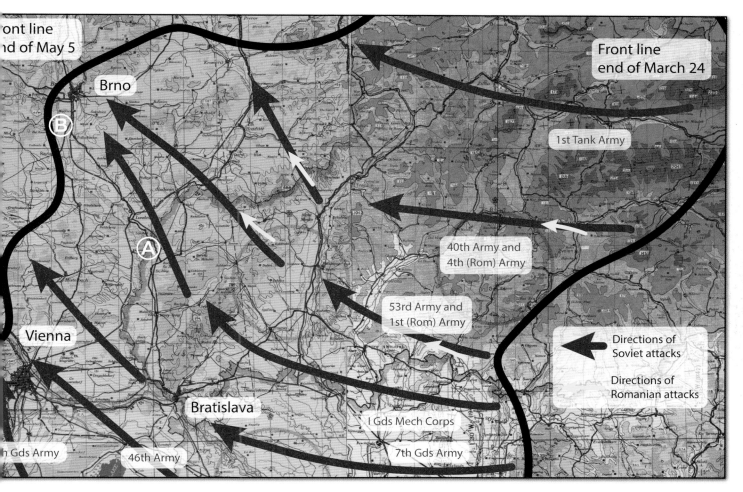

Front line
end of May 5

Brno

(B)

Vienna

(A)

Bratislava

h Gds Army

46th Army

Front line
end of March 24

1st Tank Army

40th Army and
4th (Rom) Army

53rd Army and
1st (Rom) Army

I Gds Mech Corps

7th Gds Army

Directions of
Soviet attacks

Directions of
Romanian attacks

list was small—around 960 Soviet and about 300 German troops died, with both sides losing around 30 tanks each.

Most of Brno was liberated on April 26, 1945, when armored vehicles of the Soviet Sixth Guards Tank Army broke in from the east and the Mechanized Cavalry Group penetrated from the south. There were still small outposts of Germans in place until May 5, however. Much of the Red Army was diverted off to advance towards Prague to assist the uprising, but the First and Fourth Romanian armies continued fighting their way along the line of the Morava River until the end of the war, liberating several more towns as they did so.

Although the Bratislava–Brno Offensive did not last very long, overall it had been a costly one: almost 17,000 Soviet troops killed, and nine German divisions had been wiped out. Strategically though, it achieved its aim of allowing the Red Army to move up and threaten Heeresgruppe Mitte's southern flank—and ensuring that Czechoslovakia and Austria would have a sizable Soviet presence at the end of the war.

The day after the Bratislava–Brno Offensive finished, the Prague Offensive (which is fully detailed in the chapter on Czechoslovakia) began, running May 6–11, 1945. Although the military mainstay was provided by the Red Army, it also involved troops from Romania and Poland who faced opposition from the Germans, Hungarians, and Slovakians as well as—at least in the short term—troops from the renegade Russian Liberation Army.

The Soviet 2nd Ukrainian Front—of which the twelve infantry divisions and three cavalry divisions of the First and Fourth Romanian armies were part—was ordered to advance on Prague from the southeast. Their opposition was what was left of 1. Panzerarmee and 8. Armee. Fighting in the city continued after German forces elsewhere had surrendered.

Between Romania switching sides in August 1944 and the end of the war, around 538,000 of her troops fought with the Allies—around 167,000 of whom became casualties.

Above: *The 2nd Ukrainian Front's advance to Bratislava and Brünn (Brno). Starting on March 24, Bratislava fell on April 4 and Brno on April 26. Soviet casualties were around 17,000. A identifies Lanžhot and B Orechov where sPzAbt 503 Feldherrnhalle fought (see text). sPzAbt 503 was redesignated Feldherrnhalle (unit insignia* **Right***) on December 21, 1944, and attached to Panzerkorps Feldherrnhalle. 503 had played an important role at Debrecen, and took part in Unternehmen Konrad, Südwind, and Frühlingserwachen. It retreated through Czechoslovakia, withdrawing via Budweis where, on May 10, they destroyed their vehicles including the last two Tigers, and tried to reach American lines. Those that did were handed back to the Soviets (Schneider).*

Right: *A German sniper poses for the camera in his Wehrmacht-style camouflage suit. His Kar98k has a ZF39 scope.*

Below: *Summary justice. The excesses of the Nazis, their genocidal treatment of the populations of Europe, and the executions for assisting guerrilla operations or in retaliation for deaths of occupying forces, shouldn't hide the fact that there were many more deaths as the Nazis retreated and the communists moved in. The Soviets allowed few of the old regimes to stay in place, executing thousands, and sending many others to labor camps. The takeover by the Soviets in Romania was essential for Stalin as it took away opposition for the postwar occupation of Northern Bukovina and Bessarabia, the latter becoming the Soviet Republic of Moldova. It also saw a revival of Romania's indigenous—and very small—communist party. It had been outlawed during the war, had fewer than 1,000 members, of whom 800 were in prison. In December 1947, with King Michael's forced abdication, the communist takeover was complete and Stalin had another buffer state.*

Above and **Left:** *Brno fell on April 26, 1945, to Soviet and Romanian troops. On May 30 the Brünner Todesmarsch (Brno Death March) began as the Germans were expelled from the city. Elsewhere some 500,000 German-speakers were expelled from the country in the first wave. While the expulsion cannot be compared to the death marches forced on so many by the Nazis in the last weeks of the year, nevertheless over three million "ethnic Germans"—a mixture of the Sudetenland Germans who lived in Czechoslovakia and those, such as the Germans from Silesia, who had fled the Red Army—were forced to leave Czechoslovakia and march to the German and Austrian borders over the next few years.*

Above: *The Bulgarian Parachute Druzhina was formed in 1943. Uneasy allies of the Germans, the Bulgarians trained at Fallschirmschule 3 at Braunschweig-Broitzem where they were mistrusted by their trainers. When Bulgaria switched sides in late 1944, the unit was quickly involved and on October 18, 1944, played an important role in the battle of Stracin, Yugoslavia. They suffered high casualties (35 KIA, 65 WIA of the c. 400-man unit). Here they are seen brandishing their MP38s and 40s.*

Opposite, Below: *Troops of the 3rd Ukrainian Front roll into Sofia, the capital of Bulgaria, to a variety of salutes. The infantry are riding atop a Lend-Lease British-made Valentine Mk IX armed with a 57mm gun. The Valentine enjoyed a reputation for reliability and durability with its Soviet crews, although its main armament lacked penetrative power.*

Bulgaria

Following in Romania's footsteps from a month earlier, the Bulgarian government was overthrown on September 9, 1944, following mass civil unrest, in a coup d'état by a communist coalition known as the Fatherland Front. Backed up by sympathetic units of the Bulgarian Army and partisans from the People's Liberation Revolt Army, the new government led by Kimon Georgiev immediately aligned itself with the Allies. Their situation was helped by the fact that the Red Army had entered the country unopposed the day before—and the fact that the Soviet Union had declared war on Bulgaria on September 4 forced the takeover. (The Bulgarians had not declared war on the Soviet Union; indeed, they had only done so on Britain and the United States in 1941.) The Red Army reached Sofia on September 16 and there remained a Red Army presence in the country until 1947. The new government signed an armistice in October, giving up all territorial gains. They had been reluctant Axis allies, but they played an important role in the Balkans, particularly Serbia (see p. 139).

On hearing the news of the successful coup, partisan units emerged from the hills and assumed power in the towns and villages. In most places this was peaceful, but in some there were fierce clashes between army and police forces still loyal to the old government. Once power had been secured, the new regime abolished the police and replaced it with a militia composed of a mix of partisans and civilians. They also emptied the prisons of thousands of political offenders, closed down concentration camps, and arrested many prominent members of the old government. Several of these were executed a few weeks later. Fascist organizations and their literature were also banned, and a wave of terror swept the country as the communists' enemies were purged. Those who were not killed—and somewhere between 20,000 and 40,000 died in the first four months alone—were placed in labor camps. The Russian involvement in the country ensured its alignment when the war ended.

TSAR BORIS III
(1894–1943)

Bulgaria's position in World War II was ambiguous. Allied to Germany from March 1941, it declared war on the Great Britain and the United States, but not on the USSR. It didn't join in the "Barbarossa" invasion and the king was put under great pressure by the Germans to introduce the Final Solution into Bulgaria. In those territories he gained from the Germans—Macedonia, and Thrace—the Final Solution was adopted, and some 17,000 went to their deaths. His regime has been rightly castigated for its antisemitism, but it is also incontrovertible that the Jews of Bulgaria were not deported, although many were placed in labor battalions. Here (**Left**), King Boris III visits Adolf Hitler's headquarters, March 26, 1942. Boris died, possibly of poisoning, in 1943 and his infant son took over.

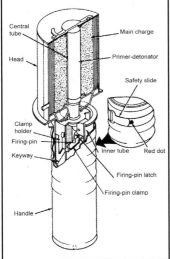

RGD-33 DEFENSIVE/OFFENSIVE STICK GRENADE

Weight (with frag jacket)	1.7lb
Weight (w/o frag jacket)	1.1lb
Length overall	7.5in
Dia. of head w/o frag jacket	2.2in
Time delay	3.2–4sec
Effective bursting radius (with frag jacket)	15yd
Max lethal radius (w/o frag jacket)	10yd
Average throwing range	30–40yd

Before the end of the month, the First Bulgarian Army (which numbered around 30,000 men), along with the Second and Fourth armies, was heavily engaged in fighting Axis forces along the border with Yugoslavia. In doing so, the Bulgarians had support from both Yugoslav guerrillas and Red Army units.

First Bulgarian Army in Hungary and Austria

For most of the period 1939–44 the Bulgarian Army's main task was the occupation of Serbia and Thrace. Traditionally, Turkey had always been Bulgaria's primary concern and during the war, there was a clear threat that Turkey would join the Allies. To cover this eventuality, Bulgaria had deployed a Screening Army (after 1941, the "Screening Front") with its HQ initially at Nova Zagora and then at Simeonovgrad (Maritza). From 1939 the border was given a concrete foundation by the Krali Marko line of fortifications. These increased in number and were extended to include by 1944 the Macedonian, White Sea (Aegean), Southeastern (facing Turkey), and Black Sea defense lines. The army was not particularly well equipped: most units were horse-drawn and there were few modern AFVs—a total of only about 120 tanks, mainly PzKpfw 38(t)s, PzKpfw IVs, and French Renault R-35s.

The Bulgarian role changed when the country left the Axis and former enemies became "friends." The change of sides meant an enormous influx of extra men into the country's military—within three months, the First Army alone had tripled in size, reaching just short of 100,000 troops. This represented a useful and much-needed supplement to the Soviets' advance, and extensive use was made of the Bulgarian armies by the Red Army in the push into Hungary and Austria in early 1945. After suffering many privations and losses due to the harsh winter conditions and heavy fighting they had experienced, in March 1945 the Soviets donated a vast quantity of equipment to help make them a more effective military force. This included 65 T-34 tanks, 370 transport vehicles, 410 field guns, 115 anti-aircraft guns, 370 mortars, around 30,000 small arms, plus 344 aircraft.

The First Army (130,000 men commanded by Col-Gen Vladimir Stoichev) saw action in March 1945 in Hungary, defending against *Unternehmen Frühlingserwachen* (see map 2, p. 127) as part of Marshal Tolbukhin's 3rd Ukrainian Front. The Bulgarians were positioned on the River Drava, and fought Heeresgruppe E's attack north from Serbia. The fighting centered on three villages—Drávaszabolcs, Drávapalkonya, and Drávacsehi. The Bulgarian defense was brave and held firm helping to stymie German ambitions.

The Bulgarian Army losses during the war amounted to 40,450 men—31,910 while fighting alongside the Soviets between September 1944 and May 1945—8,337 dead, 9,155 missing, and 22,958 wounded.

ВПЕРЕД, НА ЗАПАД!

СМЕРТЬ НЕМЕЦКИМ ОККУПАНТАМ!

Czechoslovakia 5

Parts of Czechoslovakia were under German control for seven long years. After the appeasement of Munich sacrificed the Sudetenland, the country was divided into the Protectorate of Bohemia and Moravia (German), the Slovak client state run by the Hlinka Slovak People's Party, and the Carpathian area that Hungary annexed. The Slovak State sent troops to the invasion of Poland and Russia, and was involved in deporting or murdering 58,000 Jews before the deportations ceased in late 1942. They resumed after the Slovak National Uprising in 1944 (see pp. 164–165) when Hitler occupied the country. The total number rose to as many as 106,000. In the Protectorate, some 30,000 Jews realized early enough that they should emigrate. Those that stayed faced the same fate that so many others in the areas under German control suffered. Of a prewar Jewish population of about 118,000, less than 10 percent survived.

At the start of 1945, the German defense line ran along the Slovakian–Hungarian border and then north toward Warsaw. By the end of January, the Soviets had advanced brilliantly—as we saw in Chapter 2—to the banks of the Oder. The eastern half of Slovakia had fallen and the 4th Ukrainian Front had fought through the Tatra Mountains and, along with the Romanian Army, threatened the Protectorate itself. The thrust to Bratislava and Brno is covered in Chapter 4 (see pp. 152–157); that to Vienna in Chapter 6. The crucial advance to Prague—and the importance to this for the postwar political map of Europe is covered in this chapter.

When the war ended, the "ethnic Germans" who were seen as the reason for the German takeover of the country in 1938–39, were expelled as they were from so many central European states. By the end of 1946, some 1.6 million had been deported to West Germany and 800,000 to East Germany—although a total figure of three million is given to include other Germans expelled from neighboring countries who passed through Czechoslovakia. Many of these people died during the process, although the figure of around 270,000 put out in 1958 by the West German government has since been shown to be an over-assessment.

Continued on p. 166.

Opposite: *"Death to the German invaders!"—Nikolai Dolgorukov and Boris Efimov 1942 poster shows Mannerheim (Finland), Hitler, Mussolini, Horthy (Hungary), Goebbels, Antonescu (Romania), Himmler, and Goering.*

Above: *Plaque to the victims of the Prague Uprising.*

Slovak National Uprising

The armed uprising in Slovakia had been carefully planned but when it started on August 29, 1944, it immediately ran into trouble. Its air force decamped to join the Red Air Force in Poland and the Slovak Army's two strongest divisions were quickly disarmed before they could change sides. The Germans sent over 40,000 Waffen-SS troops who suppressed the uprising in a violent counteroffensive. The biggest problem is that the Soviets wouldn't support what it saw as being an uprising with western links. The Soviet-led partisans wouldn't coordinate with the Slovaks and the Soviet Army—which had planned to cross the Dukla Pass, the lowest pass in the Carpathians between Poland and Slovakia, quickly—was halted by XXIV. Panzerkorps. The Russian and Czech troops attacked through the Kapisovka valley which was the scene of an immense battle that took place between September 8 and October 28, 1944. It pitted Soviet Thirty-eighth Army and First Czechoslovak Army from Ivan Konev's 1st Ukrainian Front—getting on for 400,000 men and 1,000 tanks—against General Gotthard Heinrici's army group, composed of 1. Panzerarmee and elements of First Hungarian Army—some 100,000 men and 350 tanks. The Germans were able to hold off the Soviet attacks while crushing the Slovaks. On October 28, the uprising was over and the Nazis embarked on reprisals that saw over 90 villages and 5,000 people killed, with thousands more sent to the camps.

Below right: *Men of the Hlinka Guard, Slovakia's equivalent of Nazi Germany's para-military SA. In 1944 units of this group were deployed against the Slovak uprising. Then, subordinated to Einsatzgruppe H, they continued the deportation of Slovakian Jews.*

Bottom right: *The uprising in Slovakia and the ongoing partisan operations that sprang up across Eastern Europe led to many German and allied troops being deployed in security operations behind the front line. Here one such unit searches a suspects house.*

Below: *Soldiers from the 18. SS-Freiwilligen Panzergrenadier-Division Horst Wessel during the uprising. Note their SS camo jacket with rank attachment stripes.*

Opposite, Above: *The Dukla Pass Memorial—a PzKpfw IVJ (left) locked in combat with a Soviet T-34/85, one of eight of the Soviet tanks to be found on this battlefield.*

Below: *This battlefield map shows the Soviet advances between October 25 and 27, 1944, in the "Valley of Death," through the Arpad Line by LXVII Rifle Corps and IV Guards Tank Corps. The defense by German 357. and 68. Infanterie-Divisionen created heavy casualties. There's a Russian graveyard and memorial at Svidník and a German one at Hunkovce.*

KEY		
Situation 25.10.1944	*SZ*	*Rifle Corps*
Situation at the turning point 25.10.44	*CSAZ*	*Czech Army Corps*
Situation 25.10.44 evening	*sd*	*Rifle Division*
Situation 26.10.44 evening	*pd*	*Infantry Division*
Attack of Soviet rifle troops	*gsd*	*Guards Rifle Division*
Attack of Soviet tank units	*gtz*	*Guards Tank Corps*
Enemy counterattack	*gtbr*	*Guards Tank Brigade*
	gmbr	*Guards Motorized Rifle Brigade*

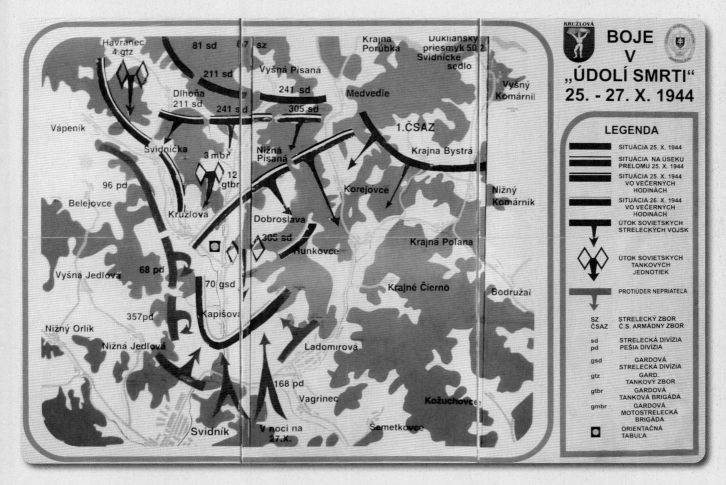

The President of Czechoslovakia, Edvard Beneš, and his government in exile in England were eventually returned to power with Soviet assistance—and the "fall" of Czechoslovakia to communism in 1948 was partly a result of a careful propaganda onslaught that started before the war ended. The Czechs already had mixed feelings about the western Allies—had they done enough in 1938 to help withstand the Nazis? Stalin had opposed the Munich Agreement that Britain and France had signed. Added to this, the Soviets pushed the myth that the Americans had stood aside rather than assist the uprising (much as the West suggests that the Red Army failed to help the Warsaw Uprising). This had an element of truth: Patton had been close enough to act but Eisenhower had forbidden it and stuck to the agreement at Yalta—something the Soviets didn't tell the Czechs. The Russian liberation—complete with false casualty figures—predisposed the Czechs to the communists. Inept American diplomacy in the immediate postwar years saw the country increasingly aligned with Moscow. The country would pay the penalty for 50 years, 1949–98, before the Velvet Revolution saw communism overthrown.

Prague Uprising

The Red Army's robust advances toward the west encouraged the citizens of Prague to rise up and attempt to push the hated Nazi occupiers out. Led by

Above: *Germans in front of the National Museum. While elsewhere they were surrendering, in Prague the Germans were still fighting to hold open a route to the west for the men fleeing from the Soviets. Using civilians as human shields, murdering any resistance fighters who they caught, they fought until May 8.*

Below: *StuG III knocked out by the insurgents with a Panzerfaust on the afternoon of May 6, on the corner of Old Town Square and Paris Street.*

the Czech resistance, on May 5, 1945, they did just this, attacking with whatever weapons they could bring to hand. Many street barricades were erected which blocked the Germans' ability to strike back at the rebels. To further frustrate their efforts, the Russian Liberation Army (ROA), which had previously been on the Axis side, switched allegiance and began fighting alongside the Czechs. Desperate radio appeals for help from the Allies were answered by Stalin who ordered his grand offensive to start a day earlier than planned.

The uprising was so successful that three days later a ceasefire agreement was agreed and formally signed by both sides. Although this allowed the remaining German forces to withdraw, some of the more fanatical elements of the Waffen-SS continued to fight until overwhelmed the next day by Red Army troops. Despite the uprising only lasting for a few days, the fighting during the short period had been especially brutal, and the casualty list was long and bloody.

Above: *German Hetzer TDs in Prague.*

Left: *This Hetzer was destroyed by the defenders of the Old Town Hall with a Panzerfaust on May 8.*

Below left: *Prague, Old Town— celebration of the 65th anniversary of the end of the war in Europe. The insurgents found a number of Hetzer TDs in the BMM (Böhmisch-Mährische Maschinenfabrik AG—what the Germans called the Czech CKD) factory in northeast Prague, most without main guns. These were put to use during the siege. This preserved example is marked with a Czech flag and further down: the names of Czech Radio (CS— Ceský— rozhlas) who were injured (zranéni) on left and on right "They died for freedom" (padli za svobodu).*

The uprising started on May 5 after a broadcast from Czech Radio that continued on air throughout the fighting, which became very difficult for the insurgents after the Russian Liberation Army pulled out as the Soviets got closer. How many died? It's almost impossible to be precise, but around 1,000 German soldiers and men of the Waffen-SS, 1,500 Czech (police and resistance fighters), 300—probably fewer—from the Russian Liberation Army (see p. 17), and at most 30 Soviet soldiers. Civilian deaths were around 3,000.

Prague Offensive

Lasting from May 6 to May 11, 1945, this was the last significant military action of the European war. As part of these closing stages, the Soviets were pushing into Austria and Germany from the east and southeast, while the Western Allies had already occupied much of the rest of Germany. The 1st, 2nd, and 4th Ukrainian Fronts were ordered to capture the remaining parts of Czechoslovakia from the clutches of the Heeresgruppe Mitte (GFM Fedor von Bock) and Heeresgruppe Ostmark (Generaloberst Lothar Rendulic). The former had been created on January 25, 1944, by renaming Heeresgruppe A; the latter formed on April 2 from Heeresgruppe Süd.

Five different German armies confronted the Red Army—1. Panzerarmee, 4. Panzerarmee, 7. Armee, 8. Armee, and 17. Armee. Although the German military situation was getting increasingly confused and desperate with some units being mostly made up of cadets and staff from training colleges, there were still enough battle-hardened troops left to pose a serious challenge to the advancing Soviets. Cadets and training units became regular elements of late-war German defenses, and they proved to be fanatical and tough opponents. However, few of the German units had their full complement of troops, heavy weapons, or transport. Fuel was in short supply as was ammunition. Movement by rail was almost impossible, and Allied aircraft ruled the skies.

1. Panzerarmee was located in the area around Olomouc to the northeast of Brno—it possessed five corps of well-equipped troops, including several Panzer and other mechanized divisions. 4. Panzerarmee was arrayed to the north of the cities of Dresden and Bautzen blocking the route to Berlin from the south. It was another strong outfit—which had just beaten the Soviet Fifty-second and the Second Polish armies, and was composed of five Panzer or mechanized divisions and 13 other divisions. 7. Armee—which was holding part of western Czechoslovakia, had been badly mauled by the U.S. Sixth

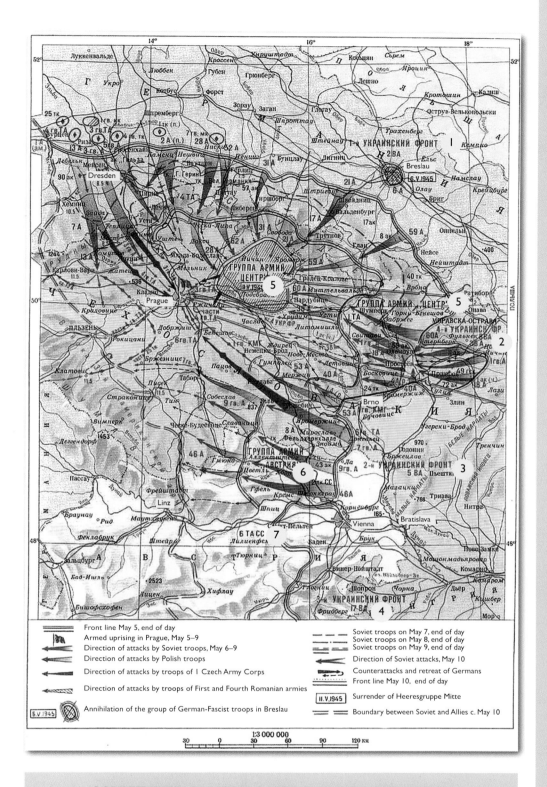

Front line May 5, end of day
Armed uprising in Prague, May 5–9
Direction of attacks by Soviet troops, May 6–9
Direction of attacks by Polish troops
Direction of attacks by troops of 1 Czech Army Corps
Direction of attacks by troops of First and Fourth Romanian armies
Annihilation of the group of German-Fascist troops in Breslau

Soviet troops on May 7, end of day
Soviet troops on May 8, end of day
Soviet troops on May 9, end of day
Direction of Soviet attacks, May 10
Counterattacks and retreat of Germans
Front line May 10, end of day
Surrender of Heeresgruppe Mitte
Boundary between Soviet and Allies c. May 10

1:3 000 000

SOVIET AND ALLIED LOSSES, PRAGUE OFFENSIVE

Unit(s)	Strength May 6, 1945	Total losses	Average daily losses
1st Ukrainian Front	806,400	23,383	3,897
2nd Ukrainian Front	613,400	14,436	2,406
4th Ukrainian Front	350,900	11,529	1,922
Second Polish Army	69,500	887	148
First and Fourth Romanian armies	139,500	1,730	288
Czechoslovak Army Corps	48,400	533	89

Source: G. F. Krivosheev (1997).

PURSUIT

Jochen Peiper talked about the speed of the Soviet pursuit of retreating German armies.

"The Red Army adopted all the German principles of this phase of battle and applied them with ever-mounting success. Once the enemy HKL [Hauptkampflinie, main line of resistance] has been broken, the pursuit elements, mostly small in numbers, are committed along a broad front. A standard formation could not be recognized. They mostly consisted of packs of five to twenty vehicles (sometimes up to eighty) joined by one to two companies on trucks. Typical were always the numerous anti-tank guns and mortars towed along. Often every combat vehicle had its own anti-tank gun attached.

With the mission 'gaining of space' those groups moved westward as rapidly as possible. Their immense range played a decisive role. On principle, they did not engage our rearguards. If they encountered resistance it was sidelined, and the original direction was maintained. Considering our utter lack of reserves, it is understandable that there was nothing here to stop these wolfpacks spreading panic and fear, they chased the fleeing service units and shook the entire rear out of its complacency. Once the attack objective—or rather pursuit objective—was reached, the Russian established himself in a village and prepared for defense. Whenever the German headquarters located in the rear succeeded in improvising an attack by hastily gathering up service units, after only a few hours they would encounter a well-prepared all-around defense and were unable to accomplish anything. During the next night, the Russian main body worked its way toward its advanced guard, we used a system of desperately helping out each other."

Army Group in heavy fighting in central Germany. As a result it had retreated to the east where came under the command of Heeresgruppe Mitte and now instead faced the Soviets. In the previous months it had suffered substantial losses and could only field one Panzer division, one Volksgrenadier division, and four other under-strength divisions.

8. Armee, part of Heeresgruppe Ostmark, was the most southerly being located in southern Moravia. It had its right flank covered by 6. SS-Panzerarmee who were north and west of Vienna and composed of a Panzer division, a motorized division, and six other divisions. 17. Armee was made up of one Panzer division, one mechanized division, and nine others; these were arranged in three corps spread in a curve from the southwest of Breslau down to the southeast, ending in the Ostrava region.

As an inherent part of their advance on Prague from the north, the 1st Ukrainian Front had to fight its way through Dresden and Bautzen, as well as force its way across the Ore Mountains. A huge assembly of manpower and equipment, it was made up of 71 rifle divisions and three cavalry divisions, along with nine tank and mechanized corps. Among these were six artillery and one rocket launcher divisions, along with one Polish artillery division. Most of these troops—including the 3rd and 4th Guards Tank armies, were to the north of Dresden, but others ranged eastward over a wide area toward Breslau. Their main enemy would be 4. Panzerarmee.

The 2nd Ukrainian Front—which was to spearhead the assault on Prague with the Sixth Guards Tank Army—had easier terrain to cross, but needless to say, it—especially the better roads—was heavily defended. It was comprised of 37 rifle, six cavalry, four artillery, and one rocket launcher divisions, and four tank and motorized corps. Fighting with them were the First and Fourth Romanian armies which comprised 12 infantry and three cavalry divisions. These forces were up against German 1. Panzerarmee and 8. Armee which were distributed in and around Brno.

Continued on p. 176.

Opposite, Above: *The color party of a unit in I Czech Corps. The design is similar to flags of the Austro-Hungarian Army. The lion of Bohemia features above the motto Pravda Vitezi (Truth Wins). The men's dress is a mix of British and Soviet issue.*

Opposite, Below: *Monument to the fighters of the 1st Czech Tank Brigade—the first tank to enter Ostrava during its liberation on April 30, 1945. Today, Ostrava is the capital of the Moravian-Silesian Region.*

Opposite, Inset: *Standard of First Czechoslovak Army—the motto is "We shall stay true."*

Below: *Panzergrenadiers and PzKpfw V Ausf G Panthers on the march in Lower Silesia. The two Red Army operations in Silesia (Lower, February 8–24 and Upper, March 15–31) protected the southern flank of Zhukov's advance to Berlin.*

I CZECH ARMY CORPS

In 1939 men of the Polish Army's Czech and Slovak Legion captured by the Soviets were interned. In February 1942 they were formed into the 1st Czechoslovak Independent Field Battalion—although there were insufficient numbers to man the unit without a significant quantity of other Czech internees and men from Hungary, Poland, Ukraine, and Ruthenia. The unit fought well. In May 1943 the battalion was enlarged to brigade size and in April 1944, it became an army corps with two infantry and one tank brigade, and a light parachute brigade (total strength 17,000 troops). Most of the corps fought at the Dukla Pass (see p. 165), and then was reassigned to the 4th Ukrainian Front and later helped liberate Slovakia and Moravia. The 2nd Parachute Brigade fought in the Slovak National Uprising and when that failed stayed with the partisans. At the end of the war, the unit became the First Czechoslovak Army. (See also the 1st Czechoslovak Armored Brigade that fought on the Western Front, see p. 233.)

Above and **Opposite, Above:** IS-2 heavy tanks from the 1st Tank Brigade of the 4th Ukrainian Front in the center of Prague, May 10, 1945. Note the DShK 12.7mmm commander's MG (**Above**).

Right: A Czech unit's staff officer writes orders in the lee of an abandoned Panther tank during the last weeks of the war. Czech personnel used Czech military ranks and insignia, and nominally were under the Czechoslovak government in exile, although all operational dealings were with the Red Army.

Opposite, Below: Memorial postcards of the Union of Friends of the USSR in Czechoslovakia showing views of the victory parade on May 17 that included I Czech Army Corps personnel.

The 4th Ukrainian Front—which was to take on 1. Panzerarmee—was made up of 34 rifle divisions and one tank corps including the Czechoslovak Army Corps of four infantry and one tank brigades; they also had two artillery divisions. It faced a hard task though, as there were few roads in the hilly area around Olomouc through which it had to pass and this consequently contributed to its slow rate of progress. Elsewhere, 17. Armee had its hands full facing six further armies including the Second Polish Army on the eastern end of the advancing Soviet forces.

By this stage of the war there was little doubt in the minds of the majority of the Germans as to the likely final outcome, even among the most fanatical of their numbers. Not only were they facing an immense horde of Red Army forces from the north, south, and east, but on their west were the massed armies of the United States, the UK, Canada, and other associated countries. Many still fought desperately though—no longer with the sole thought of winning, but in the hope that it would buy some time for their loved ones to escape to the west. Having fought the Soviets since *Unternehmen Barbarossa* began in June 1941, they knew just how the Red Army soldiers would behave toward their civilians. Indeed, many of the German troops were also planned to head west when their situation became untenable, rather than face becoming prisoners of war in Russia.

The offensive began on May 6, 1945, when Konev sent the Third and Fourth Guards Tank armies as well as three combined-arms Guards armies southward against 4. Panzerarmee. They were later joined by other units and by the end of the first day Dresden was almost within their grasp. On the same day the 4th Ukrainian Front started a drive to the west against 1. Panzerarmee in order to take the city of Olomouc.

Below: *The development of new weapons in 1944 led to a flurry of new equipment entering the battlefield in 1945. In the west the U.S. Army's M26 Pershing and British Comet were rushed into combat; in the east there were also developments. One of those was the SU-100, a distinct improvement on its predecessor, the SU-85, or the German equivalents. Peiper said of it: "The best model which appeared at the front only in March 1945 was the assault gun SU-100. Having an operating radius of about 350km, it has an extremely low silhouette and a 10cm cannon with a large capacity for carrying ammunition. The performance of the gun is superb. At 1,000m it shot the Panther through the armor and according to Russian reports it can fight the Königstiger successfully at 2km." This one is preserved in Penza, Russia.*

Left: *Most famous for its cucumbers, Znojmo (Znaim in today's Czech Republic) was a collecting point for knocked-out vehicles that were cut up for scrap postwar—including as many as three Tiger IIs from sPzAbt 503 and two from sPzAbt 509. Southwest of Brno, most of these would have been destroyed by their crews as they retreated or by 2nd Ukrainian Front in its advance toward Prague. There were three sPzAbt in Czechoslovakia in the last months of the war: 503—the most successful of the Tiger Abteilungen in terms of kills, it claimed 1,700 enemy kills for the loss of 252 of its own—had been involved deployed north of Vienna in April 1945 and ended up retreating to Budweis; 507, after fighting in the west, was deployed to Milcowicz in May equipped with Hetzer TDs; and 509—the latter actually deployed just south of the Znojmo on May 6 with 13 Tiger IIs. It had nine left when ordered to surrender and destroyed those before doing so.*

Center left: *This IS-2 of Soviet Sixth Guards Tank Army was knocked out in Znojmo in late 1945. Built in much larger numbers (3,850) than the Tigers I (c. 1,347) and II (c. 489), armed with a 122mm main gun, it was certainly a match for the German tanks. They were deployed in similar fashion, although Soviet heavy tank battalions were smaller.*

Below left: *For all the heavy tanks, it was the workmanlike StuG III that bore the brunt of the Wehrmacht's battles. Here, the crew apply winter camouflage to a StuG III Ausf G in a Czech town. Note the Zimmerit paste, Schürzen plates, and Saukopf (pig's head) mantlet on the 7.5cm StuK 40 L/48 main gun. Behind an SdKfz 10/5 mounting a 2cm on a Demag D7—2 cm FlaK auf Fahrgestell Zugkraftwagen, 1t.*

Above: *Wenceslas Square, Prague, May 10, 1945. Soviet troops enjoy the applause of the crowd. The fact that the Red Army was the first of the Allies in Prague, along with the feeling that the west had let them down in 1938–39, pushed Czechoslovakia postwar into the communist camp. The tactical symbol on the back of the truck identifies it as being from 41st Guards Tank Brigade (VII Mechanized Corps).*

Right: *The Soviet campaign medal "For the Liberation of Prague" was established on June 9, 1945. Nearly 300,000 were awarded.*

Opposite, Above: *Marshal Konev was hailed as a hero when the Soviets entered Prague. However, his involvement in suppressing the Hungarian revolution in 1956 and planning the similar entry into Czechoslovakia in 1968 has left him an ambiguous legacy.*

Opposite, Below: *Could a Tiger do this? The Russian tanks were rugged—this IS-2 has lost a road wheel.*

Meanwhile, the siege of Breslau—which lasted for two months—ended with the surrender of 40,000 German troops; this freed up more Red Army soldiers for the push to the west. On the other side of Czechoslovakia, the U.S. Army was also making good progress—pushing the German 7. Armee back along a wide front.

On May 7—the second day of the offensive—the Red Army continued to storm its way to both the west and the south. The 1st Ukrainian Front's Third Guards Army took the city of Meissen, while the Thirteenth Army and the Fourth Guards Tank Army got as far as the start of the Ore mountain range. Dresden also came under attack from its Third Guards Tank Army and Fifth Guards Army with the Second Polish Army pushing toward the same target to help with the assault. The 2nd Ukrainian Front was also hard at work, advancing to the northwest, along a line that was 15 miles (25km) wide, and the 4th Ukrainian Front ground relentlessly toward Olomouc.

Things were so bad for the defenders by this stage that General Jodl knew any further fighting would be futile and surrendered all German forces. Most of those that he still had communication with complied with the order to cease fighting by 01:00 on May 9. At this, all the U.S. troops in the region took up defensive positions and waited for the agreement to take full effect. The Red Army, on the other hand, continued to push hard though—taking Dresden and Olomouc as well as forcing their way into Prague on May 8. Vast numbers of German troops attempted to make it to what they saw as the safety of the U.S. lines, but a mix of Red Army troops, Czech freedom fighters, and maddened civilians made this extremely difficult. Most ended up in Soviet hands as prisoners of war.

Jochen Peiper said of the Soviet attackers, "While our service units constituted a tremendous burden, growing bigger year by year like a traveling circus, the complete absence of it lent to the Russians an extraordinary mobility and independence. Ammunition and fuel were the only things they carried with them or behind them. Main supply routes which had become completely impassable during the mud and rain periods, he used to bridge with a human chain. The entire population including children stood in a row up to 10km long one behind the other and the shells were forwarded by a long chain of hands—the same way gasoline barrels were rolled through the landscape. Since one lived principally off the land, one also did not know regular resupply. The soldier carried a rucksack improvised from an old bag. The contents were bread, pieces of sugar and tobacco; besides that a lot of ammunition. By this, the fellows are independent from bases for weeks."

1 IS-2 of 78th Guards Heavy Tank Regiment of the 76th Guards Heavy Tank Brigade (as identified by this tactical marking).

2 An SU-85 in Prague. Each tank corps had light (SU-76) and medium (SU-85 or SU-100) SP regiments.

3 Soviet tank corps had three tank brigades of 65 tanks each—T-34/85s (as here, note the stand-off turret armor) and IS-2s.

4 The movement of the Soviet 63rd Guards Tank Brigade (of X Guards Tank Corps of the Fourth Guards Tank Army of the 1st Ukrainian Front) from Berlin to Prague took four days—May 5–9, 1945.

5 An image of contrasts—trucks and tanks combined with horse-drawn artillery. The T-34/85 is having its track adjusted to the rear of two Soviet command trucks with wooden offices behind the cabs. Both the German and the Soviet armies made big use of horses—often more mobile than vehicles in muddy conditions.

1 An eight-man German tank-hunting section, its leader checking the sky for enemy aircraft. The second man carries a Panzerschreck, nicknamed the "stove pipe." He's followed by the loader with extra rounds. The third man is carrying a Panzerfaust anti-tank launcher over his right shoulder.

2 By 1944 the Waffen-SS was conscripting German Volksdeutsche from across Eastern Europe and Ukraine into their own units. This group is one such formation. Captions on such images often identify the men's racial origin, this one does not, nor is there any unit badge to clearly identify them. The soldier in the foreground looks if he's just scrumped some onions.

3 The German retreat was not to be hampered by broken down vehicles as this image shows. The truck is unceremoniously being pushed off the road to allow those behind free passage. Most of the heavy tank losses in this period were caused by crew demolition—after vehicles had run out of fuel or mechanical issues that couldn't be rectified by the roadside.

4 A German railroad security section deploys for the camera. Allied bombing and partisan sabotage of the rail network was an increasing problem, as the Wehrmacht depended on the railroads for resupply in the east where the road network was often poorly developed. The rail wagon carries a selection of emergency repair items.

5 People of Prague greet a I Czech Army Corps' T-34/85. Postwar, the Czech Corps would become the First Czechoslovak Army

За честь жены, за жизнь детей,   За наши нивы и луга—
За счастье родины своей,   Убей захватчика-врага!

Austria 6

As the Soviets pushed inexorably on toward the west with the end of the war in clear sight to all, what exactly was going to happen after the hostilities finally ceased was still far from clear. Stalin knew that the more ground he held, the better his position would be when he sat down at the negotiating table with the likes of Roosevelt and Churchill. Austria—which at that stage was at the Red Army's fingertips—would be an important bargaining point, and was therefore a very attractive goal. Its capital, Vienna, thus became a city of great importance to the advancing Ukrainian Fronts, and hence the Vienna Offensive was born.

Launched on March 16, 1945, the Soviet campaign was faced by the 6. SS-Panzerarmee which had withdrawn to the Austrian-Czech border area after being badly mauled in *Unternehmen Frühlingserwachen* (see p. 127). This had only ended the previous day, and knowing that the Red Army was hard on their heels, its commander Sepp Dietrich hastily tried to organize sufficient defenses to hold them off. Since there are only some 15 miles (25km) between the border and Vienna, they had very little space in which to operate.

A shortage of manpower, time, and equipment meant that many of the exhausted troops were quickly overrun. Since the 2nd Ukrainian Front held the area to the east of Vienna, the 3rd Ukrainian Front—which was arranged to the south in Hungary, was able to advance quickly, knowing that its right flank was safe. On April 2 it overran the towns and cities of Wiener Neustadt, Eisenstadt, Neunkirchen, and Gloggnitz which lay relatively close to the capital. Once on its outskirts, they encircled it, besieging those trapped within.

While the main Axis defense strength lay in the German II. SS-Panzerkorps—which not only incorporated the 6. Panzerdivision, but also such other battle-hardened troops as 2. SS-Panzerdivision *Das Reich* and the 3. SS-Panzerdivision *Totenkopf*, they also assembled more or less any other troops who were able to stand up and fight. These included men from the city's own garrison as well as crews from anti-aircraft batteries.

A main assault on the city—which lies alongside the River Danube, was launched by the Red Army at 07:30 on April 6. The weight of the attack soon saw the German defenders broken up into small groups, who nevertheless

Opposite: *"For the honor of your wife, for your children's life,*
For the happiness of your Homeland,
For the fields and meadows of the motherland
Kill the invading enemy!"
L. F. Golovanov's 1942 poster.

Above: *Many Germans committed suicide before the Soviets arrived.*

Opposite: *The Vienna Offensive.*
General der Infanterie Rudolf von Buenau was in charge of the German defense initially. His view on the task ahead was, "the idea of a successful or even prolonged defense of Vienna had to be rejected from the beginning, and measures taken accordingly. Reich Defense Commissioner von Schirach, the Commander-in-Chief of the 6. SS Panzerarmee, SS-Oberst- gruppenführer Dietrich, and I agreed about this at our first meeting April 4, 1945." He went on to sum up the battle:

"The course of events during the battle of Vienna proved the correctness of the original estimate of the situation. I did not have the authority to decide whether the battle of Vienna should or should not take place. When the battle was ordered, the only possibility, for command and troops, was wholehearted fighting. Commendation is due to the field division and the Hitlerjugend battalion; in the case of other units commendation must be qualified or even denied altogether.

Seen as a whole, the battle of Vienna was regrettable from a human point of view, however, it tied down very strong Russian forces, and made the establishment of a new front line south of the Danube possible. It also made possible, under enormous difficulties, the evacuation of some 9,000 wounded from the battle area and their removal westward."The overlays on this map show the advance of the Guards tank and mechanized corps between April 1 and 13 as they advanced on Vienna.

Right: *A column of T-34/85s heads through Sankt Pölten, west of Vienna.*

fought ferociously to hold their ground. By the evening it was clear to General Rudolf von Bünau—commander of the city working under SS-Obergruppenführer Wilhelm Bittrich—that they would not be able to do so for much longer. He ordered most of the bridges to the east to be blown up.

Meanwhile, Marshal Fyodor Tolbukhin, commander of the 3rd Ukrainian Front, had a message broadcast to the population of Vienna stating that the Germans wanted the city to be destroyed by turning it into a battleground similar to the remains of Budapest. He then appealed for them to help his men liberate it from the Nazi oppressors to prevent this happening. Whether it worked or not cannot be said with any certainty, however, many citizens did just that, doing mostly manual jobs such as moving ammunition and other stores.

The Soviets pushing up from the south included the Fourth Guards Army and components of the Ninth Guards Army, who attacked the outskirts of the southern and eastern parts of the city. Staunch defense by 2. and 3. SS-Panzerdivisionen only managed to hold them off for a day, though. On April 8, the Soviet Sixth Guards Tank Army and much of the Ninth Guards Army started assaulting the western suburbs where such important features as the main railroad station were located. These attacks proved successful, and were

Relative strength of forces at the beginning of the Vienna offensive between Lake Balaton and the Danube on March 16, 1945

	Divisions	Tanks and assault guns	Troops
2nd and 3rd Ukrainian Fronts	77	approx. 1,250	1,171,800
Heeresgruppe Süd	25	772	270,000

Losses in the Vienna offensive offensive (March 16–April 15, 1945)

	Tanks and assault guns	Cannon and grenade launchers	Troops (KIA, WIA, or MIA)
2nd and 3rd Ukrainian Fronts and First Bulgarian Army	603	764	177,745
Heeresgruppe Süd	1,345	2,250	130,000 (prisoners only)

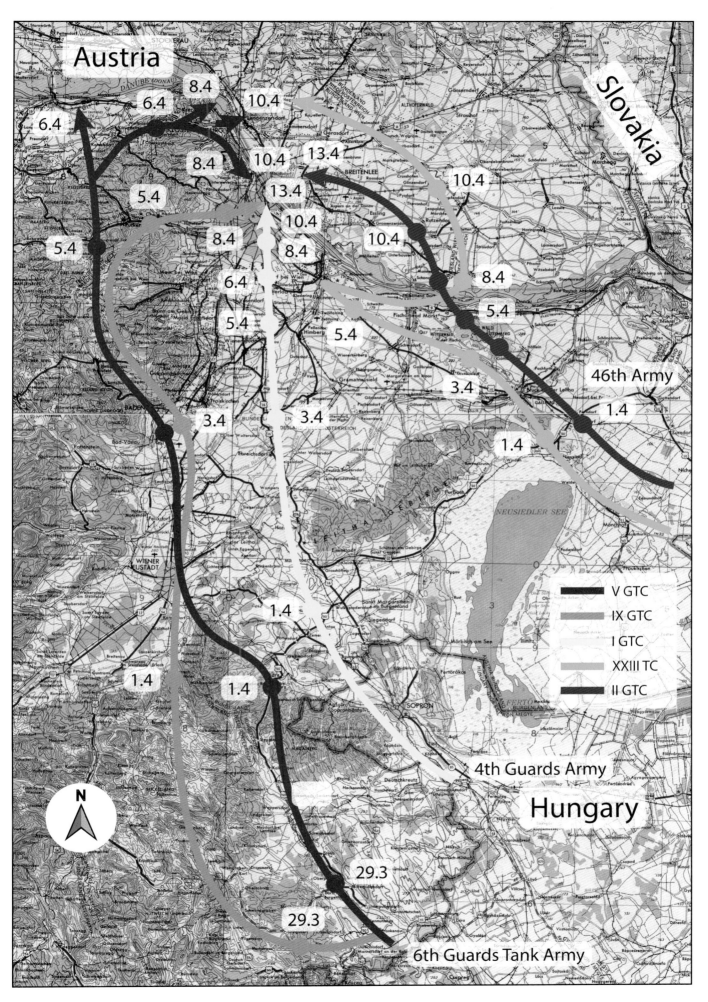

Austria

Slovakia

8.4
6.4
6.4
10.4
8.4
10.4
13.4
5.4
10.4
8.4
5.4
13.4
10.4
10.4
8.4
8.4
8.4
6.4
5.4
5.4
5.4
3.4
3.4
3.4
1.4
1.4
1.4
1.4

46th Army

V GTC
IX GTC
I GTC
XXIII TC
II GTC

4th Guards Army

Hungary

29.3
29.3

N

6th Guards Tank Army

Above: *A Soviet column in the streets of liberated Vienna. In the foreground is a ZiS-3 76.2mm M1942 divisional gun. Each field artillery regiment had three batteries, one of 122mm howitzers and two four-gun batteries of 76.2mm guns in close support of infantry (tanks), and especially for direct fire. Their main missions were antipersonnel and antitank.*

Right and **Below right:** *A convoy of German armored vehicles ambushed by Soviet artillery on the border of Hungary and Austria. The first in the German armored vehicles convoy is a Jagdpanzer IV/70(A). It's followed by PzKpfw V Panthers, this one having been knocked out by an antitank gun. The "A" stands for Alkett, the company that designed the StuG III. It and Vomag produced a redesign of the Jagdpanzer IV with a PaK 42 L/70 gun. The Vomag design allowed a lower silhouette, consequently nearly 1,000 of the (V) version were built, against nearly 300 of the (A).*

quickly followed by others in the eastern (defended by 6. Panzerdivision) and northern areas (defended by the Führer Grenadier Division). The latter of these was taken by the Forty-sixth Army, who by linking up with other units pushing northward on the western side, managed to isolate central Vienna.

While this fighting was going on, some of the other troops of the 3rd Ukrainian Front navigated around Vienna and assaulted toward Linz and Graz. This was not only to continue the general advance, but also to help cut off any German forces which attempted to escape from Vienna to the west.

Although cut off from any prospect of significant outside help, the defenders caught in the central area continued to fight from building to building, gradually being pushed back from day to day. Determined to bring matters to a close, the Soviets continued to pour more troops into the city. Overnight on April 11, the Fourth Guards Army crossed the canals and got across the Reichsbrücke Bridge, one of the main eastern crossings of the Danube. Two days later, it was fully secured when troops of the 80th Guards Rifle Division and the 7th Guards Airborne Division established themselves on both sides of the bridge.

The last vestiges of the German defense holed up in the center surrendered later that day, although some units which were still mobile fought their way out to the west to avoid capture. These included many of the remaining elements of 2. SS-Panzerarmee, such as 2. SS-Panzerdivision *Das Reich* which withdrew in its last 36 or so armored vehicles as well as surviving parts of the 6. Panzerarmee. Fleeing toward Graz and Linz, the remnants of these once proud fighting forces were utterly exhausted by the continuous fighting and were thus able to do little more than perform minor stalling operations as they pulled back.

The retreating Germans were unable to pause for any much-needed rest though, as the Soviet Ninth Guards, Forty-sixth, Twenty-sixth, Twenty-seventh, Fifty-seventh, and First Bulgarian armies were hot on their heels, all keen to close with their foe and finish the job. After mopping-up operations had come to a close, the Vienna Offensive finally finished on April 15, 1945.

Although Vienna had largely survived as a city, many of its best architectural features had been destroyed, and the remaining inhabitants had to endure the depredations of the Soviet troops many of whom raped and pillaged their way through the following weeks before order was restored. In the meantime a Provisional Government was set up in Vienna headed by Austrian politician Karl Renner who was effectively a Soviet puppet; one of his first public tasks was to declare full secession from the Third Reich.

Above: *Just over 277,000 of the Medal "For the Capture of Vienna" were awarded.*

Below left: *The SU-76M (see p. 35) proved a versatile and long-lived AFV. A regiment of 76.2mm or 85mm self-propelled artillery supported assault divisions in the attack, and its light footprint and mobility helped in the close-support role.*

FLAK TOWERS (Flaktürme)

There were eight pairs of massive flak towers built in Germany, three in Berlin, two in Hamburg, and three in Vienna. They fulfilled two prime requirements: they were armed with Luftwaffe antiaircraft guns and they also provided large air-raid shelters. Each of the Flak towers had two elements: a Gefechtsturm—fighting tower—and a Leitturm, fire-control tower. There were three "generations" of fighting tower, each with slightly different dimensions and armaments. Since the war, a number have been destroyed, but all six of Vienna's are still visible, their locations shown on the aerial photograph (Opposite, Center left)

Above and **Opposite, Top** and **Bottom:** The 3rd generation G tower at Augarten is damaged, but still extant. It was usually armed with 8 (4 x 2) 12.8cm guns and 32 (8 x 4) 20mm guns.

Below: The Stiftskaserne 3rd generation G tower is used by the Austrian Army; the L tower is an aquarium.

Opposite, Center: The Arenbergpark 2nd generation G towers were usually armed with 8 (f4 x 2) 12.8cm guns and 16 (4 x 4) 20mm guns.

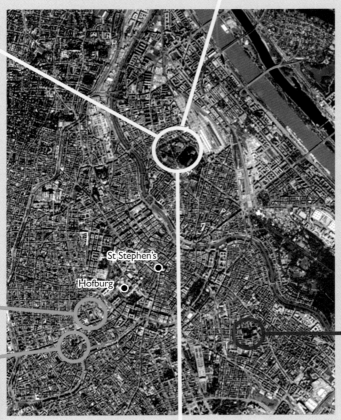

St Stephen's

Hofburg

Right: *Street fighting in Vienna. The Maxim machine gun has had its armored shield removed to reduce its weight. The crewman nearest the camera is armed with a 7.62mm M38 carbine that was shorter than a rifle by 8.4in (21.3cm) making it easier to wield in an urban environment.*

Below right: *BM-13 Katyusha rocket launchers let fly a salvo in an industrial area on the outskirts of Vienna. Although not an accurate weapon, it was an excellent destroyer of morale simply for the weight of shot discharged and the sheer noise generated.*

Opposite, Above: *An armored Soviet river gunboat of the Danube Naval Flotilla in action. The front turret is that of a T-34 tank with a 76mm gun. Vessels such as this supported land forces in Vienna when the Reichsbrücke was captured intact.*

Opposite, Center: *Soviet soldiers from I Mechanized Corps of the 3rd Ukrainian Front are attacking covered by machine-gunners on an American-made M3 Scout Car. On the right is the nose of a German SdKfz 251, the most-produced German personnel carrier of the war. Designed by Hanomag, the 251 was produced in many variations carrying mortars, flamethrowers, infantry guns, AA guns, antitank guns, and rockets. There were radio versions, and observation/spotting versions—it was a versatile vehicle. The Soviet mechanized corps were resuscitated in 1942 into all-arms units designed to exploit breakthroughs.*

Opposite, Below left and **right:** *M4 Sherman medium tanks were supplied under Lend-Lease Act and equipped a number of mechanized corps. In these photos IX Guards Mechanized Corps of Sixth Guards Tank Army (**left**) on the road in Austria on March 17, 1945; and 334 of 20th Guards Tank Regiment, I Guards Mechanized Corps, in Vienna.*

Opposite, Above and **Below:** *A Soviet mortar team, with another to the rear, take position in the Heldenplatz surrounded by the façade of Vienna's Hofburg Palace. Prior to the battle, the plinth behind the aimer's head supported the equestrian statue of Archduke Charles—seen back in position in the modern photo. The extreme elevation of the mortar barrels suggests the target is close by.*

Above: *Urban warfare, with an explosion illuminating the scene. A group of Soviet infantrymen advances toward a gap in an overgrown wall passing over broken ground. The sweat on the men's tunics stands out clearly.*

Center right: *An interesting image. It is possible that these are Czech infantry judging by their British style gaiters. If Czechs, then this will be I Czech Army Corps. These submachine gunners armed with PPSh-41 weapons appear to be following an armed civilian guide. The central figure wearing the dark Kubanka (fur hat) may be a Kuban Cossack cavalryman as this is their headgear. The top would be red with a cross of white.*

Below right: *Karl Renner (center, waving) a veteran left-wing Austrian politician, contacted Marshal Tolbukhin, commanding the operation to take Vienna, regarding Austria's future. With Stalin's blessing Renner formed a provisional government in late April 1945. This image is one of a series commemorating that event. The Soviet officer to the left is Vienna's military governor, General A. Blagodatov.*

Right: *Their faces tell it all, a mixture of fear and anticipation. A group of German infantrymen watch for the advance of the Red Army by the side of a railroad bridge. They appear to be unarmed and are possibly waiting for the order to blow the bridge.*

Below: *Two Tiger Is move into ambush positions during the spring of 1945. The chronic fuel and resupply situation limited the effectiveness of such fighting vehicles. Nevertheless, they still gave a good account of themselves up to the end. Both are early production models.*

Above: A German outpost. Pinned to the tree are photos of loved ones that will inspire this man to defend his family against the waves of "Jewish-Bolshevik Untermenschen" (sub-humans) that threatened to overrun the Reich and Western Civilization.

Left: A column of late production SdKfz 251 halftracks waits for the order to move off. In the muddy conditions seen here, the vehicles' cross-country abilities would have been impaired due to the poor weight distribution caused by the narrow tracks and the interleaved/overlapped road wheels becoming fouled by mud or snow.

Below left: A visit to Austrian local forces in southern Styria by SS-Obergruppenführer Hans Juttner (saluting). He was Himmler's deputy Chef der Heeresrüstung und Befehlshaber des Ersatzheers (Chief of Army Armaments and the Replacement Army). He is accompanied by Gauleiter (regional party leader) Dr. Siegfried Uiberreither head of the Styrian Volkssturm. Troops such as these were expected to die for the Führer in glorious last stands.

ДОЙДЕМ ДО БЕРЛИНА!

Germany 7

The speed of the Soviet advance to the Oder had left the Red Army 50 miles from Berlin by February 15, wth a foothold on the west bank. Their two-month pause on the river had then allowed the Soviet armies to clear the "Baltic Balcony"—Pomerania and Prussia, and to advance through Silesia, Hungary, Slovakia, and Austria, clearing the flanks for the final thrust to the German capital. It had also given time for Soviet armies to close in on the countries Stalin wanted to dominate postwar. But with the Western Allies themselves nearing Berlin—Ninth (U.S.) Army reached the Elbe on April 12—it was time to take the major prize. The Red Army's advance was kick-started.

On April 15, when Vienna fell, the Third Reich—Hitler's Thousand-Year Reich—had less than a month to go. It had shrunk to a north–south sliver of Germany, Czechoslovakia, and Austria, its borders squeezed by the invading Allied armies. However, it shouldn't be thought that the last weeks of the war were a procession. In some ways the most surprising thing about that period is that so much of the apparatus of the Reich still functioned. For example, 3./ sPzAbt 502 received eight Tiger IIs from the factory at Kassel on March 31. In February, 1,675 tanks were sent to units in the east. Hitler may have moved paper armies in his bunker, but in the real world soldiers were still fighting and dying for the cause. They would continue to do so in their thousands—many at their own hands rather than falling into the arms of the Soviets.

The hiatus on the Oder had given the Germans some time to prepare their defenses. Heeresgruppe Weichsel (Vistula) had been set up under Himmler, but he'd proved so useless that Guderian had convinced him to step down. His replacement was General Gotthard Heinrici, known for his defensive skills. Heinrici decided that he'd defend the high ground rather than the river line. The forces at his disposal were impressive on paper, although in reality they weren't in good condition: 3. Panzerarmee (Hasso von Manteuffel), 21. Armee (von Tippelskirch), and 9. Armee (Busse)—it was the latter that was arrayed on the Seelow Heights and would bear the brunt of Zhukov's attacks. Against the million Soviets and Poles and 3,000 tanks, the Germans had between 80,000 and 110,000 men, 500 tanks, and 300 8.8cm Flak guns to be used in the antitank role. It was the last real obstacle before Berlin.

Opposite: *"Let's get to Berlin!" Leonid Fedorovich Golovanov's 1944 poster shows a frontnik preparing for the final march to Berlin.*

Above: *Braving the icy cold waters of the Oder River, Soviet combat engineers work to repair a bridge that has recently been hit by German fire. The image is taken from the bank behind the Küstrin Bridgehead.*

Oder-Neisse Line

Opposite, Above: *Map of the battle at the Gedenkstätte Seelower Höhen—the Seelow Heights Museum and Memorial.*

Opposite, Below: *On what appears to be a pleasant day an ISU-152 self-propelled gun is ferried across a German river. The five-man crew are dressed in the tankers' dark overall. Weighing in at a little over 45 tons, it was safer to ferry such behemoths individually than risk collapsing a temporary bridge. The Germans nicknamed them "Dosenöffner"—tin opener—due to their ability to burst open armor or bunkers.*

April 16, 1945—the day after the Vienna Offensive came to an end—saw the launch of a fresh Soviet campaign with Berlin as its target. It started with the crossing of the Oder–Neisse rivers, and then expanded into the creation of a classic pincer movement around Berlin. There were four separate thrusts, all of which began on the same date and opened well before dawn with a heavy artillery and Katyusha rocket barrage along the whole front.

The northernmost of the pushes—the Stettin–Rostock Offensive—was undertaken by Marshal Konstantin Rokossovsky's 2nd Belorussian Front. It swept to the north of Berlin and on April 20 drove a wedge through the northern components of the Heeresgruppe Weichsel—mainly 3. Panzerarmee which had the task of defending the banks of the River Oder. After several days of intense fighting, the Soviets overcome these forces, and on April 25 moved to the south of Stettin through the Randow swamp. Then part of the front headed north toward Rostock to establish a Soviet presence on the Baltic coast and the rest moved west toward British 21st Army Group. Their part of the operation was not concluded until May 5.

Meanwhile, Marshal Georgy Zhukov's 1st Belorussian Front set out on the Seelow–Berlin Offensive, which saw the heaviest fighting of the entire campaign. Held by the German 9. Armee under General Theodor Busse, the Seelow Heights comprise, as its name suggests, high ground ranged around the town of Seelow. They form a natural defensive barrier some 55 miles (90km) to the east of Berlin, and rise above the flood plain which borders the River Oder, over which the Soviets crossed as soon as the artillery barrage ended. Reinforced for what was obviously going to be a tough assault, the 1st Belorussian Front discovered to its cost that the attack had been anticipated by Generaloberst Gotthard Heinrici, and the German forces had been carefully prepared with many Flak 88s, acquired from all over Germany, to back up the defenders. When the Red Army troops reached the first line of trenches, they were empty—the

Below: *German paratroopers dig in dressed in their jump suits and distinctive helmets. Having fought at the Seelow Heights, during the Battle for Berlin the remnants of 9. Fallschirmjäger-Division was tasked with defending the northwest of the city where they faced Third Shock Army.*

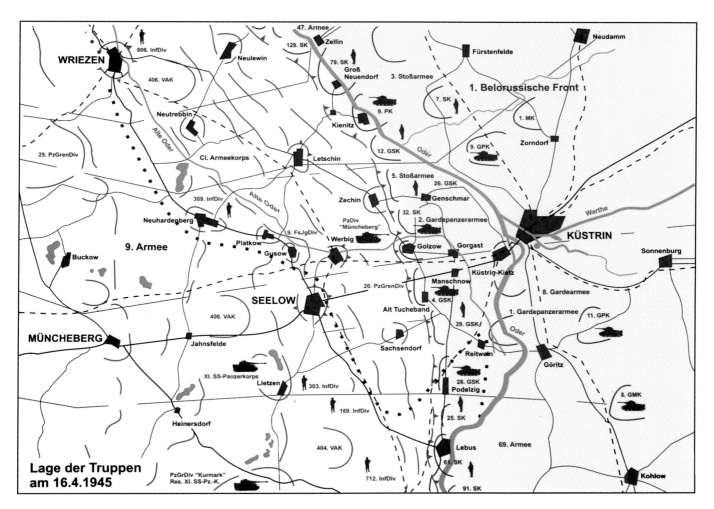

Lage der Truppen
am 16.4.1945

Above: *Routine maintenance on a PzKpfw V Panther was vital if these precision-engineered machines were to perform to the optimum. By 1945 this sort of essential work was well-nigh impossible due to the lack of spares and time. Tanks that could have been recovered and repaired were now often abandoned for lack of fuel and spares.*

huge weight of munitions expended over the previous hours had been wasted, and when the German counterattack came it was severe, costing the Soviets enormous casualties.

Another major issue proved to be that the ground which they had to cross was unduly soft—this meant that the heavy armor struggled to make any headway across it. As a result the infantry lacked the immediate support it needed to tackle the entrenched defensive positions.

Overall, progress was far slower than anticipated, and in order to try and break through, Zhukov had to send in his reserves which he had hoped to use instead for later exploitation. A combination of blood and artillery saw his men slowly grind their way forward, and by the end of the second day, the 1st Belorussian Front had reached the third line. They finally broke through it on April 19, by which time the Germans had been thoroughly beaten. Their tenuous situation left 9. Armee as well as the northern flank of 4. Panzerarmee at severe risk of being encircled by parts of the 1st Ukrainian Front.

The third element of the offensive saw the Cavalry Mechanized Group of the 1st Ukrainian Front begin the Cottbus–Potsdam Offensive Operation. This started with a drive to the south of Berlin designed to destabilize the previously secure position of the Germans around the Seelow Heights area, as it left their right flank dangerously exposed. Once the town of Forst had been taken, they swept north across the flatter terrain to the west of the capital. There they confronted the southern components of the Heeresgruppe Weichsel, as well as troops from GFM Ferdinand Schörner's Heeresgruppe Mitte. These proved to be easier opponents than those that Zhukov was having to deal with, however, and progress was far swifter allowing them to round the western edge of the capital and link up with the 1st Belorussian Front, thus cutting Berlin off from the rest of Germany (see map p. 207). This part of the offensive concluded on April 27.

The mission assigned to the southern part of Konev's 1st Ukrainian Front was the Spremberg–Torgau Offensive Operation. The front's role was to cross the Neisse river and drive west to meet the Americans coming the other way and thus cut off all communications and supply routes to the Heeresgruppe Mitte from the south. Like the other parts of the Oder–Neisse offensive, its start followed on from the massive opening artillery barrage when they crossed the Neisse before dawn. The resistance they met was much lighter than that encountered elsewhere, and the push ended on April 25 with the famous meeting at Torgau, when the Soviet 58th Guards Rifle Division met the 69th Infantry Division of the First (U.S.) Army near Torgau, Germany.

Above: *The two unwounded crew of a Tiger I looking rather downcast as their comrades have been moved into the nearby ambulance. The effects of a small-caliber Soviet anti-tank round can be seen on the armor plate between the two men. The availability of Tigers for the defense of the Oder had been severely disrupted by the speed of the Soviet Vistula-Oder offensive. sPzAbt 424 (sPzAbt 501 had been renamed on December 21)and 507, fielding at least 90 Tigers between them, couldn't stem the attack although they gave a good account of themselves. 501 was destroyed around Lisow and Kielce in Poland about 50 miles west of Sandomierz. Usually put down to an ambush on January 13 by IS-2s, Polish and Russian research identifies that it wasn't an ambush, that only*

12 Tigers (7 Tiger Is and 5 Tiger IIs) were knocked out by 61st Guards Armored Brigade (of X Armored Corps of the Soviet Fourth Armored Army); the rest were destroyed between January 13 and 16 in the Kielce area, some by the actions of their own crews when they ran out of fuel. In the north, 22 of 507's Tigers made it back to the east bank of the Vistula but had to be destroyed for lack of ferries. Only seven of 507's Tigers were operational on February 1.

Below: *A group of German infantrymen waiting for a cup of ersatz coffee being prepared in the background. They are dressed in the M1943 Marsh-pattern camouflage suit and look surprisingly happy.*

Below: *Two maps showing the two phases of the battle of Bautzen. The first shows the Poles advancing to the southwest with 9th Infantry Division in the van. Elstra is 25 miles from Dresden.*

In the first phase the Germans hit the unprotected flank of Second Polish Army—Swierczewski had omitted that element of the advance—and, after hard street-to-street urban fighting, relieved the German troops in Bautzen

In the second phase, Konev's reinforcements have taken position and the German thrusts are turned back. Swierczewski's errors were glossed over as he was a political high flier—he ended up in the communist Polish postwar government. He was killed in 1947 in an ambush by Ukrainian insurgents.

Bautzen: The Last Victory

Zhukov's 1st Belorussian Front broke through at Seelow, and Konev's 1st Ukrainian Front thrust further south. German 9. Armee was trapped between them as the Halbe Pocket formed (see next page). Alongside Konev's front, to the south, Second Polish Army headed for Dresden. The Poles were commanded by General Karol Swierczewski—callsign Walter. Between April 21 and 28 it was subjected to a major counterattack by Heeresgruppe Mitte's 4. Panzerarmee and 17. Armee. Swierczewski may well have been drunk: he was certainly incompetent, as he allowed a portion of his force to continue toward Dresden before they were called back. The Germans took Bautzen and General Konev had to send eight divisions from his 1st Ukrainian Front to reinforce the Polish positions. Swierczewski was relieved of command, the line was held. The Poles paid the price: some 22 percent of the army, the official casualty figures being 4,902 KIA, including 2,798 MIA, and 10,532 WIA. The German losses were high but probably not as high as the 6,500 originally suggested. Tactically, it was a success, but the German attack failed in its attempt to break through to Berlin.

April 21–22, 1945

- Position of Second Polish Army April 22
- Position of Soviet units April 22
- Position of German units April 22–23
- Direction of German offensive April 21–23

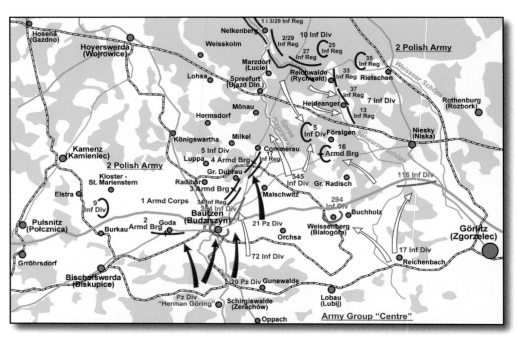

April 23–28, 1945

- Position of Second Polish Army April 23
- Position of Soviet units April 23
- Position of German units April 22–23
- Direction of German offensive April 24–28

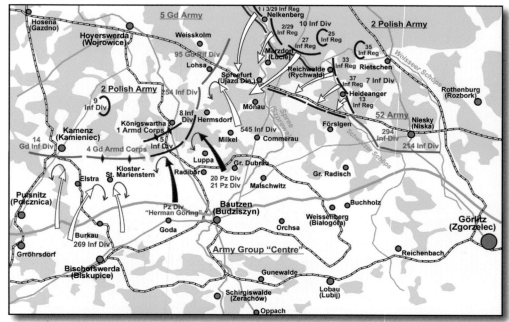

Right: *Men of Fallschirm-Panzerdivision 1. Hermann Göring in Kleinvelka, a suburb of Bautzen, inspect 5100 Tadeusz, an IS-2 of I Polish Armored Corps. Note at left a Lend-Lease British Universal Carrier. Both vehicles carry Polish eagles.*

Center right: *Grenadiers in Bautzen. In the background, a PzKpfw IV Ausf J. After linking up with the Bautzen garrison on the evening of April 24, the division rounded the city and attacked to the northwest.*

Below right: *Here, a knocked-out Polish ISU-122 SP gun among the damage. Polish armor losses were said to be around 200 out of over 500. As an example, 4th "Dresden" Armored Brigade lost 30 of 65 T-34s and 55 of 325 tank crew.*

FALLSCHIRM-PANZERDIVISION 1. HERMANN GÖRING

With antecedents back to the 1930s, the unit grew in size to become a division in May 1944. It fought in Italy, where it was involved in a number of atrocities. It moved to the Eastern Front in July 1944 and fought around Warsaw, helping to put down the rising. In October 1944 it fought in East Prussia and, in January 1945, was trapped in the Heiligenbeil Pocket. Evacuated by sea to Pomerania, in April it moved to Silesia, then Saxony. After Bautzen, it fought near Dresden but wasn't able to escape to the west and was captured by the Red Army.

Opposite, Inset: *The Halbe Pocket developed as 9.Armee was encircled by the thrusts of the 1st Belorussian and 1st Ukrainian fronts.*

Opposite, Below: *Based on Soviet maps, this shows the contracting pocket. Very few escaped from the cauldron to the west, where 12.Armee had fought to within 40 miles of Halbe.*

Halbe Pocket

As a direct result of the Soviet's outflanking maneuvers after crossing the River Neisse, German 9. Armee—commanded by General Theodor Busse—had attempted to withdraw north to Berlin. Their troops were unsuccessful, however, as the Red Army blocked their way and then encircled them in the Spree Forest to the southeast of Berlin on April 24. It must be remembered that by that stage of the war the German troops had long experience of being isolated in pockets of one kind or another while fighting in Russia, and so neither morale nor leadership suffered immediately.

Although nominally an entire army, those caught by the Red Army were merely a shallow reflection of their previous establishments. They had fewer than 80 tanks left—about 14 of which were Tiger IIs, and somewhere between 150 and 200 other armored vehicles. Not many days before there had been 800 or so. They also had around 1,000 field guns. 9. Armee at this stage was made up of the remnants of XI. SS-Panzerkorps, V. SS-Gebirgskorps, and V. Armeekorps, as well as men from the Frankfurt Garrison.

Desperately short of supplies, the beleaguered troops appealed for help from the air. Despite repeated attempts over two days to provide air drops—on April 25 and 26—the pilots simply could not work out where their men were in the endless sea of greenery, and few were successful. Those in the pocket hoped to escape to the west in order to join forces with the German 12. Armee which was located to the southwest of Berlin. After that, they intended to surrender to the U.S. Army, which was close by.

Since the forest is primarily a vast area of pine trees and countless lakes, there were few roads along which any vehicles could pass. This meant that the Germans' only choice was to travel through the village of Halbe. Before they could do this, however, they would first have to force their way through Konev's 1st Ukrainian Front which had established three formidable lines of defense to prevent just that. To make matters worse, Zhukov's troops of the 1st Belorussian Front were also attacking from directly behind them.

In order to block the only significant escape routes to the west, Soviet Marshals Konev and Zhukov placed the Third Guards Army and the Twenty-eighth Army along the Berlin to Dresden autobahn which marked the line they would have to cross. These troops included huge numbers of tank and other mechanized forces backed up by the 1st Guards Breakthrough Artillery Division—its name reflecting its role of providing artillery concentrations for offensives.

In an effort to support 9. Armee's breakout attempt, 12. Armee pushed to the east and north on April 24, attacking Fourth Guards Tank Army, catching them unawares. Much of Soviet unit's rear area was overrun before order was restored. The German plan was that when the two armies met, they would combine in a drive northward to reach Berlin. General Busse intended that 9. Armee would be led out of the forest by the Tiger IIs of the SS-sPzAbt 502, and that the tail of the evacuation would be protected by a rearguard.

The first break-out attempt by 9. Armee took place late on April 25: two Kampfgruppen—that of Oberst Hans von Luck, made up of the 21. Panzerdivision, and that of SS-Standartenführer Rüdiger Pipkorn, which comprised the 35. SS- und Polizei-Grenadier-Division. Neither succeeded in getting through, and their fight to escape continued the next morning, but the Soviets then launched a massive counterattack backed up by around 500 air sorties by the IV Bomber Air Corps and I and II Air Assault Corps. The weight of the attack smashed both Kampfgruppen, and around 5,000 German prisoners were taken, along with many field guns and mortars. About 40 tanks and self-propelled guns were also destroyed. Von Luck was captured the next day, while Pipkorn was killed. German aerial resupply operations were ineffective.

UNITS CAUGHT IN THE HALBE POCKET

The question of who exactly was trapped in the pocket, and what happened to them, is not straight-forwardly answered. Few of the units were anything like up to strength. Wilhelm Tieke talks of elements of XI. SS-Panzerkorps, V. SS-Gebirgskorps, and V.Armeekorps

The intelligence report of HQ 1st Ukrainian Front on the actions of the enemy for the period from April 15 to 30, 1945, talks about "The encirclement of the units and formations of 9.Armee in the southeast region." The units identified are:

- *169., 214., 275., 303., 342., and 712. Infanterie-Divisionen*
- *32. SS-Freiwilligen Grenadier-Division "30. Januar"*
- *Division Raegener*
- *391. Sicherungs-Division*
- *36. Waffen-Grenadier-Division der SS*
- *35. SS- und Polizei-Grenadier-Division*
- *23. SS-Freiwilligen-Panzergrenadier-Division Nederland (niederländische Nr. 1)*
- *Panzergrenadier-Division Kurmark*
- *21. Panzerdivision divisional group*

- *Additionally, five brigades, four separate infantry and two artillery regiments, six detachments of artillery divisions, and up to 40 different battalions, totaling up to 90,000 soldiers and officers, over 1,400 guns, up to 100 tanks and TDs, and up to 500 mortars.*

Also identified as being present:
- *SS-sPzAbt 502*
- *Fahnenjunker Regiment 1239*

The Tigers of 1. and 2./SS-sPzAbt 502 played an important role in spearheading (seven tanks of 2./) and as rearguard (seven of 1./) to the breakout on April 27. Schneider (2005) reports that the last Tiger (SS-Untersturmführer Klust of 1./) was abandoned on May 1 near Elsholz.

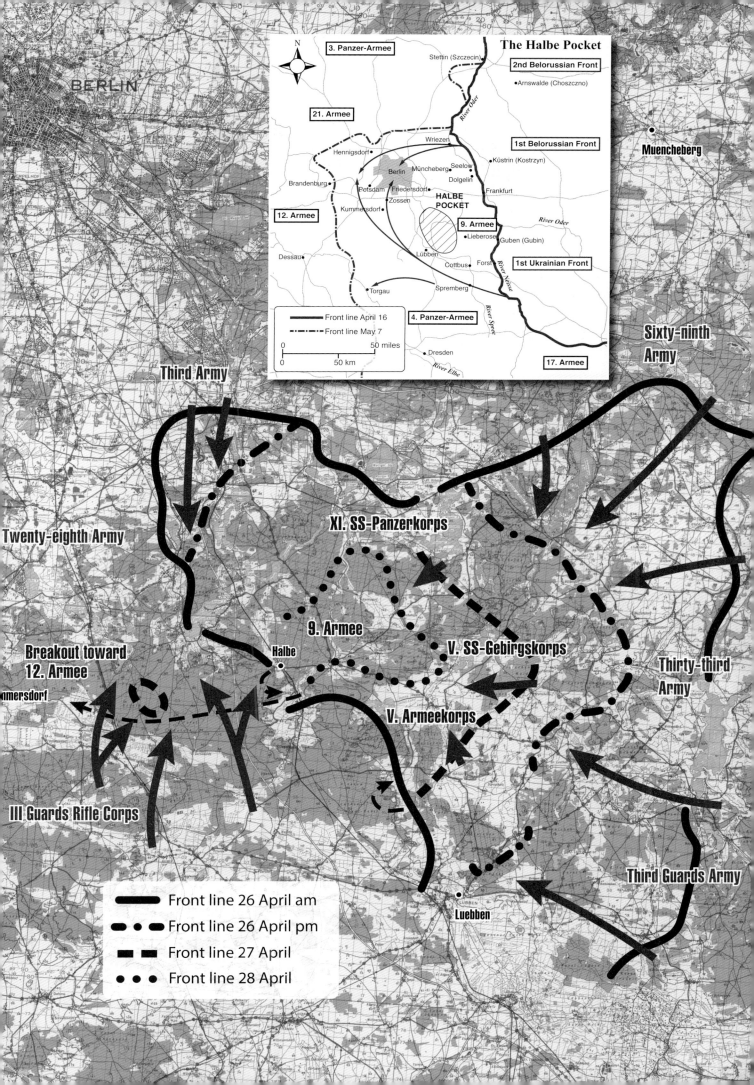

BERLIN

The Halbe Pocket

3. Panzer-Armee

Stettin (Szczecin)

2nd Belorussian Front

Arnswalde (Choszczno)

21. Armee

Wriezen

Hennigsdorf

1st Belorussian Front

Müncheberg

Seelow

Küstrin (Kostrzyn)

Brandenburg

Berlin

Dolgelin

Potsdam

Friedersdorf

Frankfurt

12. Armee

Kummersdorf

Zossen

HALBE POCKET

River Oder

9. Armee

Lieberose

Guben (Gubin)

Dessau

Lübben

Cottbus

Forst

1st Ukrainian Front

River Neisse

Torgau

Spremberg

4. Panzer-Armee

River Spree

Dresden

17. Armee

River Elbe

Front line April 16

Front line May 7

0 — 50 miles

0 — 50 km

Muencheberg

Third Army

Sixty-ninth Army

Twenty-eighth Army

XI. SS-Panzerkorps

9. Armee

Halbe

V. SS-Gebirgskorps

Breakout toward 12. Armee

mmersdorf

V. Armeekorps

Thirty-third Army

III Guards Rifle Corps

Third Guards Army

Luebben

Front line 26 April am

Front line 26 April pm

Front line 27 April

Front line 28 April

**OPERATIONS OF
ENCIRCLED FORCES
German Experiences in
Russia**

*(Department of the Army
Pamphlet No. 20-234 of 1952)*

*Combat in pockets has its own
fundamental rules. Whatever
circumstances may determine the
length of the battle, it will always be
advisable to seek an early decision. To
make this possible, the commander of
an encircled force must, on principle,
be granted full freedom of action. The
notion that pockets must be held at
all costs should never be applied as a
general principle. Hitler's adherence
to this mistaken concept resulted in
the loss of many German soldiers.
Another principle that has proved
itself in the German experience is the
delegation of authority by the pocket
commander to three subordinate
command elements within the pocket;
one to maintain the defensive effort;
another to prepare and conduct the
breakout; and a third to be
responsible for organization, traffic
control, and the maintenance of
discipline inside the pocket.*

*So long as the encirclement has
not been completed—or before the
enemy ring has been reinforced—an
immediate break-through offers the
best chance of success.*

*The tactical measures leading up
to the breakout are the following :
a. Emphasis on defense; all weapons
committed in support of the fighting
along the perimeter.
b. Establishment of clear channels of
command.
c. Stabilization of the defense.
d. Reinforcement of the combat
element at the expense of the service
units.
e. Evacuation of nonessential
personnel; destruction of excess
equipment.
f. Gradual change of emphasis from
the defense to preparations for the
breakout attack.
g. Formation of a breakout force.
h. Shortening of the defense
perimeter; further strengthening of
the sector selected for the breakout.
i. Deceptive maneuvers culminating in
a diversionary attack.
j. Breakout.*

A second escape attempt was launched on April 26 when the Germans realized that the Soviets had left a gap in the blockade. When the Germans attacked it, many got through before Red Army troops were able to close the breach. The Soviets used their air power to good effect again, with 2,459 sorties flown, of which 1,683 were bombing runs. The Germans were severely hampered by the terrain—their tanks and other armored vehicles were unable to operate in the forests because the ground was too soft. This left them more or less entirely dependent on using the roads, but that then left them open to attack from the air, against which they were unable to defend themselves.

Those troops who had managed to break out thus far did so in a westerly direction—when Hitler was told they were heading away from Berlin though he was livid with rage, but despite issuing orders for them to come to his aid, he got no response. Due to the convoluted nature of the ground, the density of the trees, and the smoke from numerous fires, it was possible for small groups of men to move unseen. As a result, a few more managed to break through Soviet lines the next day, but the majority were again repulsed.

One of the Soviet tactics was to fire high-explosive shells into the forest at treetop height—these created enormous showers of lethal wooden splinters which would kill or injure anyone who wasn't well sheltered. Since the ground was composed of loose sand it was virtually impossible to dig foxholes, so few were able to achieve much in the way of protection.

On the evening of April 27 the final, and ultimately successful, breakout attempt was launched during the night from around the village of Halbe. Spearheaded by the Tigers of SS-sPzAbt 502, over the next five days the German troops forced their way toward Beelitz and a rendezvous with 12. Armee. But although the spearhead temporarily overcame the 50th Guards Rifle Division and established a route to freedom, it came at a high price in casualties and equipment lost (by the time the last Tiger was abandoned at Elsholz, 8 miles south of Beelitz, all 14 had been destroyed in battle or by their own crews). The Soviets quickly reinforced the flanks and saturated the area with Katyusha rockets and artillery fire. Nevertheless, the Germans still somehow kept the corridor open even though they were in near total disarray. Troops from different formations were often completely mixed up, and to complicate matters the Waffen-SS and Wehrmacht men were at each other's throats. Communications between most of the units had failed, and despite being on home territory, they had almost no maps of the area. The breakout reached Sperenberg on the 29th, and Kummersdorf on the 30th. By May 1, it was all over.

The outcome had been a foregone conclusion due to the overwhelming superiority of the Soviet forces which included somewhere around 280,000 men, of 1st Belorussian Front in the north and 1st Ukrainian Front in the south. They had also sent in II Guards Cavalry Corps which specialized in crossing through forests and other tough terrain. Of the 80,000 or so Germans involved, somewhere between 25,000 and 30,000 managed to break through and link up with the 12. Armee, while the rest were killed or taken prisoner.

Those German soldiers who had managed to escape from the pocket were hotly pursued by Red Army forces, and some were encircled again by the Fourth Guards Tank Army just before they reached the relative safety of the 12. Armee lines. Those that did reach 12. Armee—along with several thousand civilians—managed to surrender to the 102nd Infantry Division, Ninth (U.S.) Army, which had stopped its advance on the west bank of the River Elbe. Many crossed on the badly damaged Tangermünde bridge, but when Soviet forces arrived on May 7, no further crossings were permitted.

The fighting during the battle of Halbe had been so confused that precise casualty figures still cannot be established. The Russians claimed 60,000 Germans were killed and perhaps as many as another 120,000 taken prisoner. The Red Army lost tens of thousands in the struggle, and at least 15,000 civilians were also killed.

Weary and unkempt this was the face of much of Hitler's final defenders—exhausted determination.

Berlin: The Last Rites

By March 1945, the Red Army had advanced to within 40 miles (60 km) of Berlin, but it did not move any farther at that stage since there were still unsecured flanks which needed protecting. As it was clear that it would arrive sooner rather than later, a set of plans for the defense of the city entitled "Basic Order for the Preparations for the Defense of the Reich Capital were drawn up on March 9. Codenamed *Unternehmen Clausewitz*, it stipulated that the city was to be divided into nine different zones within four concentric rings. These were composed of an outer exclusion zone around the city's limits, an outer defense zone reaching inward from there to the city's main ring road, and an inner defense zone extending from the road toward the center where the final zone was the citadel.

Since the citadel, which was designated as zone Z (*Zitadelle* in German) contained so many vital parts of the remaining infrastructure—including the Reichskanzlei (Chancellery) and the Führerbunker, it received its own dedicated defense unit called the Kampfgruppe Mohnke. This was named after its commander, SS-Brigadeführer Wilhelm Mohnke, a trusted and seasoned veteran of the battlefield. The battle group was made up of a hastily thrown-together assembly of around 2,000 troops drawn from various 1. SS-Panzerdivision *Leibstandarte* SS Adolf Hitler (LSSAH) elite formations. These included troops from the LSSAH Flak Bataillon and the LSSAH Ausbildungs-und Ersatz Bataillon, together with 600 men from the Begleit-Bataillon Reichsführer-SS (previously Himmler's bodyguard unit) and 800 men from the LSSAH Wach Bataillon 1, Hitler's own personal guard.

The creation of *Unternehmen Clausewitz* also saw martial law being imposed on the civilian inhabitants—this established the death sentence for a variety of offenses, including anything remotely perceived as defeatism. Actual construction of the required defense positions began on March 20 under the control of General Gotthard Heinrici, who was commander of Heeresgruppe Weichsel at the time, although he was dismissed shortly afterward on April 29 for disobeying what he considered to be nonsensical orders.

Continued on p. 214.

Opposite: *The Brandenburg Gate after the battle. Note the ruins of the Reichstag on the right.*

Left: *T-34/85s of XII Guards Tank Corps (1st Belorussian Front). Second Guards Tank Army was the first unit to enter Berlin. Its three corps were IX and XII Guards Tank, and I Motorized. XII Guards' tactical insignia can be seen on the turret. It had three Guards tank brigades (48th, 49th, and 66th).*

Below left: *Heading for Berlin, Red Army troops are exhorted onward by a sign at the side of the road: "The more German tanks are destroyed, the closer is the victory." Above that, "Forward to victory!"*

Below: *A battery of ISU-122s rests in a municipal housing estate in Berlin. The crews are fraternizing with a group of workmen, maybe in the Wedding district. It is possible that the workmen are imported laborers from France or elsewhere. The scene is particularly notable for the lack of damage.*

KEY

Red Zone boundaries. They were commanded by:

A Obstlt Erich Bärenfänger;
B Oberst Clausen;
C Oberst Mootz;
D Gen-Maj Schreder;
E Obstlt Romhild;
F Oberst Eder;
G Oberst Schaefer;
H Obstlt Rossbach;
Z Obstlt Seifert.

Yellow Outer restricted zone

Blue Outer defense ring

White Inner defense ring

Orange Flaktürme (Flak towers):
1 Berliner Zoo;
2 Friedrichshain;
3 Humboldthain.

DEFENDING BERLIN

With Guderian dismissed, the OKH simply a mouthpiece for Hitler, and it being seen as defeatism to prepare plans to defend Berlin, there was little chance that the commander of the Berlin Defensive Area was going to be able to meet his requirements. Hitler had promised sufficient ground forces. When the moment that they were needed came, few were available. Had Hitler been prepared to allow his forces leeway to move tactically, he could have effected a more sensible defense of Berlin. Rather than letting 9. Armee be trapped in the Halbe Pocket, he could have moved the full army back to the city. Instead, he moved LVI. Panzerkorps and that allowed 9. Armee to be surrounded.

Reymann issued Grundsätzlicher Befehl für die Vorbereitungen zur Verteidigung der Reichshauptstadt (Basic order for the preparations to protect Berlin). When Hitler announced "Clausewitz," it meant that the Soviets were getting close and Berlin became a Festung. "Kolberg" meant an enemy attack. The nine sector commanders took command of all Wehrmacht troops and Volkssturm units in their sectors: "The capital of the Reich is to be defended to the last man and to the last cartridge … every block, every house, every floor, every hedge, every shell hole is to be defended to the end!" The OKH and OKW left the city, as did various ministries. The problem with the defense lines was that they needed at least 100 battleworthy divisions; the Commander of the Defense Area had 60,000 Volkssturm troops, one-third of whom were unarmed, 20–30 artillery batteries, and the city's permanent AA units. None of this stopped the Soviets and the overlapping jurisdictions meant that there was no firm control over the disparate units. When Weidling took over the defense on April 24, he had at his disposal 45–60,000 troops (including 1. Flakdivision) with 50–60 tanks, plus the Volkssturm and Hitlerjugend. Of this total, 13–15,000 were from LVI. Panzerkorps:

- Panzerdivision Müncheberg (a third of unit lost in fighting)—allocated to sector B.
- 18. Panzergrenadier-Division (largely intact)—in reserve; then to sector E after 20. PzGr-Div was cut off.
- 20. Panzergrenadier-Division (had sustained heavy losses)—sector E.
- 11. SS-Panzergrenadier-Division Nordland (largely intact)—sector C.
- 9. Fallschirmjäger-Division (heavy losses)—sector A.

On top of this, Kampfgruppe Mohnke (LSSAH) had about 2,000 men, and on April 24, reinforcements —350 mainly French volunteers—from 33. SS-Grenadierdivision Charlemagne arrived.

Around the inner defense ring, at the intersection of important roads, tanks without running gear were dug in. They belonged to 5. Panzerkompanie (bo) "Berlin" (bo = bodenständig = immobile), which was allocated 10 Panthers and 12 PzKpfw IVs.

Left: This 5. Panzerkompanie (bo) "Berlin" PzKpfw V Ausf D is on the intersection of Badstraße and Pankstraße. Cobblestones surround it, as do spent shellcases..

Below left: T-34/85s of VII Guards Tank Corps (1st Ukrainian Front, Third Guards Tank Army). Awarded the Order of Lenin for bursting through the German defenses on the Neisse and later "Berlin" for its work in the German capital, the corps was commanded by Maj Gen Vasily V. Novikov. Its main striking power was its three Guards tank brigades, 54th, 55th, and 56th, and 23rd Motorized Guards Rifle Brigade. Maj Semyon Vasilyevich Khokhryakov, commander of 209th Tank Battalion (54th Bde) was one of the few to receive the Hero of the Soviet Union award twice. His battalion was ambushed 60 miles from Berlin on April 17 and he was killed in action. VII Guards Tank Corps is identified by the double concentric circles after the number 313. The other corps of Third Guards Tank Army used one (VI Guards Tank) and three (IX Mechanized) rings.

Below: A mixed column of Soviet armor in Berlin. At the front a T-34 with an 85mm gun followed by an SU-85. Both leading vehicles have their hatches open suggesting little fear of sudden attack. The white bars on the turret may be a form of keeping score, although rings around the barrel were more common.

Once the operations to clear the threats to the Soviet's flanks had been concluded and the armies south of Berlin rendered powerless (as detailed elsewhere in this book), the Red Army began the first phase of taking the city on April 16. This involved encircling it to prevent both any escapees getting out or any kind of support getting in. On paper, the Germans had significant units arrayed for its defense, however, they were all understrength and incapable of withstanding the Red Army for long. The 20. Infanterie-Division was disposed to the west, the 9. FJ-Division to the north, Panzerdivision Müncheberg to the northeast, 11. SS-Panzergrenadier-Division *Nordland* was arrayed in the southeast as well as to the east of the main airport at Tempelhof, and in the center were the reserves of 18. Panzergrenadier-Division.

With the encirclement mostly completed, on April 20 the 1st Belorussian Front launched an artillery assault on the city center while at the same time attacking from the north and east. Simultaneously, the 1st Ukrainian Front smashed through the Heeresgruppe Mitte and moved into the southern suburbs.

By April 23, things were going very badly for the defenders—among other terrors, the shelling which began on the 20th had not stopped, and did not do so until the city finally surrendered. This barrage actually dropped more tonnage of explosives on the unfortunate inhabitants than that dropped by all the combined efforts of western allied bombers throughout the entire war. The same day the last connections between the 9. Armee and Berlin were severed when the Fifth Shock Army as well as the First Guards Tank Army attacked from the southeast. They had fought their way as far as the main ring road by the following evening.

In desperation, Hitler appointed General Helmuth Weidling to take over the reins of control as Kampfkommandant of the defense of Berlin from Generalleutnant Hellmuth Reymann. He had only been in charge for about a month, but the Führer felt he was not being sufficiently hardline and wanted a harsher regime implemented. Before accepting the job, however, Weidling stipulated that if he was to take on the role, he would not take any interference from Goebbels or any other high ranking Nazis. Although this condition was granted, he had no proper army left to organize. There were only remnants of both Wehrmacht and Waffen-SS troops along with various inexperienced and often elderly Volkssturm, police officers and members of the Hitlerjugend left. These numbered a total of around 45,000 men. Against the massed forces

Above: *1943 Wehrmacht recruitment poster published by the OKH—"From Hitlerjugend to officer in the army—Your destiny!" The propaganda art is by Wolfgang Willrich, a German war artist known for his portraits of winners of the Knight's Cross.*

Below right: *During the final hours of the battle for Berlin, Soviet troops were naturally wary of ambush. Here a unit can be seen entering an underground railroad station on Frankfurter Allee. The sign gives directions to a nearby air raid shelter. Thousands of Berliners sought refuge underground during the fighting.*

Opposite, Above: *A cheerful young soldier carrying a rifle, hand grenade, shovel, and a Panzerfaust 30, whose effective range was 30m. The wooden box strapped to his back contains four more warheads for the Panzerfaust.*

Opposite, Below: *Some of Berlin's youngest defenders drawn from the Hitlerjugend were simply disarmed and taken prisoner, as is the case here. The youth in the front row to the left does not seem too downhearted that for him the war is over.*

"A thirteen-year old boy manned a machine gun against advancing Allied tanks on the Rhineland frontier, while his mates passed the ammunition.

An execution squad composed of 14–16 year olds shot Polish civilian hostages.

Eleven years of Nazi indoctrination, at a most susceptible age, in the Hitlerjugend has done its work.

The Hitlerjugend is not a Boy Scout or Girl Guide organization. It is in no respect comparable to any organization for young people known to the Western World.

It is a compulsory Nazi formation, which has consciously sought to breed hate, treachery and cruelty into the mind and soul of every German child. It is, in the true sense of the word, 'education for death'.

Under no circumstances should the Hitlerjugend be taken lightly or be considered a negligible factor from an operational or occupation point of view.

Both the SS and the Wehrmacht have long since appreciated this. From mere liaison with the Hitlerjugend, their relationship with the HJ has passed through the stage of supervision and has finally resulted in complete domination.

The Hitlerjugend has became a Wehrmacht replacement pool, a manpower reservoir for auxiliary war services, and a means of strengthening the increasingly pernicious hold on the German people of the most ruthless of all Nazi organizations, the SS.

A few courageous young Germans have sought to escape from the tentacles of the Hitlerjugend, and some underground cells composed of such young people are known to exist.

But it must not be forgotten that this 'Junior Army' is ready to take the field either individually, in small groups, on a larger, more organized scale, or as saboteurs, informers and even franctireurs in defense of Nazism, its fanatical creed."

Top: *Moltke Bridge with the Reichstag in the background. The bridge saw heavy fighting as SS and Volkssturm troops barricaded it at both ends. On April 28 units of the Soviet Third Shock Army forced their way across in sufficient numbers to hold their own, withstand the inevitable counterattacks, and allow others to join them.*

Above and **Right:** *One of many flag-raising groups making their up the steps of the Reichstag. Almost every unit within sight of this symbol of Germany's defeat had detailed a group of veterans to plant the Red Banner on the Reichstag's roof. Very quickly several were in competition. On the plans for the capture of Berlin the Reichstag building was referred to as Objective 105. This is a reproduction of the official Victory Banner (housed in the Central Museum of the Armed Forces, Moscow). The Cyrillic says "150th Rifle, Order of Kutuzov 2nd class, Idritsa Division, LXXIX Rifle Corps, Third Shock Army, 1st Belorussian Front."*
It was raised by Alexei Berest, Mikhail Yegorov, and Meliton Kantaria.

Opposite, Above and **Inset:** *Postwar views of the Reichstag in 1945 and again in 2012.*

Opposite, Below: *The battle for the Reichstag, April 30–May 2, 1945. The Reichstag may not have been used since its burning, but it still symbolized Germany and its capture was emblematic.*

of the Red Army though, Weidling's troops stood no chance, and little by little they were gradually wiped out.

By April 26, Eighth Guards Army and the First Guards Tank Army had advanced as far as Tempelhof Airport where they came up against a furious defense from Panzerdivision Müncheberg which had moved southward and were fighting alongside the *Nordland*. To counter this, the Soviets put five armies up against them—the Fifth Shock Army, the Eighth Guards Army, the First Guards Tank Army, and Third Guards Tank Army. The weakened defenders were completely outmatched and inexorably driven back toward the center, eventually seeking refuge around the Hermannplatz.

As the Red Army closed in on the citadel, vicious combat took place from house to house and was often hand-to-hand. The SS units recruited from foreigners were particularly determined defenders as they knew that the Soviets would give them little chance of survival if taken prisoner. Much of the heaviest action took place around the Reichstag, the Moltke bridge, Alexanderplatz, and the Havel bridges at Spandau. When the damaged Moltke bridge was taken in the middle of the night of April 29/30 by the Soviet Third Shock Army, troops poured across and began occupying the area, storming the buildings they encountered.

The Soviet advance slowed when it became out of range of its artillery's reach, but by April 30 engineers had finished repairing the relevant bridges, and the guns were brought in closer to help clear the way. At 06:00 an attack was launched on the Reichstag, but it was strongly defended with the support of heavy artillery from the zoo's flak tower. They kept the Soviets out until

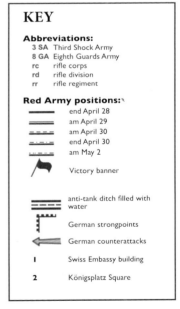

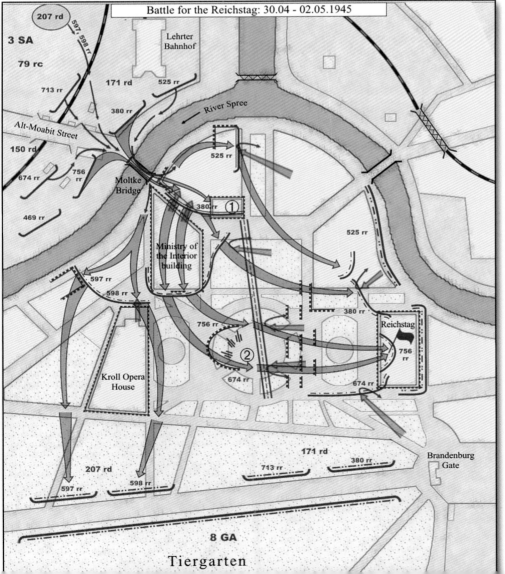

Battle for the Reichstag: 30.04 - 02.05.1945

207 rd

3 SA

79 rc

Lehrter
Bahnhof

597, 598 rr

713 rr

171 rd

525 rr

380 rr

River Spree

Alt-Moabit Street

525 rr

150 rd

674 rr

756 rr

Moltke
Bridge

380 rr

①

Ministry of
the Interior
building

525 rr

469 rr

380 rr

597 rr

598 rr

756 rr

380 rr

Reichstag

756 rr

②

Kroll Opera
House

674 rr

674 rr

171 rd

Brandenburg
Gate

207 rd

713 rr

380 rr

597 rr

598 rr

8 GA

Tiergarten

KEY

Abbreviations:

3 SA	Third Shock Army
8 GA	Eighth Guards Army
rc	rifle corps
rd	rifle division
rr	rifle regiment

Red Army positions:

	end April 28
	am April 29
	am April 30
	end April 30
	am May 2
	Victory banner
	anti-tank ditch filled with water
	German strongpoints
	German counterattacks
1	Swiss Embassy building
2	Königsplatz Square

Above and Below: *One of Hitler's final appearances was in the Reichskanzlei garden on March 20, 1945, when he met HJ members who had been awarded medals: Erwin Scheideweg is at 1; "Willi" Hübner (**Above** and 2) was a messenger in Lauban, Upper Silesia and was awarded the Iron Cross (2nd class)—see p 96. 12-year-old Alfred Czech (3) rescued wounded soldiers in Goldenau, Silesia. Reichsjugendführer of the HJ Artur Axmann (obscured by Hitler in this photo) gave them their medals before Hitler greeted them. They lunched with Hitler before leaving.*

the evening, but even then, fighting continued for another two days. The heavy fighting continued wherever any defenders were left—the Gestapo headquarters on Prinz-Albrechtstraße were briefly taken by the Soviets, but a fierce counterattack by the Waffen-SS caused them to temporarily relinquish the building. By this stage it was obvious even to Hitler that it was all over, a fact that was brought home to him when Weidling came and told him that the defenders were almost out of ammunition. He even gave permission for the survivors to attempt to breakout to try and reach the western allies' front lines.

Hitler completed his will at 04:00 that morning, and soon after a brief marriage ceremony was held where he finally took his mistress, Eva Braun, to be his wife. That afternoon, he and his new bride committed suicide; their bodies were then taken out into the bunker's grounds and cremated to prevent them falling into Soviet hands. Hitler's will stipulated that Admiral Karl Dönitz would become President and Goebbels the new Chancellor of the Reich.

Gradually, the defenders—of whom there were only about 10,000 left, were constricted into a small area. The Hermann von Salza battalion still had a few Tiger tanks left though, and these mounted a staunch defense along the eastern side of the Tiergarten, in an attempt to keep the 3rd Shock and the 8th Guards Armies at bay. Early on the morning of May 1, General Hans Krebs tried to negotiate a surrender with General Chuikov, commander of the Eighth Guards Army, but the Soviets insisted that if any such thing was going to be accepted, it had to be unconditional. Unfortunately, Krebs was still subordinate to Goebbels, who would not countenance such an action. When the Propaganda Minister and his wife killed their children and then themselves later that day though, the way was open for a final capitulation.

When the actual surrender was agreed it was deliberately delayed overnight by General Weidling to give Berlin's remaining garrison a chance to breakout while it was still dark. They attempted to do so in three directions, but two of these failed completely, while most of those who chose to go through the Tiergarten and then across the Charlottenbrücke managed to get through

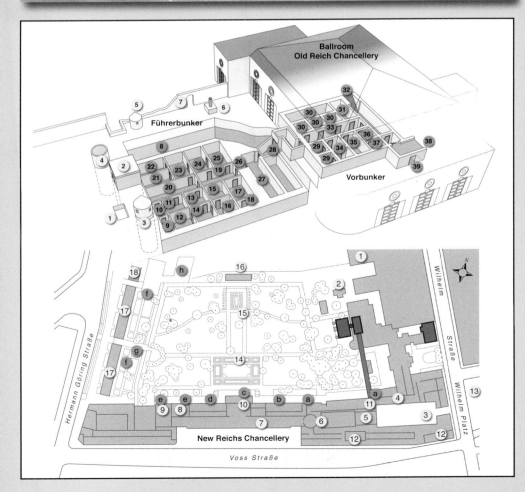

REICHSKANZLEI

OLD CHANCELLERY
Above ground (yellow)
1 Incineration pit where Hitler/Eva Braun's bodies were burned
2 Staircase to garden exit
3 (and **Left**) and 4 Ventilation and guard towers (4 under construction)
5 Ventilation intake
6 Generator/air conditioning exhaust
7 Old Chancellery garden wall

Below ground (brown)
8 Reinforced concrete ceiling
9 Stair to guard tower
10 Cloakroom
11 Conference/map room
12 AH's bedroom; 13 AH's office
14 AH's sitting room
15 Eva Braun's bedroom
16 Dressing/bathroom
17 Lavatories
18 Electrical switching room
19 Corridor/lounge
20 Conference room
21 Goebbels' bedroom
22 Doctor's quarters
23 Goebbels'/doctor's office
24 Switchboard/Bormann's office
25 Generator/ventilation plant
26 Gas doors
27 Hall/lounge
28 Stair to Vorbunker
29 Storeroom
30 Goebbels' family
31 Canteen
32 Stair to Foreign Ministry
33 Conference room/corridor
34 Pantry
35 Kitchen
36 Water supplies
37 Boiler room
38 Stair to old chancellery
39 Tunnel to new Reichskanzlei

NEW CHANCELLERY
Above ground (yellow)
1 Garage
2 Kempka's house
3 Ehrenhof (Court of Honor—main entrance) (**Center left**)
4 Pantry
5 Mosaic Hall
6 Round Hall
7 Marble Gallery
8 Cabinet room
9 Reception room
10 Hitler's office
11 Dining room
12 Entrances
13 Balcony
14 Fountain
15 Garden
16 Greenhouse
17 Security detail accommodation
18 Entrance to deep garage

Below ground (brown)
a Sleeping quarters and offices of adjutant and staff
b Civilian bunker
c Medical aid post
d Workers
e Ready rooms and canteen
f Garages
g Bunker for drivers
h Workshop bunker

the immediate Soviet front. Very few got much further though, being either captured or killed by the next lines of encirclement.

General Weidling, together with his supporting staff surrendered unconditionally at 06:00 hours on May 2 after which he ordered the remaining troops to stop fighting and give themselves up. Most did so—including around 350 men from the flak tower, however, some fanatical SS soldiers would not give in and continued resisting until the buildings they were in were flattened by the Soviets. That evening, General von Manteuffel, commander of 3. Panzerarmee surrendered to the British; General von Tippelskirch, commander of the 21. Armee surrendered to U.S. forces, followed by General Walther Wenck of 12. Armee on the afternoon of May 7. Likewise, 2. Armee under Von Saucken surrendered to the Red Army on May 9 (the latter electing to stay with his men and refusing evacuation by air).

All these capitulations were relatively local arrangements though—in order to legitimize the overall position and end the war in Europe legally a formal Instrument of Surrender was drawn up for signature. After a brief fiasco whereby an early version of the surrender document was signed in Reims, it was shortly after agreed that this would only be a temporary measure and that a full and slightly amended text would be formalized in Karlshorst, Berlin at the Soviet Military Administration.

Eisenhower therefore ordered that the heads of the three German armed services would be flown from where they were being held at Flensburg to Berlin. They got there early on May 8, 1945, and then after waiting for the

Left: *The original caption states that the target is the Air Ministry on Wilhelmstraße. By this stage of the battle heavy artillery was deployed simply to batter any pockets of resistance into submission in an effort to reduce Soviet casualties. The artillery piece is a 203mm BR-4 howitzer.*

Center left: *Loading rockets onto the guide rails of a Katyusha launcher, these men look happy with their task. This is the BM-13-16, the last number indicating the number of rockets that can be loaded. The truck is a Studebaker US6. The far-side vehicle's armored protection for the cab has been raised for the driver's benefit.*

Below left: *With its gun barrel marked with the words, "Death to Hitler," this 152mm M1937 howitzer fires into central Berlin. At maximum elevation of 65 degrees, as it appears here, the shell will not be traveling far.*

Below: *Soviet medal issued to those who took Berlin.*

Right: *Generalfeldmarschall Wilhelm Keitel signing the definitive Act of Military Surrender in Berlin early on the morning of May 9, 1945. The signatories were:*

Allied:
Zhukov (Red Army)
Tedder (Allied Expeditionary Force)
Spaatz (USAAF, witness)
de Tassigny (French Army, witness)

German:
Keitel (Wehrmacht, Heer)
von Friedeburg (Kriegsmarine)
Stumpff (Luftwaffe).

Below right: *The Russian names on the milepost translate into the local villages:*
18 Werneuchen
14 Tiefensee
14 Werftpfuhl
Wriezen 13
Ihlow 9
Grunow 6
Sternebeck 4
25 Altlandsberg
10 Strausberg
8 Gielsdorf

And that places this group of German troops at Plötzel, east of Berlin. They are eating while they await processing before transport to PoW camps in the Soviet Union. This scene was common throughout Eastern Europe during the last weeks of the war. Many of the tradesmen among them would spend their years of captivity rebuilding shattered Soviet cities. Many wouldn't return home till the 1950s. Many died in captivity—Russian historian Grigori F. Krivosheev (1997) puts the figure at over 380,000 of the 2.7 million PoWs. Western figures suggest nearer a million died. It's worth mentioning that, in comparison, between 1941 and 1945 it's estimated that between 3 and 3.6 million of the 5.7–6 million Russian PoWs of the Third Reich died in captivity.

Allied delegation to arrive, the document was signed that evening. Even as final preparations were underway, however, arguments were still raging. De Gaulle, for instance, demanded that General de Tassigny sign as representative of the French High Command. This then raised the issue that if France was going to be a signatory, then so should the United States—but the Soviets insisted that there should only be a maximum of three Allied signatories.

Tempers were not smoothed over until it was agreed that France—represented by General de Tassigny as General Commanding in Chief First French Army, and the United States by General Carl Spaatz as General Commanding United States Strategic Air Forces, would sign as witnesses. The primary Allied signatories were those of Air Chief Marshal Tedder, on behalf of Eisenhower as the Supreme Commander Allied Expeditionary Force, and Marshal Georgy Zhukov as Supreme High Command of the Red Army.

On the German side, the three signatories were GFM Wilhelm Keitel, Generaladmiral Hans-Georg von Friedeburg, and Generaloberst Hans-Jürgen Stumpff. Keitel did so as Chief of the General Staff of the German Armed Forces (Wehrmacht) as well as representative of the German Army, while von Friedeburg signed as Commander-in-Chief of the German Navy, and Stumpff as the representative of the German Air Force.

It is not possible to establish any precise casualty figures for the Berlin offensive, however, it is thought that more than 80,000 Soviets were killed and over 280,000 became wounded or sick. Nearly 2,000 tanks and other mechanized armor were lost. The Germans lost far more though—estimates suggest that around 100,000 were killed and nearly 480,000 captured. It is thought that about 125,000 civilians were killed, with about two million rapes being committed by Red Army troops who also undertook widespread looting. The rebuilding of Berlin's shattered infrastructure began almost straight away along with attempts to provide food for the population, but despite this, many still faced starvation.

ПОБЕДА

ПОБЕДОНОСНОЙ РОДИНЕ-СЛАВА!

Aftermath 8

The fighting didn't stop immediately—although many of the belligerents laid down their arms, some battles continued. The Soviets improved their position in Czechoslovakia by moving into Prague on May 8/9—but the last shots weren't fired until May 11 by which time the Soviet advance had reached the U.S. Army lines. German units continued to force their way westward to surrender to the Western allies rather than the Soviets. There was serious fighting in Yugoslavia, as Chetnik and Partisan settled scores; the Courland Pocket didn't receive the capitulation order until May 10; the Georgian uprising on Texel in the Netherlands saw Germans fight men of the Georgian Legion in a bloody battle that didn't end until May 20 when Canadian troops arrived.

Even after the final battle had been fought, the dying continued. In the liberated concentration camps disease, malnutrition, and hunger continued to kill thousands. Political retribution against those who fought for Nazi Germany—whether voluntarily or not—was rife. And then there were the repatriations agreed at Yalta: the British returned 40,000 Cossacks, many of whom had fought on the German side, to Russia with their wives and children—straight to execution or the gulags; Croats and Slovenes were returned to Yugoslavia and death.

The final organization of the zones of occupation saw territory changes and political pragmatism at work. The Western powers don't like to talk about it, but they were partners in awful crimes that were perpetrated on a range of peoples postwar. Poland had lost a fifth of its population (half of this Jews; many of the others killed by Stalin or ethnic cleansing in Ukraine). Its exiles had fought with distinction in the skies and on land for the Allies. Stalin kept the parts of Poland he had annexed in 1939 and the borders were shifted westward to the Oder–Neisse line in compensation, reducing the country's size by 20 percent and displacing millions who, in their turn, turfed out the ethnic Germans who were sent westward or used as forced labor. The Nazis had resettled 1.3 million Germans in Poland. By 1950 the expulsion of Germans from Poland was over 3 million and some 400,000 died. The Polish government in exile was ignored and a Soviet puppet government emplaced. Elsewhere, the Saar became a

Opposite: *"Glory to the victorious Motherland!" Alexei Kokorekin's 1945 poster—victory for the red star over the Kremlin.*

Above: *The Allies produced many medals for those who served during the war. This is the one that was awarded to Poles fighting in the west or east, for armed forces or partisans—including the French Resistance—from July 21, 1945.*

French protectorate until a referendum saw it rejoin the then West Germany in 1956. Austria was also divided into zones until 1955.

The perpetrators of the Final Solution and all the abominations of the Nazi regime were prosecuted—but not many went to trial. Within five years many of those imprisoned were free as the Western Allies found it easier to run the country using the experienced administrators of the Nazi regime. Denazification and non-fraternization were the order of the day, but the catastrophic destruction meant that short cuts were imperative.

The political map of Europe was set for fifty years by the position of the Allies' front lines in May 1945. As agreed at Yalta, in the west the Elbe was where the advance stopped—with the final dash to the Baltic "saving" Denmark from the possibility of Soviet occupation. The east disappeared behind the Iron Curtain other than Yugoslavia that managed to remain unaligned. Germany itself and Berlin were divided into four zones, each coming under one of the main Allies. The war had ended with a new political order, two superpowers vying against each other, and as the new war—the Cold War—started, so the border would become an area of friction.

Above: *Fraternization the American way—although his Russian partner may be worried about the "Hell on Wheels."*

Above right: *The "Handshake of Torgau" was photographed the day after the actual event. It shows 2Lt William Robertson (First (U.S.) Army) and Lt Alexander Silvashko, who met on the destroyed bridge over the Elbe.*

Below: *German PoWs rest on their way to imprisonment in the USSR. They were usually guarded by units of mounted NKVD men. The last German PoWs returned in the mid-1950s. Their treatment was significantly better than had been handed out to their Red Army counterparts.*

Below right: *Front und Heimat (Front and Home: The German Soldier's Newspaper) suggests "Every German a freedom fighter— Werewolf attack!" and "Fanatics, not fatalists."*

Opposite, Above: *The demarcation line on May 8 was blurred in Czechoslovakia as fighting continued. The Germans were trying to reach American lines to surrender. Prague was taken on May 9 and fighting continued sporadically till mid-May.*

Opposite, Below: *Luckily, the threat of a southern redoubt didn't materialize and the German forces laid down their arms and surrendered.*

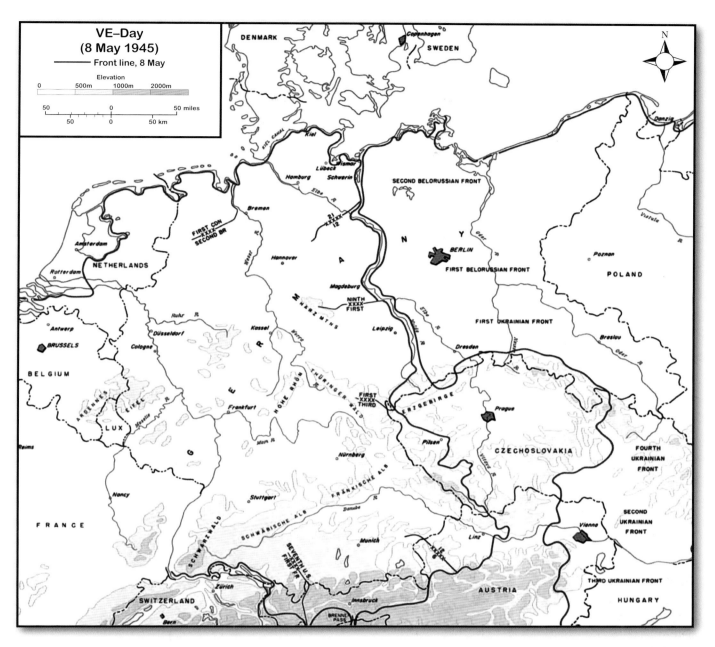

VE–Day
(8 May 1945)

— Front line, 8 May

Elevation

0   500m   1000m   2000m

50   0   50 miles

50   0   50 km

DENMARK

SWEDEN

Copenhagen

Kiel Canal

Kiel

Lübeck

Wismar

SECOND BELORUSSIAN FRONT

Hamburg

Schwerin

Danzig

Elbe R.

Bremen

Oder

FIRST CDN
XXXX
SECOND BR

2
XXXX
12

N

BERLIN

FIRST BELORUSSIAN FRONT

Poznan

POLAND

Amsterdam

NETHERLANDS

Hannover

A

Magdeburg

Weser R.

NINTH
XXXX
FIRST

Elbe R.

FIRST UKRAINIAN FRONT

Oder R.

Rotterdam

Ruhr R.

Kassel

Leipzig

Dresden

Breslau

Antwerp

BRUSSELS

Düsseldorf

Cologne

R

Neisse R.

ERZGEBIRGE

Prague

CZECHOSLOVAKIA

BELGIUM

E

HOHE RHÖN

THÜRINGER WALD

FIRST
XXXX
THIRD

Pilsen

Vltava R.

FOURTH
UKRAINIAN
FRONT

ARDENNES

EIFEL

Frankfurt

G

Main R.

Nürnberg

LUX

Moselle R.

Reims

Nancy

FRÄNKISCHE ALB

FRANCE

Stuttgart

SCHWÄBISCHE ALB

Danube R.

Munich

Linz

Vienna

SECOND
UKRAINIAN
FRONT

SCHWARZWALD

SEVENTH US
FIRST FR

Zürich

Innsbruck

AUSTRIA

THIRD UKRAINIAN FRONT

HUNGARY

SWITZERLAND

Bern

BRENNER
PASS

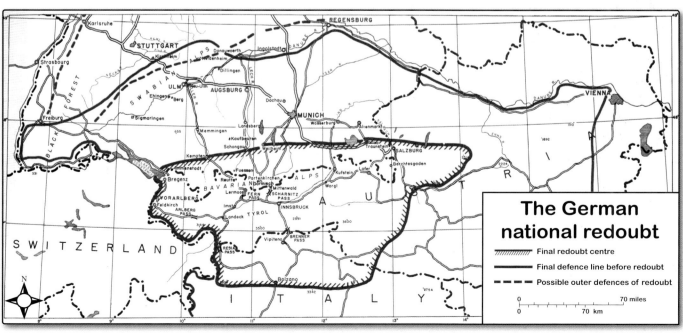

KARLSRUHE

REGENSBURG

STUTTGART

ALPS

Donauwoerth

Ingolstadt

DANUBE

Strasbourg

SWABIAN

Heidenheim

NECKAR R.

Dillingen

LECH R.

BLACK FOREST

ULM

Neu-Ulm

AUGSBURG

VIENNA

Freiburg

Ehingen

Berg

Dachau

DANUBE

Sigmaringen

Munich

ENNS R.

Memmingen

Landsberg

MUNICH

Wasserburg

Altenmarkt

Kaufbeuren

Schongau

Weilheim

Traunstein

SALZBURG

Kempten

ALPS

Immenstadt

Reutte

Fuessen

Partenkirchen

Lofer

Berchtesgaden

A

Bregenz

Lermoos

FERN
PASS

Mittenwald

SCHARNITZ
PASS

Kufstein

Wörgl

U

VORARLBERG

Feldkirch

Garmisch

INNSBRUCK

Landeck

TYROL

ARLBERG
PASS

BAVARIA

I

SWITZERLAND

Imst

BRENNER
PASS

RESIA
PASS

Vipiteno

ALPS

T

R

ITALY

Bolzano

The German
national redoubt

///// Final redoubt centre

—— Final defence line before redoubt

--- Possible outer defences of redoubt

0   70 miles

0   70 km

Displaced Persons

Europe in 1945 was teeming with people who were miles from home—if they still had one—displaced by the fighting, by ethnic cleansing, and by changes to the government and political leanings of their original countries. Many were ill with rickets, dysentery, intestinal and chest infections, tuberculosis, diphtheria, typhus and skin infections; all needed to be fed, clothed, and housed until they could be returned or found a home. This process took a decade; the rebuilding much longer. In Germany where up to half the homes in over sixty cities had been destroyed, much of the initial work fell to women, the so-called *Trümmerfrauen* (rubble women).

By the end of 1945 seven million DPs had returned home but there were still a million in West Germany alone, some scared to go back to now communist countries, others having returned after poor treatment in what used to be their home areas. From October 1945 the newly created United Nations got involved in the form of UNRRA (UN Relief and Rehabilitation Administration) and later the International Refugee Organization. Camps were created and used until 1952. Two events in 1948 helped: the creation of the state of Israel on May 14 and the U.S. Displaced Persons Act in June—the latter allowing 200,000 European refugees into the United States. Many of the 250,000 Jews left in Germany went and by 1952 there was only one camp, Föhrenwald, which remained open until 1957.

Above: *This memorial remembers Frankfurt Zeilsheim. A camp for forced laborers during the Nazi era, it became a camp for displaced persons after the end of the war, finally closing in 1948.*

Above right: *A common sight across Eastern Europe, DPs making their way home or to a safe haven. This group seem to be well-dressed and healthy when compared to many others in a similar position.*

Right: *This Monument to the Displaced in Budafoki Lutheran church garden remembers the 15,000 people who were expelled from Budapest between May 21 and July 18, 1951. The two outer walls show a stylized wagon—the usual method of transport.*

Left: *New arrivals at Displaced Persons Camp F in the Salzgitter region of Lower Saxony, 1946. They have brought with them whatever possessions they have been able to hang onto and await housing.*

Center left: *Displaced in their own cities. War damage meant many people had to make do with temporary shelters. The Nazis' scorched earth policies laid waste to cities, towns, and villages and left the western regions of the USSR devastated for several years.*

Below left and **Below:** *Wolfstein internment camp near Neumarkt in the Upper Palatinate was set up in 1942 as a transit camp for foreign workers. The memorial stone lies near an information board that talks starkly of 814 men, 447 women, and 287 children who died far from home. From 1945 to 1949 it served as a warehouse for the Displaced Persons Camp Neumarkt and as a supply warehouse for the U.S. Army. From 1949 it was used for displaced persons from the German eastern areas, especially Silesia and the Sudetenland. The barracks were torn down step by step and houses were built instead. The war cemetery is the biggest in south Germany with 5,049 burials from East and South Europe.*

Above: *Emaciated but recently liberated, Red Army PoWs. Many such men were, if healthy enough, drafted into second-line units where they gained a reputation for the brutal treatment they meted out to German civilians.*

Right: *Incensed by what they found at Volary in the present-day Czech Republic, on May 11, 1945, men of 5th (U.S.) Infantry Division made the Sudeten German civilians who lived nearby, walk past the bodies of thirty Jewish women. They had been starved to death by German SS troops during a 300-mile death march across Czechoslovakia from Helmbrechts concentration camp to Volary. The bodies were exhumed by Germans directed by U.S. medical orderlies and were later placed in coffins and reburied with dignity.*

Above and **Left:** The 1st Czechoslovak Independent Armoured Brigade Group (CIABG) was British equipped and trained and fought with 21st Army Group. A company of some 150 men was sent to take part in the Third (U.S.) Army's liberation of Czechoslovakian soil, raising the Czechoslovak flag in the city of Cheb on May 1, 1945. A few days after the war finished, CIABG journeyed back to Czechoslovakia. At the end of the month, as much of the CIABG as possible went to Prague for a Victory Parade on May 30. With the Jan Hus memorial in the background, men of the unit receive medals from Maj Gen Ernest N. Harmon, CG XXII (U.S.) Corps, in Old Town Square, Prague, October 1945.

Opposite, Above: *Initially, the relationship between the great powers was cordial and the niceties were performed, but soon politics reared their ugly head. Churchill had talked about an Iron Curtain and had pushed the Americans to consider the divisions of Europe but they had, at times, been more worried about what they saw as British attempts to revive colonialism. However, as it became clear postwar that there were but two superpowers and Britain was bankrupt, so the political rhetoric between the U.S. and the USSR ramped up. Things quickly deteriorated when access issues between the zones of occupation led to the Berlin Airlift of 1948–49.*

*Made worse by events such as the shooting down of an unarmed RAF Lincoln in 1953 and the Soviet invasion of Hungary in 1956, the early 1960s saw the Cold War heat up considerably when the Berlin Wall was built in August 1961. That year the Soviets tried to force recognition by the western Allies of the East German state by using East Germans rather than Soviet policemen to check the passports of diplomats visiting the east. This led to the farcical—but hugely dangerous—pointblank standoff of tanks at Checkpoint Charlie (**Opposite, Below**), swiftly defused by Kennedy and Khrushchev. The wall lasted from 1961 to 1989, and up to 200 people died trying to cross it. They were remembered in an unofficial memorial of January 2005 (**Opposite, Center**).*

The official demolition of the wall started in June 1994 and five months later, Germany was reunified. There are many memorials to the wall, reconciliation, and reunification in Germany, and pieces of the wall can be found all over the world.

Above left and **Left:** *The Kaiser Wilhelm Memorial Church, Berlin was built in the 1890s. Badly damaged by a bombing raid, it was going to be demolished until stopped by popular consent. Today the Gedächtniskirche complex (built 1959–63) includes a new church, a separate belfry with an attached chapel, and the damaged spire of the old church. Its ground floor became a memorial hall.*

Right: *One of the icons of Berlin, the Brandenburg Gate was built 1788–91 at one end of Unter den Linden leading to the Royal Palace. This postwar shot shows Allied vehicles—note the British roundel on the rear of the jeep.*

Below right: *A lone IS-2 tank parked on the Pariser Platz below the Brandenburg Gate. It displays the white air recognition turret stripe and a red star imposed over a polar bear—the insignia used by the 7th Guards Separate Heavy Tank Brigade which had served in Finland and Norway in fall 1944. The IS-2 in Berlin were drawn from several units and operated in groups of five with infantry and engineer support.*

Below: *A wrecked Tiger I stands forlorn in the Tiergarten. It is the last tank of 3. Kompanie I./Panzerdivision Müncheberg which had been issued with five of this model in early March 1945 when the division was formed. It was lost no later than April 30. A Soviet soldier can be seen peering in through the driver's hatch.*

Opposite: *Then and now—the Brandenburg Gate and Unter den Linden.*

236

Remembrance 9

The events of the last six months of the Great Patriotic War—as it is called in many countries that used to form the Soviet Union—were cataclysmic and sudden. For so long under the cosh, for so long fighting in their own motherland, for so long treated as second-class adversaries and subhuman by their enemy, suddenly the boot was decidedly on the other foot. The Red Army's overwhelming manpower helped, but don't let postwar obfuscation by beaten German generals take away from the skill and courage shown by the Soviets. Just as the Americans, British, and Canadians learned on the job, so did the Red Army—even though it had one arm tied behind its back from the start thanks to Stalin's cull of officers in the prewar years. It is certainly unsurprising that Russians remember their role in World War II as a great victory: it was. They faced down the bulk of the Axis forces and—helped by the extraordinary Lend-Lease assistance of its Allies and the prodigious efforts of its own industry—stopped them in their tracks, pushed them back, and beat them.

Opposite: *"Glory to victorious warrior!" Viktor Klimashin's 1945 poster extols the Red Army soldier who is held in as much esteem in his country as any GI or Tommy is held in theirs.*

Above: *Detail from the cemetery of Soviet soldiers at Katowice.*

They did so and then ensured that if they were to be invaded again from the west, there would be a tripwire of buffer states in the way of the invader. For fifty years, the *cordon sanitaire* provided by the Warsaw Pact was a useful insurance policy. Whether it would actually have been able to withstand an attack from the free west is conjectural. Whether that—or a similar Russian invasion of the west—was ever really on the cards is also a matter for debate.

What isn't debatable is that the Soviets overstayed their welcome. Fifty years of communism enabled the states that fought for the Axis to reinvent themselves. It has been all too easy to turn the narrative toward the many failings of the Soviet-influenced regimes and trumpet the Red Army's depredations of the last months of the war—thus downplaying the decisions that took many not just into alliance with Hitler but the enthusiasm with which they followed the Nazi plan, and all that entailed when it came to ethnic cleansing and genocidal attacks on Jews, gypsies, Poles, and other Slavs. The anti-Soviet feelings that lead to Russian statues or cemeteries being defaced or moved are understandable—particularly for a youth that

THE DISPARITY BETWEEN EAST AND WEST

The following table, based on German orders of battle, gives a comparison of German divisions in eastern Europe, exclusive of Finland and the Balkans, with those in western Europe, exclusive of Norway, Denmark, and Italy:

	East	West
June 1944	140	60
October 1944	120	50
January 1945	136	73
April 1945	130	65

grew up with the privations of the Eastern Bloc, so easily compared with the economic and personal freedoms in the west. Certainly some of the memorials and statues, have political connotations and served to justify Soviet rule and the debt due to the liberators. A good example of this is the Tiergarten memorial in Berlin. It's big and it was built very shortly after the war ended very near the Reichstag and the Brandenburg Gate. It's inscription reads "Eternal glory to heroes who fell in battle with the German fascist invaders for the freedom and independence of the Soviet Union." It remembers the Soviet losses throughout the war, but particularly the 80,000 men and women of the Soviet armed forces who died in the battle of Berlin. 80,000 dead—for comparison, the bloodiest battle in Europe fought by the U.S. Army was the battle of the Bulge in which 19,000 were killed. This is not to belittle their or any other nation's death toll, but politics shouldn't hide the immense sacrifice the peoples of the Soviet Union made against fascism. Poles, Bulgarians, Romanians, and many other peoples died fighting for the Red Army, but the greatest toll was on the Soviet people themselves.

Above: *Detail from the Soviet memorial at Manschnow just west of Kostryzn (Küstrin).*

Above left and **right:** *The Soviet War Memorial at Tiergarten (**left**) is one of several war memorials in Berlin. This is one of the kneeling soldier figures at the larger site of Treptow Park.*

Below: *Russian war memorial in Komenského sady, Czech Republic.*

Finland and the Baltic states

Above: *Salaspils on the Daugava River east of Riga was a Nazi labor camp. The memorial's giant statues remember the 2–3,000 who died there, including 600 children.*

Right: *The Rumbula massacres took place on November 30 and December 8, 1941. About 25,000 Jews—most from Latvia plus 1,000 from Germany—were killed by Einsatzgruppe A with help from the Arajs Kommando, plus support from other such Latvian auxiliaries.*

Poland

Above: *The Warsaw Uprising Monument—sculpted by Wincenty Kucma—was unveiled in 1989; the architect was Jacek Budyn.*

Right: *In September 1943, at least 500 people from Ostrówki north of Lublin—half of them children—were murdered by members of the Ukrainian Insurgent Army and local villagers. The same day a further 529 were killed in Wola Ostrowiecka (then in Poland, today in Ukraine). The cross and plaque were put on the pole by a survivor.*

Below: *This memorial in the People's Park Friedrichshain, Berlin, remembers Polish soldiers who died during the war.*

Hungary

Right: *Monument in Budapest to the local partisans.*

Below right: *Dombóvár, about 40 miles south of Lake Balaton, is the site of this unusual memorial combining a bronze foot, helmet, and hand. The work of Péter Raab Párkányi and Sándor Ruttkay (designer), it is in memory of the victims of World War II*

Below: *This controversial memorial in central Budapest is dedicated to "all the victims" of Hungary's German occupation. Hungary is depicted as the Archangel Gabriel being attacked by a German imperial eagle—opponents say it minimizes the nation's role in the Holocaust. Some 450,000 Jews were sent to their deaths during the occupation.*

Czech Republic and Slovakia

Above: *Designed by Ján Svetlík, and constructed 1957–60, the Slavin Monument in Bratislava, Slovakia, is a traditional memorial to the Red Army soldiers who fell while taking the city in April 1945.*

Right: *Originally the memorial in Hrabyne was named for the Ostrava Operation (in which I Czech Army Corps took part), today it's the National World War II Monument.*

Below: *The Slovak National Uprising, August 29–October 28, 1944, is remembered in Bratislava.*

The Balkans

Right: Monument to Romanian soldiers fallen in World War II, Romanian Military Cemetery, Constanta, Romania.

Below: Russian heroes' cemetery with the Soviet war graves from the Second World War near Vladeni, Romania.

Below right: Part of the relief at the Cemetery of the Liberators of Belgrade.

246

Above: *Monument to the Novi Sad Partisan Detachment, Cenej, Serbia.*

Left and **Below left:** *The Monument to the Red Army in Sofia, Bulgaria is a good example of the ambiguity that surrounds Soviet memorials. It was erected in 1954 on the tenth anniversary of the "liberation" of the city. Polarizing views, the right wingers want it gone; those friendly to Russia don't. Meanwhile, it is "dressed" with political colors and slogans, much to Russian fury.*

248

Opposite, Above: *Dudik Memorial Park in Vukovar, eastern Croatia is dedicated to those executed by the Independent State of Croatia—mainly Yugoslav Partisans and ethnic Serbs. This monument at the Dudik Memorial, built 1978–80, was designed by Bogdan Bogdanović.*

Opposite, Below: *Monument to World War II dead on Solta Island, Croatia.*

Left: *On April 26, 1944, the Jewish community of Murska Sobota was sent to Auschwitz by the Germans. This Holocaust memorial was unveiled on January 29, 2010.*

Below left: *Monument to the Fallen Soldiers of the Kosmaj Detachment, Serbia. "On the second of July 1941, at this place, the Kosmaj/Sava-area Partisan regiment was formed. At the end of July, this regiment expanded to become two regiments of Kosmaj and Sava. In all four years of the war, within the gates of Belgrade, the rifle of freedom never ceased to fire. Over 5,820 fighters and allies of the resistance died for freedom, of which 3,411 young men and girls (along with 16 fighters from this regiment) were proclaimed to be national heroes."*

Above: *Aruncuta, Cluj, Romania (Catalog of heroes).*

Austria and Germany

HIER RUHEN
ÜBER 400 OPFER
DES BOMBENKRIEGES
1944 — 1945

Opposite, Left: *Vienna's Soviet War Memorial was unveiled in 1945 and remembers the 17,000 Soviet soldiers who died in the battle of Vienna. Austria was occupied by the four major powers until 1955. The Soviets are not remembered kindly in Austria, both for the excesses on taking Vienna and the continued problems while in occupation.*

Opposite, Above: *Vienna was bombed 52 times during the war—heavily in March and April. This memorial remembers the victims.*

Opposite, Below: *The reestablishment of the Republic of Austria in Vienna through the Austrian Declaration of Independence took place on May 15, 1955. Excerpts from the declaration and the names of the signatories are remembered on the stone of the Republic.*

Left: *The Friedland memorial (Friedland-Gedächtnisstätte) was commissioned by the German Federation of Homecomers, PoWs, and Relatives of the Missing.*

Below: *German soldiers' graves and chapel in Baden-Baden. The German War Graves Commission (Volksbund Deutsche Kriegsgräberfürsorge) is responsible for their upkeep, and all other German war graves in Europe and North Africa.*

GLOSSARY

Abt *Abteilung* = detachment or battalion (German). Could also mean department. Usually battalion-sized, but an *Armeeabteilung* (eg *Serbien*) was bigger

a.D *außer Dienst* = retired (German)

AOK *Armeeoberkommando* = Army Higher Command. Usually commanded by a Generaloberst, the AOK came between army group (Heeresgruppe/Armeegruppe) and Korps. It controlled several army corps and had its own army troops

Arko *Artilleriekommandeur* = artillery commander of an allocated artillery unit from the Heerestruppen pool

Armee(n) army(ies) in German

Armeegruppe *see Heeresgruppe*

Bde brigade

Belorussian Also Bielorussian, White Russian, and, more recently, Belarussian/Belarusian. Complicated since the collapse of the USSR and the creation of the Republic of Belarus, in this book Belorussian is used to refer to the two fronts, 1st and 2nd created in February 1944

Bn battalion—*Bataillon* in German

CGS Chief of the General Staff

CMG Cavalry-Mechanized Group (Russian) see p. 150

Div division—*Divisionen* (pl in German). Sizes of divisions varied across countries and different times of the war. The Soviet divisions were smaller than those of the German or Western Allies—Soviet corps were closer in size. A 1944 comparison:

German	Russian
Inf div (12,772 men)	Rifle div (9,375)
Tank div (14,727 men)	Armd corps (10,500)

DShK *Degtyaryova-Shpagina Krupnokaliberny* = Degtyaryov-Shpagin large calibre

GPMG general-purpose machine gun

Festung(en) fortress(es) in German—areas based on a city that were to be defended at all costs and were likely to be encircled. Resupply by air (often gliders) was expected, but not always available

FHO *Fremde Heere Ost* = Foreign Armies East. OKW intelligence organization

FJ *Fallschirmjäger* = German paratrooper

FJR6 6th Regt of 2nd FJR Div

Flak *Flugzeugabwehrkanone* = AA gun (German)

Front Soviet term roughly equivalent to the Western Allies' army group.

Gebirgsjäger mountain troops (German)

GFM *Generalfeldmarschall* = Field marshal (German)

GR *Grenadier Regt* (German infantry)

Heer The German Army

Heeresgruppe In German, this is not the same as an *Armeegruppe*, although both can be translated as army group. The *Heeresgruppe* is more like the Allies' army group and is made up of *Armeen*. The *Armeegruppe* is usually made up of elements of various armies and named after the leader

Hitlerjugend (HJ) Hitler Youth—see box on p. 215

HiWi *Hilfswilliger* = volunteers (German) see p. 17

HMC howitzer motor carriage

Honvédség The Hungarian Army

Kessel German word for cauldron. It was used militarily to mean encircled forces; thus, *Kesselschlacht*, cauldron battle—the attempt by the attackers to eradicate the encircled pocket and the defenders to break out

KG *Kampfgruppe* = battle group (German), combinations of ground troops that happened to be available at a given time. Usually named for their commander. Also *Kampfgeschwader* = battle wing (Luftwaffe unit)

KO knocked out. If used about armored vehicles this didn't necessarily mean that they were destroyed. Battlefield recovery, refurbishment in battlefield workshops, and reuse in battle was frequent on both sides

KONR The Committee for the Liberation of the Peoples of Russia (renegade Russians)

KwK *Kampfwagenkanone* = tank gun (German)

Korps corps (German). Various types in the Wehrmacht. In the Heer, mostly Armee-, Gebirgs- or Panzerkorps; Waffen-SS mainly infantry/armored with one or two exceptions (eg Gebirgs-, Kavallerie-Korps); Luftwaffe had Flieger- (Air), Flak- (AA), Fallschirmjäger- (para), and Feld- (field = infantry) Korps

le/sFH *leichte/schwerer Feldhaubitze* = light/heavy field howitzer (German)

LSSAH *Leibstandarte-SS Adolf Hitler* = 1st SS-Panzerdivision

m *mittlere* = medium (German)

L/M/H MG light/medium/heavy machine gun

Mitte middle or center (German)—so *Heeresgruppe Mitte* = Army Group Center

MLR Main line of resistance; in German *Hauptkampflinie*

MV muzzle velocity

NDH *Nezavisna Država Hrvatska* = Independent State of Croatia

Nord north (German)

NOVJ *Narodnoosvobodilna vojska Jugoslavije* = People's Liberation Army of Yugoslavia (Croatian)

OB West *Oberbefehlshaber West* = C-in-C West (German)

OSS Office of Strategic Services

OKH/L/M/W *Oberkommando des Heeres/der Luftwaffe/der Marine/der Wehrmacht* = German Army/Airforce/Navy/Armed forces High Command

Ostbataillone Eastern battalions = usually PoWs who fought for the Germans (see p. 17)

Ostlegionen Eastern legions = usually volunteers or conscripts who fought for the Germans (see p. 17)

Panzerfaust, Panzerfaüste (pl) German hand-held antitank weapon that came in 30m, 60m, 100m, and 150mm versions

PzGr *Panzergrenadier* = motorized infantry (German)

PaK *Panzerabwehrkanone* = antitank gun (German)

portyanki footcloths (Russian). Both Soviet and German soldiers used them both in preference to socks or under them. (See illustration **Below**)

PPS *Pistolét-pulemyót Sudayeva* = Sudayev's SMG (PPS-42/43) in Russian

PPSh *Pistolét-pulemyót Shpágina* = Shpagin's SMG (PPSh-41) in Russian

PzGr *Panzergrenadier* = armored infantry (German)

Pionier military engineer (German)

Red Army Soviet Army (see box p. 4)

Regt regiment

ROA *Russkaya osvoboditel'naya armiya* = Russian Liberation Army (renegade)

RONA *Russian Army of National Liberation* (renegade)

S-mine *Schuh-mine* = anti-personnel mine (German)

SdKfz *Sonderkraftfahrzeug* = special purpose vehicle (German)

SG *Schlachtgeschwader* = close-support wing (German)

(SS-) sPzAbt *(SS-)schwere Panzer-Abteilung* = (SS-) heavy tank battalion (Tiger I and II)

SOE Special Operations Executive

SP self-propelled

SPAAG SP AA gun

SPW *schwerer Panzerspähwagen* = heavy armd recon vehicle (German)

Sqn squadron

Above: *This medal was awarded "For the Victory Over Germany in the Great Patriotic War 1941–1945." Established on May 9, 1945, nearly 15 million were issued.*

Stavka The *Stavka Verkhovnogo Glavnokomandovaniya* (Supreme GHQ) was the High Command of the Red Army. Taking its name from the Russian for tent, it had gone through various forms before being instituted on August 8, 1941, with Stalin at its head. From February 17, 1945, the Stavka was composed of: Marshals of the Soviet Union I.V. Stalin (the President and Supreme C-in-C), G. K. Zhukov (People's Commissar for Defense, assistant) and A. M. Vasilevsky (People's Commissar for Defense, assistant), Generals N.A. Bulganin (a member of the State Committee for Defense and People's Commissar for Defense, assistant) and A. I. Antonov (CGS), Admiral N. G. Kuznetsov (People's Commissar of the Navy of the USSR)

StuG *Sturmgeschütz* = assault gun. StuG III on PzKpfw III chassis; StuG IV on the PzKpfw IV. The StuG III had been designed as an infantry-support vehicle but in the later war both were used as in the anti-tank role

Süd south (German)

TD tank destroyer—could mean towed antitank guns or tracked (eg, U.S. Army M10, M18, or M36)

UNRRA UN Relief and Rehabilitation Administration

Ustaša (pl *Ustaše*) The Croatian fascist organization that ruled the country during World War II.

VG Division *Volksgrenadier* Division = "People's" rifle division (German). A late-war designation, most VGDs were built around a cadre of experienced officers and NCOs. Some fought very well

VVS *Voyenno-voz-dushnyye sily* = Military Air Forces in Russian = Soviet Air Force

BIBLIOGRAPHY

Online sources include:

http://ww2today.com Day-by-day coverage of the war with photos and articles; always interesting.

http://www.history.army.mil The U.S. Center of Military History is a wonderful location for the official histories and much more.

http://www.tracesofwar.com/ Indispensable site!

https://forum.axishistory.com/viewtopic. php?f=55&t=252970&start=45 for the Lisow/Kielce battles. And much else as well. Great site.

http://www.niehorster.org/index.htm for excellent ORBATs.

http://wio.ru has tons of info on Russian tactical markings.

https://waralbum.ru is the go-to site for visual information on the Russian war machine in World War 2.

https://wwii.germandocsinrussia.org/de/ nodes/8769-akte-8-unterlagen-der-ia-abtei- lung-des-verteidigungsbereiches-berlin-grunds-tzli- cher-befehl-f-r-die-vorbereitungen-zur-verteidi- gung-der-reichshauptstadt-vom-9-3-1945-nebst- russischer-bersetzung-sowie-schreiben-des-reichsf- hrers-ss#page/1/mode/inspect/zoom/4—the defense of Berlin document.

https://weaponsandwarfare.com/2010/03/04/the- organization-of-the-eastern-troops-5-may-1943/

www.jaegerplatoon.net coverage of the Finnish armed forces, their equipment and weapons.

http://www.ww2.dk Includes fantastic coverage of airfields and units.

Books, Dissertations, and magazine articles

Antill, Peter, and Dennis, Peter: *Campaign 159 Berlin 1945;* Osprey 2005.

Archer, Lee, & Auerbach, William: *Panzerwrecks: German Armour 1944–45* (various numbers); Panzerwrecks Ltd.

Archer, Lee, Kraska, Robert, & Lippert, Mario: *Panzers in Berlin 1945;* Panzerwrecks Ltd, 2019.

Axworthy, Mark & Serbanescu: *The Romanian Army of World War 2;* Osprey, 1992.

Beevor, Antony: *Berlin The Downfall 1945;* Penguin Books, 2002.

Beorn, Waitman Wade: "A Calculus of Complicity" *Central European History,* June 2011.

Bonhardt, Attila: *Armour of the Royal Hungarian Army, 40M Nimród Tank Destroyer and Armoured Anti Aircraft Gun;* PeKo Publishing Kft., 2019.

Braham, Randolph L.: "Hungary and the Holocaust: The Nationalist Drive To Whitewash The Past (Part 1)"; *East European Perspectives,* Vol 3, No 18 2001.

Buenau, Gen der Infanterie Rudolf von: *Combat in Vienna;* U.S. Army, 1965.

Eyre, Lt Col Wayne D.: *Operation Rösselsprung and the Elimination of Tito, 25 May 1944: A failure in planning and intelligence support;* Quantico, 2002.

Führer Directives and other top-level directives of the German Armed Forces 1942–1945; Washington, 1948.

Gebhardt, Maj James F.: *Leavenworth Papers 17 The Petsamo-Kirkenes Operation Soviet Breakthrough and Pursuit in the Arctic, October 1944;* Combat Studies Institute, 1990.

German Antiguerrilla Operations in the Balkans (1941–1944); Department of the Army pamphlet no. 20-243, August 1954.

Germany in the East; U.S. Army, 1949.

Glenn, Maj Russell W.: *Soviet Partisan Warfare: Integral to the Whole;* Fort Leavenworth, 1988.

Guderian, Heinz: *Panzer Leader;* Futura, 1974.

Holliday, Lt Col Sam C., and Dabezies, Pierre C.: *Irregular Warfare in a Nutshell;* Fort Leavenworth, 1962.

Isaev, Aleksei & Kolomiets, Maksim: *Tomb of the Panzerwaffe;* Helion & Company, 2018.

Karalus, Maciej, & Jerzak, Jaroslaw: *Panzers in the Defence of Festung Posen 1945;* Helion & Company, 2018.

Kaspar, Maj Edward M.: *Suffering What They Must: The Shifting Alliances of Romania and Finland in World War II;* Fort Leavenworth, 2015.

Kaufmann, J.E., & Kaufmann, H.W.: *The Forts & Fortifications of Europe 1815–1945: The Central States;* Pen & Sword, 2014.

Kopenhagen, Wilfried: *Armored Trains of the Soviet Union 1917–1945;* Schiffer Military History, 1996.

Krivosheev, G.F. [ed]: *Soviet Casualties and Combat Losses in the Twentieth Century;* Greenhill Books, 1997.

MacDonald, Charles D.: *The European Theater of Operations The Last Offensive;* CMH, 1993.

Maclean, Maj French L.: *The Unknown Generals— German Corps Commanders in World War II;* Fort Leavenworth, 1988.

Mann, Chris, and Jörgensen, Christer: *Hitler's Arctic War;* Pen & Sword, 2016.

Morzik, Generalmajor a.D Fritz: *German Air Force Airlift Operations;* Valmy Publishing, 2017.

Operations of Encircled Forces: German Experiences in Russia; Department of the Army pamphlet no. 20-234, January 1952.

Oswald, Werner: *Kraftfahrzeuge und Panzer der Reichswehr, Wehrmacht und Bundeswehr;* Motorbuch Verlag, 1975.

Peculiarities of Russian Warfare; U.S. Army, 1949.

Reinhardt, Genmaj Helmut; *Infantry organization and equipment based on German experiences in Russia;* Historical Division European Command, 1951.

Rottman, Gordon L., and Gerrard, Howard: *Warrior 123 Soviet Rifleman 1941–45;* Osprey, 2007.

Sasso, Major Claude R.: *Leavenworth Papers 6 Soviet Night Operations in World War II;* Combat Studies Institute, 1982

Schneider, Wolfgang: *Tigers in Combat I;* Stackpole Books, 2004.

Schneider, Wolfgang: *Tigers in Combat II;* Stackpole Books, 2005.

Schneider, Wolfgang: *Tigers in Combat III;* Helion, 2016.

Schlaug, Georg: "Eine Einheit, die kaum jemand kennt", *Jet & Prop* 2/00; Verlag Heinz Nickel, 2000.

Seaton, Albert and Roffe, Michael: *Men at Arms 29 The Soviet Army;* Osprey, 1972.

Small Unit Tactics Partisan Warfare; Historical Division European Command, 1952.

Soldatenblätter für Feier und Freizeit; OKW, October 1940.

Svencs, Maj Edmunds: *The Latvian Legion (1943–1945) and its Role in Latvia's History;* Fort Leavenworth, 2013.

Thomas, Nigel & McCouaig, Simon: *Foreign Volunteers of the Allied Forces 1939–45;* Osprey, 1991.

Trifkovic, Gaj: *Carnage in the Land of Three Rivers: The Syrmian Front 1944–1945;* 2016.

Tucker-Jones, A.: *Hitler's Great Panzer Heist;* Pen & Sword, 2007.

Ungváry, Krisztián: *Battle for Budapest 100 Days in World War II;* I.B. Tauris, 2006.

War Department (USA) and Bolin, Robert L.: *Handbook on USSR Military Forces:* Chapter III, Field Organization; 1946. DOD Military Intelligence. 23. http://digitalcommons.unl.edu/ dodmilintel/23

Wilbeck, Christopher W.: *Sledgehammers, Strengths and Flaws of Tiger Tank Battalions in World War II;* The Aberjona Press, 2004.

Willems, Bastiaan: "Defiant Breakwaters or Desperate Blunders? A Revision of the German Late-War Fortress Strategy," *The Journal of Slavic Military Studies,* 28:2; Routledge, 2015.

Wray, Maj Timothy A.: *Standing Fast: German Defensive Doctrine on the Russian Front during the Second World War;* Fort Leavenworth, 1982.

Yelton, David K., and O'Brogain, Sean: *Warrior 110 Hitler's Home Guard: Volkssturmmann;* Osprey, 2006.

Zaloga, Steven J.: *Armor at War Stalin's Heavy Tanks 1941–1945;* Concord, 1997.

Zaloga, Steven J., and Noon, Steve: *Campaign 293 Downfall 1945;* Osprey, 2016.

Zeimke, Earl F.: *Stalingrad to Berlin: The German Defeat in the East;* Office of the Chief of Military History, United States Army, Washington D.C., 1968.

Zgoda, Tomasz: "The Battle for Festung Posen"; *After the Battle* 188; Battle of Britain International Ltd, 2020.

Below: *Tough to the end. This German soldier is armed with a Sturmgewehr 44 assault rifle.*

CREDITS

First and foremost, grateful thanks go to Nik Cornish for his photographs and captions; to Patrick Hook for major sections of the text; to Richard Charlton Taylor for his help with captioning, particularly the sections covering weapons, and supplied a number of the German photographs, artwork, and other illustrative material. Thanks, too, to John Gibbon of the 13th Guards Rifle Division "Poltavaskaya" for the reenactment and equipment photographs.

Other photo credits are noted below. If anyone is missing or incorrectly credited, apologies! Please notify the author through the publishers.

Other thanks are due to Elly for design work and the overlays for the maps on pp. 79, 94, 98, 108, 118, 121, 141, 155, 187, 207, 212. The overlay on p. 121 is based on information found in Isaev & Kolomiet (2018); p. 187 on https://www.o5m6.de/redarmy/battleofvienna.php. The excellent modern map artwork is, as usual, by Mark Franklin. Info on map p. 125 based on work by Panzerrene50.

The contemporary maps are from various online resources, particularly those of the University of Texas, Perry-Castañeda Library Map Collection.

Finally, many thanks to the SSEES old timers who provided translation and editorial assistance—particularly Piers Hemy and, of course, Sandra.

Russian poster chapter openers

Thanks to Kirill Belyayev for his kind permission to use his material.

Photographs

13thguardspoltavaskaya.com: 23TL, TC, & TR, 24 (2–7), 25

albumwar2.com, 106T, 136 (3), 158, 174T, 181T, 188 (all), 189B, 193 (C, BR & BL), 205 (all except insignia), 216T, 218B

Author/Author's collection: 2–3, 7, 12T, 16T, 17B, 45R, 46 (both), 48 (3), 50R, 52 (5 & 6), 53 (4), 54 (3), 55 (both grenades), 57(6), 58(2), 79, 83B, 210, 217T, 227T, 233T

Battlefield Historian, 226, 228TR

Bradford's Auction Gallery, 28 (3 & 4)

Bulgarian Archives State Agency, 160, 161B

Bundesarchiv 17TR (146-1980-036-05), 42 (3, 146-1978-111-10A), 43 (4, 146-1977-120-09; 8, 1011-209-0076-02/Tannenberg/CC-BY-SA 3.0; 9, 146-1983-028-05), 57 (3, 1011-680-8282A-06), 63 (4, 1011-003-3445-33), 74 (1, 101L-110-1699-23; 2, -21; 3, 1673-08; 4, 1694-34/Faßhauser/CC-BY-SA 3.0), 83C (146-1972-093-65), 106B (183-J28536), 116 (1011-680-8282A-12A), 172 (183-H28356), 219T (183-V04744)

Nik Cornish:
From the fonds of the RGAKFD in Krasnogorsk via Stavka, 27R, 34 (1), 37C & B, 38 (1), 80T, 87, 104B, 128B, 148T, 153TL, 199, 211B, 213B, 214B, 215B, 216B, 220L, 221T & C, 223B, 236B, 253;
Courtesy of the Central Museum of the Armed Forces, Moscow via Stavka, 32T & B, 33T & B, 35 (6), 36T, 37T, 38 (2 & 4), 39 (7), 41 (C & B), 86L, 87B, 97T, 100C, 101B, 110C, 119C, 129C, 140TL, 149T, 150T, 151, 153TR, 154T & B, 159B, 161B, 173T, 192 (both), 193T, 194T, 195 (all), 201B, 221B, 228BL, 230C;
Nik Cornish at www.Stavka.org.uk, 10B, 22, 36B, 43 (6), 49 (5), 51 (8), 56 (2), 58 (1 & 3), 59 (both), 60 (T), 61(all), 62 (both), 96T, 104T & C, 105T, C, & BR, 115, 121L, 126C, 128T, 129T, 130R, 131B, 139B, 146 (C & B), 150B, 152, 153B, 156 (both), 164TR & BR, 174A, 181B, 182 (all), 183T, 196 (both), 197 (all), 200, 202, 203 (both), 209, 211C, 215T, 218T, 220R, 222B, 223T, 231C, 232T, 236C

Fortepan Hungarian Archives: 11 (Archiv für Zeitges-

chichte ETH Zürich / Agnes Hirschi), 24 (1 Inkey Tibor), 41T (Zádori Ferenc), 60B (Vargha Zsuzsa), 63 (5, Vörös Hadsereg/Red Army), 63 (6, Vojnich Pál), 117T, 117C, 118C & B (Vörös Hadsereg), 119T & B (Vörös Hadsereg), 120T, 120B (Vörös Hadsereg), 121R, 122 (Vörös Hadsereg), 123TL, 123C & B (Vörös Hadsereg), 124T, 125T (Album050), 125C (Ungváry Krisztián), 125B (Vörös Hadsereg), 126T & B (Vörös Hadsereg), 128C (Vörös Hadsereg), 129B (Lissák Tivadar), 130L (Ormos Imre Alapítvány), 177B

FreeImages.com/Krzysztof (Kriss) Szkurlatowski, 35 (5),

Germany in the East (1949), 8, 9.

Greene Media (Simon Clay): 28 (1, 2, 5–7), 29 (1–5), 30 (1–5), 31 (1, 2, 4), 52 (1–5), 53 (1–3), 54 (1, 2, 4, 5), 55 (6)

Library of Congress: 14, 15(3), 103BR, 135, 236T

MacDonald (1993): 229

Mil.ru: 20 (2T CC BY 4.0), 21(4 CC BY 4.0), 21(7 CC BY 4.0), 38 (3 CC BY 4.0), 171 (CC BY 4.0)

Anatoly Morozov / RIA Novosti 26 (2)

Museums Victoria, 231T

NARA: 20 (1), 20 (3), 43 (10), 222T, 223B, 227T, 232B, 234T

Narodowe Archiwum Cyfrowe Polish Archices: 13 (both), 16B, 17TL (Sanok Museum of History), 18 (all), 42 (1), 48 (1, 2, & 4), 49 (5 & 7), 50L, 51 (1–7, 9), 56 (2), 67, 78, 83 (all), 89C, 90BR, 98TL, 99T, 100T, 120C, 134BL (colorised by EF), 134BR, 137 (both), 139 (all except artwork), 142 (all), 143 (all), 144T & B, 146T, 147T, 159T, 164L, 255

North Korean media - pohodd.ru, 27 (4)

Petr Podebradsky 74T

RCT: 42 (2), 44, 45 (all L), 47 (both), 49 (6), 66T, 83T, 90BL, 98 (4), 102B, 105BL, 107, 110B

SA-Kuve Finnish Archive: 32C, 39 (6), 43 (5), 67, 68 (2, colored by Ruffneck88) 68 (3), 69 (all), 70 (all), 71 (all), 73B, 74B, 76B, 78 (1 and 2)

Shutterstock: 237B (Alexey Fedorenko)

Stalingrad-Berlin (1966): 72C, 81

Tom Timmermans: 4–5, 165 (both)

Unknown, 100B, 103BL, 134T, 139, 177C

USAF, 145T & C, 219C, 227B, 231B

US Army: 55 (mortars), 78 (3), 87T, 252

USAMHI, 234B

WikiCommons: 12B (Boksi CC BY-SA 3.0), 15 BC (Sakhalin Regional Museum of Local Lore), 22(2/lower, Tornado-84 evgeny CC BY-SA 4.0), 21 (5, Eduard Kosarev CC BY-SA 4.0), 21 (6T, By Time Inc.; photograph by Grigory Vayl - Life magazine, Volume 18, Number 7 (page 94)), 21(6B, Dennis Jarvis from Halifax, Canada CC BY-SA 2.0), 21(8, Andshel at Russian Wikipedia CC0 1.0), 23C (Ain92 CC BY-SA 3.0), 23B (Balcer CC BY-SA 3.0), 24 (7 Rama CC BY-SA 3.0), 31 (3, Stanislav S.Yanchenko CC BY-SA 3.0), 34 (3, Radosław Drożdżewski CC BY-SA 4.0), 39 (5) (Eric Salard CC BY-SA 2.0), 40T (Lukб̌č Peter CC BY-SA 4.0), 40B (Wistula CC BY-SA 3.0), 43 (7, REYK30 CC BY-SA 4.0), 54 (7, Balcer CC BY-SA 3.0), 56 (1, Eugeniusz Lokajski), 57 (4, Raul654 CC BY-SA 2.5; 5, Srdan Popović CC BY-SA 3.0), 68 (1, Prozaq CC BY-SA 3.0), 68 (2, Ruffneck88 CC BY-SA 4.0), 72B (SeppVei), 74C (Crown Copyright), 76TL (QuentinUK CC BY-SA 3.0), 76BL (Glasshouse CC BY-SA 3.0), 77 (Municipal Archives of Trondheim CC BY 2.0), 85 (Unknown), 88–89B (PawełMM CC BY-SA 3.0), 88T (unknown), 89T (Zbyszko Siemaszko, CAF/Warsaw), 90T (Archiwum Zakładu Historii Partii), 90T (S. Kolowca), 90C (Jarekt/Marek Tuszynski's collection of WWII prints), 91B (Fdutil CC BY-SA 3.0), 92 (1), 92 (2, Radosław Drożdżewski CC BY-SA 4.0), 92 (4, Radosław Drożdżewski CC BY-SA 4.0), 92 (5, SybilKaesedick CC BY-SA 4.0), 99BL (Unknown author, bi.gazeta.pl), 99BR (adamchemík), 102T (Fdutil CC BY-SA 3.0), 109 (Uwe Brodrecht

CC BY-SA 2.0), 110C (Pudelek CC BY-SA 3.0), 110B (Muzeum Miejskie we Wrocławiu), 111L (Logaritmo), 111R (Alexandre Lepage QC CC BY-SA 4.0), 112B (Wolfgang Staudt CC BY 2.0), 113T (Ericmetro FAL), 113BL (kallerna CC BY-SA 4.0), 113BR (Photojack50), 117B (Nikodem Nijaki CC BY-SA 3.0), 117 inset (Karsai, L6szly), 120BL (Thaler Tamas CC BY-SA 4.0), 123TR (Jakub Hałun CC BY-SA 4.0), 123 inset (Fdutil CC BY-SA 3.0), 124B (FashionStreet.hu/Gosztom Gergő CC BY-SA 4.0), 133 (Marxists Internet Archive), 134BC (George Skrigin), 136TL & TR (Unknown), 136 (1, Amazone7 CC BY-SA 3.0), 136BC (2, w:Savo Orović), 138 (2, AnonMoos), 140B (Boris Mavlyutov CC BY-SA 3.0), 141T (unknown), 141B (Copernicus Sentinel-2, ESA CC BY-SA 3.0), 145B (Unknown), 148B, 155 (Jake V), 157T (warthunder.com), 157B (VitVit CC BY-SA 4.0), 163 (Benoot Prieur - CC-BY-SA), 166T, 168 (both, Heyduk), 169C (Heyduk), 169B (Daniel Bar6nek, CC BY-SA 4.0), 173BL (Panek CC BY-SA 4.0), 173BR (ThecentreCZ CC BY-SA 4.0), 175BL & BR (Monument postcards of the Association of Friends of the USSR Czechoslovakia CC BY-SA 4.0), 176 (BíláVrána), 178T (Unknown, CC BY-SA 4.0), 178B (Fdutil CC BY-SA 3.0), 179T (Karel H6jek), 189T (Fdutil CC BY-SA 3.0), 191CL (Copernicus Sentinel-2, ESA), 190 (bothKasa Fue CC BY-SA 4.0), 191T & CR (Kasa Fue CC BY-SA 4.0), 191B (gerald-zojer), 194B (Rafa Esteve CC BY-SA 4.0), 201T (de:User:Ralf Roletschek Fahrradmonteur.de; derivative work by Maximilian Durrbecker (Chumwa) GNU FDL 1.2), 204 (both Lonio17 / Orionist CC BY-SA 4.0), 205 inset (NikNaks93), 214T (Wolfgang Willrich CC BY-SA 4.0), 216 (inset Pianist CC BY-SA 2.5), 217B (Ivengo(RUS) CC BY-SA 3.0), 221 inset (Fdutil CC BY-SA 3.0), 228TL (Yank), 228BR (Franz Eher Nachf. GmbH, Berlin, April 1945), 230TL (Gaki64 CC BY-SA 4.0), 230B (Globetrotter19, CC BY-SA 3.0), 231BR (Dalibri, CC BY-SA 3.0), 233B (Tiia Monto, CC BY-SA 4.0), 234C (Richardfabi CC BY-SA 3.0), 235T (Max Missmann), 235B (nl:User:GerardM CC BY-SA 3.0), 237T (tormentor4555, CC BY-SA 3.0), 239 (Wojciech Domagała CC BY-SA 3.0 PL), 240L (Marcus Cyron CC BY-SA 3.0), 241TL (Mike Peel (www.mikepeel.net), CC BY-SA 4.0), 241TR (Dupisingh CC BY-SA 4.0), 240–41 (Michal Klajban, CC BY-SA 4.0), 242T (Mārtiņš Bruņenieks, CC BY-SA 4.0), 242B (Avi1111 dr. avishai teicher, CC BY-SA 3.0), 243T (Adrian Grycuk, CC BY-SA 3.0), 243C (Glaube, CC BY-SA 4.0), 243B (Tim Rademacher, CC BY-SA 4.0), 244T (Rlevente, CC BY-SA 3.0), 244BL (Elekes Andor, CC BY-SA 4.0), 244BR (Gnagyrobi, CC BY-SA 4.0), 245T (Diego Delso, delso.photo, CC-BY-SA), 245C (Juandev - Own work, CC BY-SA 3.0), 245B (Doko Jozef Kotulič, CC BY-SA 3.0), 246T (Anonimu, CC BY-SA 4.0), 246L (Stoschmidt, CC BY 3.0), 246R (Pinki, CC BY-SA 4.0), 247T (Subnorns CC BY-SA 4.0), 247C (Ignat Ignev GNU FDL 1.2), 247B (Mark Ahsmann CC BY-SA 4.0), 248T (Pera detlic CC BY-SA 4.0), 248B (Adam Jones adamjones.freeservers.com CC BY-SA 3.0), 249T (Daniel Thornton CC BY 2.0), 249B (Vanilitsa CC BY-SA 4.0), 249 inset (Tare Gheorghe at Romanian Wiki), 250L (Dennis Jarvis from Halifax, Canada CC BY 2.0), 250T GuentherZ CC BY-SA 3.0), 250B (NonScolae), 251T (Simon-Martin CC BY-SA 4.0), 251B (Gerd Eichmann CC BY-SA 3.0), 253 (Fdutil CC BY-SA 3.0)waralbum.ru 19T, 96B, 108C, 113T, 167, 174T, 177T, 179B, 183B, 211 (via WikiCommons)

World War Photos: 1, 10T, 15(2), 19B, 26 (1), 27 (3), 33C, 34 (2), 35 (4), 80B, 82 (both), 86R, 91T, 92(3), 95 (all), 97B, 99C, 111C, 113C, 144C, 147B, 149B, 166B, 169T, 170, 175T, 180 (all), 185 (Eugene Khaldey), 186, 213T & C

INDEX

Below: *"Stalin sacrificed many millions of honest soldiers of the Soviet army to this war. He does not hesitate to donate many more millions!" Ukrainian-language leaflet showing Churchill, Roosevelt and the shadowy figure of international Jewry pushing Stalin to send troops to their deaths.*